Mobile Radio Handbook

Mobile Radio Handbook

Leo G. Sands

With a specially written chapter for the guidance of the English reader by W. Oliver

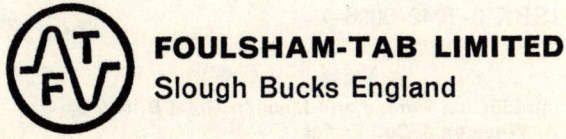

FOULSHAM-TAB LIMITED
Slough Bucks England

Foulsham-Tab Limited
Yeovil Road Slough Bucks England

Mobile Radio Handbook

Copyright © 1972 and 1974 by
Tab Books and Foulsham-Tab Limited

Reproduction or publication of the content in any manner, without the express permission of the publisher, is prohibited. No liability is assumed with respect to the use of the information herein.
Library of Congress Number 73-85404
Cat. Code No. 665

ISBN 0-7042-0093-7

Introduction Printed and Made in Great Britain by
A. Wheaton & Co., Exeter
Balance printed in U.S.A.

It is essential that the English reader should read this chapter.

When radio first started, frequencies used were relatively low, wavelengths comparatively long. Entertainment broadcasting was confined at first to medium and long wavebands. Short-wave broadcasting came much later. The short waves below 100 metres were thought to be of only very limited use and were allotted, in part, to amateur transmitters to play with (in compensation for being ousted from the medium waveband, on which in pioneer days they were allowed to experiment out of broadcasting hours).

The amateurs quickly proved that short waves (high frequencies), far from being useless, were unexpectedly but quite outstandingly excellent for long-distance communication. Very soon these high frequencies became crowded with signals of all kinds from fixed and mobile stations of every class—broadcasting, commercial W/T and R/T, shipping and coastal, aircraft and airfield, trans-Atlantic public telephone links and many other fixed or mobile transmitters.

As the years have passed, higher and higher frequencies, shorter and shorter wavelengths, have come into use. Long, medium and short-wave broadcasting continues; but VHF transmissions largely supplement or even supersede the service on "ordinary" wavebands.

As for television, the 405-line transmissions on VHF are obsolescent (at the time of writing) and it is the 625-line service on UHF (ultra-high frequencies) which is most typical of the present *and* future trends.

The tendency to explore the possibilities of higher and higher frequencies is equally typical now of two-way radio telecommunication which forms the subject of the present book. In his preface the American author outlines the development of two-way mobile radio and shows how the possibilities of higher and higher frequencies have been recognized by equipment manufacturers.

As this book originates from the United States, the author is writing mainly from the American angle, but most of the information he gives is readily adaptable to British needs, and a good deal of it is even directly applicable with little or no reorientation.

The photographic illustrations concentrate on American-made equipment; but similar apparatus is available in other countries including Britain. Many of the leading American manufacturers, mentioned in this book, have agents, subsidiaries or associated companies on this side of the Atlantic, either in Britain or in other European countries.

In the line diagrams of typical circuitry, valves indicated are American types. About a dozen type-numbers are shown, and the present writer has verified that nearly all of these are readily obtainable here at the time of writing, in the American numbering. Some, too, have British equivalents; for example, in the Mullard range, the EF95 = 6AK5; the ECC81 = 12AT7 and the ECC83 = 12AX7.

Solid-state equipment has superseded valve circuits for most purposes nowadays; but the landslide to this which occurred in some applications is not nearly so typical of others. The predictions made so confidently some years ago that everything would soon be transistorized and that valves would disappear from the scene completely have not yet materialized and very many valves are still in use for transmitting purposes especially. But some types are now scarce and expensive, so replacement is apt to be an increasing problem.

Various solid-state devices now being produced are capable of handling much higher power than was formerly the case and there can be no doubt that their advantages will become increasingly evident even in fields where valves have held sway far longer than most people thought they would.

Naturally, two-way communication involves the use of transmitters as well as receivers; and immediately one moves into the field of transmission, the question of official rules and regulations governing transmitting licences, frequency allocations, etc., looms large.

Where regulations and wavebands are discussed in this book, the information about them given by the American author is based on the rules of the United States Federal Communications Commission or FCC. This is the department that deals with official and legal matters involved in radio, TV and general telecommunication services in the States.

Here in Britain, a roughly-equivalent organization which fulfils similar duties is our Ministry of Posts and Telecommunications. This is the department which deals with the granting of transmitting licences, allocates frequencies and so on. The present headquarters address of "Minpostel" is: Waterloo Bridge House, Waterloo Road, London SE1 8UA.

One has to check the licence position carefully, because the definition of a transmitter from a legal angle is not as simple and straightforward as one might suppose.

Technically the situation is quite a complex one, but a few brief notes may help. Broadly speaking, every transmitter contains an oscillator which forms its "heart" and generates the essential radio signals that are the actual source of the transmission.

One should bear in mind that virtually every radio-frequency oscillator is, in one sense, a potential transmitter, insofar as it can, very easily in some cases, be made to radiate signals if one wishes it to do so. Moreover, unless suitable precautions are taken it may radiate signals or interference whether or not you intend it to do so.

There are millions of radio-frequency oscillators in daily use which are *not* classed as transmitters *nor* employed for intentional transmission. They are capable of radiating interference but fortunately this is usually confined to a very restricted radius around the set. Examples are the "local oscillators" found in superhet receivers—which means nearly every radio and television set on the market!—and the oscillators found in RF signal-generators, used daily in workshops everywhere for servicing, testing and adjusting sets. No transmitting licence is required for oscillators used in these limited applications; yet the basic circuitry may be, and often is, practically identical to that used in a simple transmitter, for which of course you *do* need an appropriate transmitting licence or permit from the Ministry of Posts and Telecommunications.

Merely connecting an aerial to any radio-frequency oscillator is enough to turn it into a transmitter of sorts, and transforms it instantly from a "harmless" sort of oscillator to a fully-fledged transmitting station, albeit an extremely low-powered and limited one.

In general it is illegal, and a heavily-punishable offence, to operate any illicit transmitter in this country. By "illicit transmitter" we mean any equipment used for radio communication without the appropriate transmitting licence or permit from the Ministry of Posts and Telecommunications.

One must not assume that the mere fact of being able to buy a particular set on the open market is any guarantee that it can be lawfully used in this country, or that you can be sure of being granted a licence for its use in any particular application. So it is best to check on these points before going to the expense of buying or building any equipment for fixed or mobile two-way communication.

Regarding sources of supply for equipment—transmitting and receiving sets, aerials, control-units, microphones, etc.—you can find names and addresses of manufacturers or distributors, mail order and retail firms, in the advertisement pages of the technical journals which cater for these interests.

The discussion in the present book covers a wide variety of transmitting and receiving circuits suitable for various radio communication purposes, notably in mobile services. Both valve and solid-state (transistorized) circuits are described and illustrated.

The last two chapters give useful information on testing, troubleshooting and servicing mobile transmitting and receiving gear.

There is a useful chart which gives details of trouble symptoms; causes, checks and cures are tabulated so that you can see at a glance what faults are likely, what gives rise to them, how to check the circuits, and what steps you can take to cure the various troubles. Test-gear discussed ranges from the simplest type of field-strength meter circuit to fairly advanced types of signal-generators etc.

Where ready-made sets etc. are concerned, if they are new enough to be still in guarantee, it is advisable to check on the exact terms of this before attempting any repairs or alterations which might invalidate it should you wish, subsequently, to return the equipment to the makers' service department for servicing under guarantee.

Preface

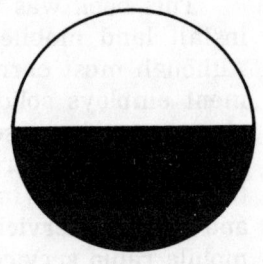

Two-way mobile radio has grown from humble beginnings shortly before World War II into a giant industry. Millions of vehicles are equipped with two-way radiotelephones, and annual industry sales of equipment (world wide) have passed the billion-dollar mark.

Although two-way radio equipment was used by police and fire departments in the 1930s, it was the wartime experience with VHF radio (150 MHz range) that expanded the use of two-way radio. The Bendix Corporation, Motorola, RCA, Raytheon, General Electric, and others demonstrated that VHF radio could meet the requirements of mobile communications with freedom from long-distance "skip" interference and with less noise than at lower frequencies.

As recently as 1949, the 450-470 MHz UHF band was not taken very seriously except by Link Radio Corporation, under the leadership of Fred M. Link, and by Philco Corporation, which developed a UHF-band mobile unit before Philco prematurely bowed out of the mobile radio business. This band has become very popular and is superior in many respects to the 150-174 MHz band.

Now, a new band in the 900 MHz region is being opened up, and it has been found to be as satisfactory in many respects as the 450 MHz band. Motorola has conducted exhaustive tests and is developing equipment for this new band.

The mobile radio field has been dominated by Motorola, General Electric, and RCA for many years. Numerous other companies have entered the field because of the great demand for two-way radio by small business enterprises and for lower-cost equipment by small-community public safety organizations. Standard Communications Corporation, for example, has introduced a line of low-cost, solid-state FM mobile radio equipment and is making significant progress in its goal of garnering a fair share of the market.

This book was written for those who sell, service, and install land mobile radio equipment and design systems. Although most currently manufactured mobile radio equipment employs solid-state circuitry, tube-type equipment is also covered because so much of it is still in use.

In addition to transmitter, receiver, and control circuits, this book contains information about antennas, power sources and supplies, servicing, test equipment, and how to operate a mobile radio service business.

The author extends his appreciation to the many companies that furnished technical information and photographs of their products, particularly Standard, Motorola, RCA, General Electric, and E. F. Johnson Company. The author is grateful to James P. Hervey, William A. Bitcon, Fred M. Link, Stuart F. Meyer, Lewis Bondon, and all of the others who were so very helpful in making this book possible.

Leo G. Sands
New York City.

Contents

1 Basic Systems — 7
Communicating Range—Effects of Power—Extended Range Systems—Relay System—Point-to-Point Radio—Radio Paging—Radio Dispatching Services—Mobile Telephone Service—Two-Way Dialing—AM vs FM

2 Transmitters — 21
Tube-Type Transmitters—Oscillators—Phase Modulator—Frequency Multipliers—RF Power Amplifiers—Booster Amplifiers—AM Transmitters—Solid-State Transmitter Circuits

3 Receivers — 46
Tube-Type Receivers—UHF Band—Solid-State Receiver Circuits

4 Control Systems — 81
Right-of-Way Systems—Multifunction Control—Troubleshooting—Monitoring—Selective Calling—Dial Systems

5 Antenna Systems — 98
Base- and Fixed-Station Antennas—Mobile Antennas—Transmission Lines—Fixed-Antenna Supports—Lightning Protection—Mobile-Antenna Installations—Fixed-Antenna Troubleshooting—Antenna Farms—Antenna Sharing—Antenna Gain and Range—Directional Gain—Power Gain and Loss

6 Power — 123
Vehicular Power Sources—Locomotives—Miscellaneous Vehicles—Reverse-Polarity Protection—Hybrid Mobile Units—Tube-Type Units

7 Servicing — 133
Field Servicing—Shop Servicing—Inoperative Receiver—Transmitter Metering—Receiver Checkout—Receiver I-F Alignment—Sensitivity Measurement—Selectivity Measurement—Bandpass Symmetry—

Troubleshooting—Relay Maintenance—Preventive Maintenance

8 Setting Up the Shop 161
Lighting—Power—Test Equipment—RF Power Meters—Field-Strength Meters—Special Mobile Radio Instruments

Index 189

Basic Systems

A two-way radio communications system consists of two or more mobile units, or a base station and one or more mobile units, or a combination of two or more base stations and any number of mobile units.

A **mobile unit** (Fig. 1-1) is a radio station on board a vehicle or other conveyance, or one carried by a person. The compact radiotelephone in Fig. 1-1 contains a transmitter, receiver, and power supply. Another mobile unit is shown in Fig. 1-2. It consists of speaker, microphone, control head, and the communications unit. The latter, designed for trunk-mounting, contains the transmitter, receiver, and power supply. Also considered a mobile unit is the hand-held portable radio station in Fig. 1-3. Self-contained batteries power the transmitter and receiver.

A **base station** is a radio station permanently installed at a fixed location and used primarily for communicating with mobile units. A **fixed station** is also a radio station installed at a fixed point, but one which is used primarily for communicating with other fixed stations. The basic components of a base station are shown in Fig. 1-4. They are the microphone and the communications unit, which contains a built-in speaker. The transmitter, receiver, and power supply are all included in the cabinet of the communications unit. An external antenna is used.

The art of communicating between mobile units, or between a base station and mobile units, is called **mobile radio**. A mobile radio system may be either one-way or two-way.

A **one-way** mobile radio system consists of a base-station transmitter and any number of portable receivers. It may also consist of portable transmitters and one or more base receivers.

A **two-way** mobile radio system may consist of two or more mobile units, each equipped with a transmitter and receiver for two-way communication. Or it may consist of one

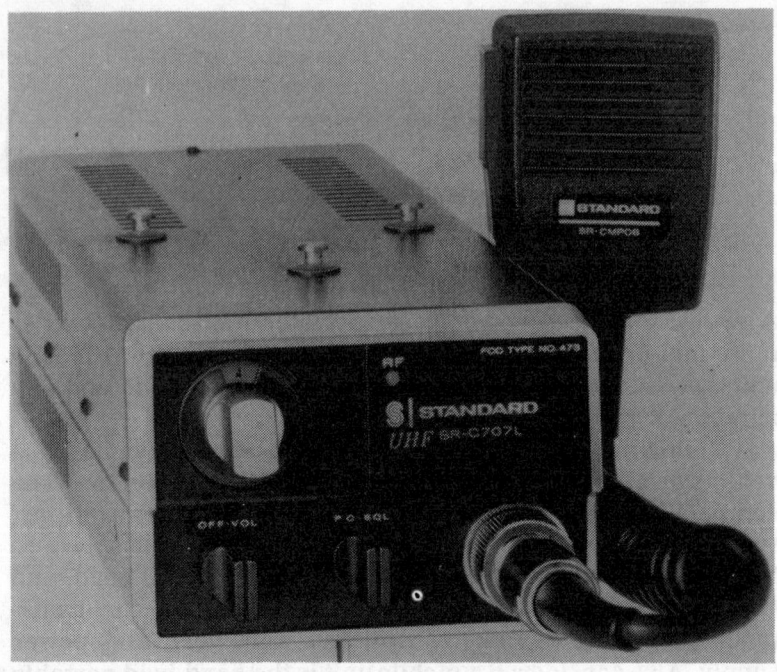

Fig. 1-1. Mobile unit.

or more base stations and one or more mobile units equipped for two-way communication with each other.

A single- or two-frequency system may be employed in mobile radio. In a **single-frequency** system (Fig. 1-5), mobile units and base stations transmit and receive on the same frequency on a **simplex basis**, mobile units and base stations

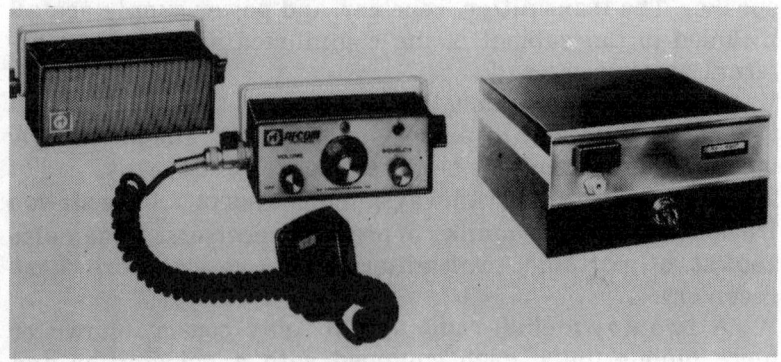

Fig. 1-2. Basic components of a mobile two-way unit.

Fig. 1-3. The portable 2-way radio.

transmit sequentially (one station transmitting and the other listening).

In many **simplex** two-frequency systems, the base stations transmit on one frequency (F1) and receive on another (F2). (See Fig. 1-6.) Mobile units transmit on F2 and receive on F1. They do not communicate **directly** with each other. Communication between mobile units is not ordinarily possible unless they have two-channel receivers that can be switched to receive on both F1 and F2, or unless the transmitters are equipped for transmission on both channels. Communication is sequential. In other words, the mobile unit cannot receive while transmitting.

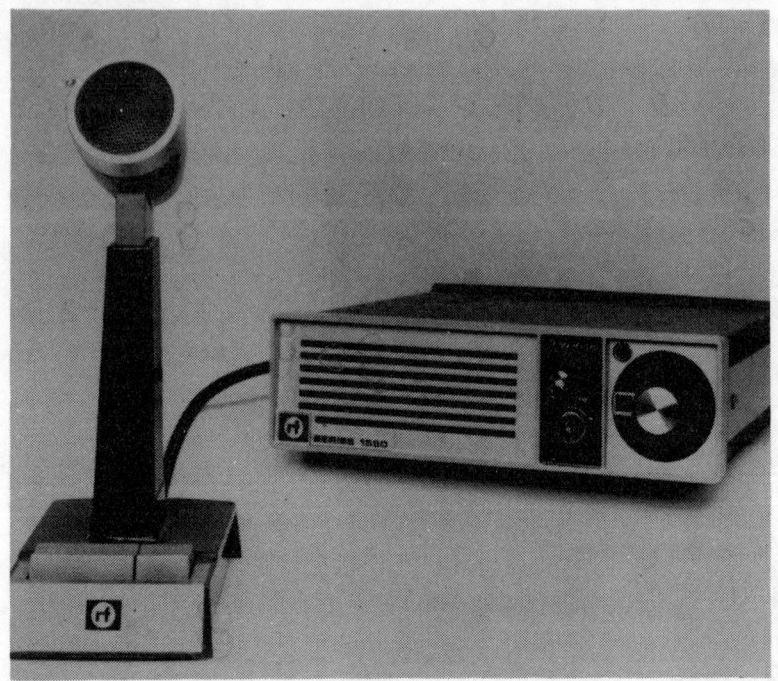

Fig. 1-4. Typical base station installation. With modern solid-state circuitry, station equipment is smaller, more compact than ever before. At one time, the station microphone plugged into a "control head" arrangement similar to those found in mobile units. Today the transceiver itself is no larger than the early control head of a fixed station. The microphone of the typical base station has two switches; the bar at the left is the normal push-to-talk button, which is a momentary-contact device, and the smaller bar at the right is a standard "locking" switch— useful for long transmissions or when the operator has to have free hands during a transmission.

In a **duplex** system, mobile units are equipped with the capability of receiving on F1 while transmitting on F2. This allows "telephone-type" operation. In a **repeater** type of system, the base-station transmitter may be so connected to the base-station receiver that signals from the mobile units on F2 are rebroadcast by the transmitter on F1. Communication between mobile units, therefore, is via the base station and is sequential.

The typical mobile radio system operates on a single-frequency basis, however, in which mobile units and base stations transmit and receive sequentially on F1. In some services, such as taxicab dispatching, direct mobile-to-mobile

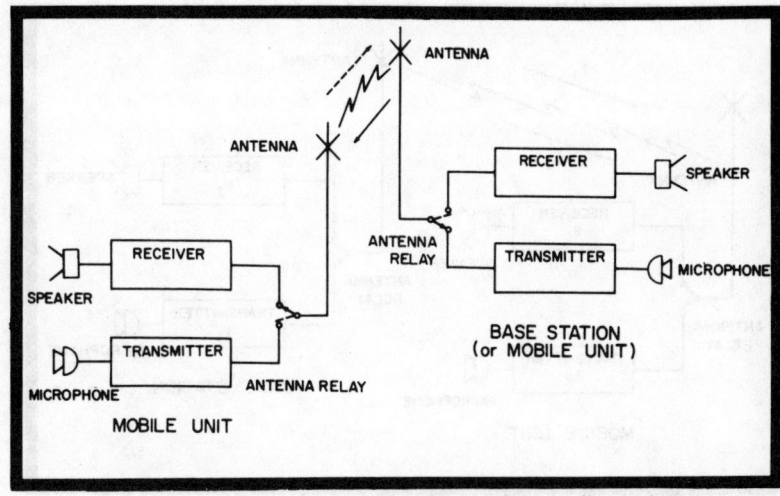

Fig. 1-5. Single-frequency simplex mobile radio system.

communication is not desirable. In fact, it is impossible because the base station transmits on F1 and receives on F2, while the mobile units do just the opposite.

When mobile-to-mobile communication via the base station is required in a two-frequency system, the audio output of the base-station receiver is fed to the audio input of the base-station transmitter, repeater fashion (Fig. 1-7). The base-station transmitter may be turned on automatically or manually.

It is sometimes desirable to limit communications so that mobile units can communicate with the associated base station only, but not with each other (as in a taxicab system). In other systems, mobile-to-mobile communication, whether direct or via the base station, is desirable.

COMMUNICATING RANGE

The base-to-mobile communicating range is considerably longer than the mobile-to-mobile range on a direct basis. This is due to the greater effective elevation of the base-station antenna.

Communicating range in VHF and UHF bands is considered line-of-sight. If the base station antenna is 100 ft above the surrounding terrain and the mobile-unit antenna is 6 ft off the ground, the communicating range is considered to be about 15 miles, based upon the following formula:

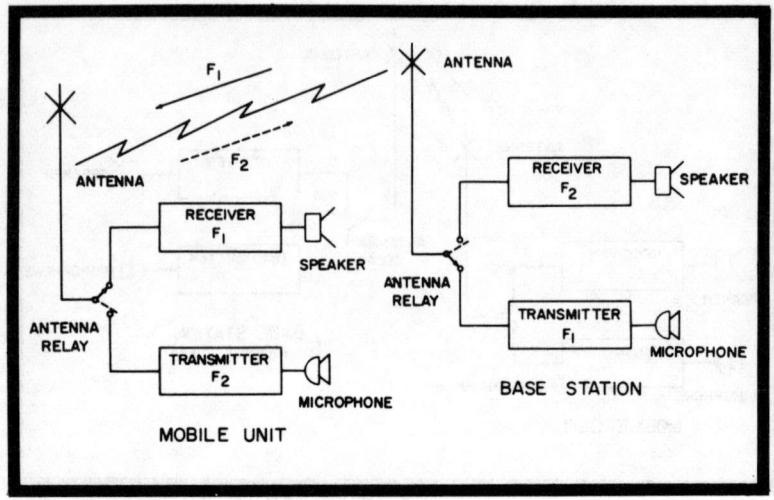

Fig. 1-6. Two-frequency simplex mobile radio system.

Range in miles = $1.23(\sqrt{H2} + \sqrt{H1})$ where,

H1 is the effective elevation of the base-station antenna;
H2 is the effective elevation of the mobile unit.

These calculations are based upon flat terrain. In hilly terrain, where the mobile unit may be elevated, the anticipated range is considerably greater. However, intervening hills and other solid objects, as well as foliage (which has an absorption effect) can greatly reduce the calculated range.

Range also depends upon frequency. When a mobile radio system is operated in the 25-50 MHz band, greater range than that in the 152-174 MHz VHF band can be anticipated. In the 450-512 MHz UHF band, the communicating range is considered to be about two-thirds that in the 152-174 MHz band.

Under typical conditions, the communicating range between a base station and mobile units operating in the 25-50 MHz band varies from 25 to 50 miles. In the 152-174 MHz band, the typical communicating range is 15 to 25 miles. In the 450-512 MHz band, communication with mobile units within a 10- to 15-mile radius of the base station is typical.

EFFECTS OF POWER

Power also affects the communicating range, but not as much as one would think. A 3-watt mobile unit in Ashland,

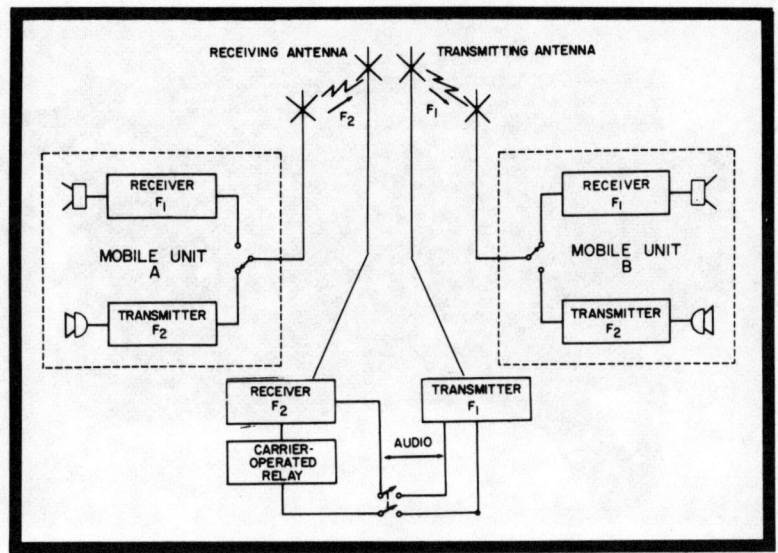

Fig. 1-7. Mobile-to-mobile communication via base station. Relay keys transmitter with each incoming carrier.

Wisconsin, operating in the 152-174 MHz band, has communicated regularly with a base station in Duluth, Minnesota—60 air miles away. However, such ranges are not common. In this situation the base station is on a hilltop, well above surrounding terrain, and part of the transmission path is over Lake Superior. Line-of-sight conditions do not exist, however, because of the earth's curvature.

A 1-watt (output) mobile unit can talk with another mobile unit or base station of the same power rating, within a radius of one to two miles when both antennas are less than 10 ft above the ground. When one antenna is raised, the range increases dramatically.

Many intraplant operations use low-power mobile radio equipment of the type shown in Fig. 1-8. This equipment is effective for only very short ranges. Intraplant systems are often operated on special low-power channels.

For community-wide coverage, however, higher power is needed. To cover a medium-sized city, mobile transmitters rated at 10 to 30 watts output are required in the 152-174 MHz (VHF) band. Mobile radio systems in the 450-512 MHz (UHF) band are also used primarily for community-wide coverage. Their transmitters are rated at 5 watts or more output. For covering larger areas, such as entire counties or even several

Fig. 1-8. Low-power radiotelephone.

small counties, mobile radio systems are often operated in the 25-50 MHz band, using transmitters rated at 30 to 100 watts output.

EXTENDED RANGE SYSTEMS

More than one base station is often used where coverage of an extended area or a long, narrow right-of-way is required. These base stations may be operated independently or they may be controlled from one or more points individually, in a group or all at once.

The base station often uses a transmitter with a power rating identical to that of the associated mobile units, since both must transmit the same distance. However, a more powerful transmitter is sometimes used at the base station. The base station can thus transmit a stronger signal which will carry farther than the signals from the lower-powered mobile units. This technique is advantageous, it is claimed, because the base station is usually in an area where less interference is apt to prevail. The mobile units move in and out of noisy areas. Therefore, the stronger signal is needed from the base station to override any noise at the mobile unit. The effective sensitivity of the base receiver is greater than that of the mobile units, because the lower noise level at the base station permits satisfactory reception of weaker signals.

Some systems use a single high-power base-station transmitter and two or more base-station receivers. One of these receivers may be at the transmitter. The others, known as satellite receivers, are located at distant points. Their outputs are fed over wire lines or radio links to the base-station control point, as illustrated in Fig. 1-9. Thus, the base transmitter blankets the area. The mobile units have to transmit only the short distance to the nearest fixed receiver.

RELAY SYSTEM

The mobile-to-mobile communicating range can be increased by employing an automatic relay or repeater station on a hilltop or with its antenna well above surrounding terrain.

The transmitter is normally off. It is turned on automatically when the receiver picks up a tone-coded signal of suitable intensity from a mobile unit. (A timer shuts off the transmitter should the system remain on after a predetermined period). When mobile unit **A**, for example, wants to talk to mobile unit **B**, the signal from **A** on F2 is intercepted by the relay station, which retransmits the intelligence to mobile unit **B** on F1. In the same manner, the signal from **B** is transmitted to the relay station on F2 and then to **A** on F1.

POINT-TO-POINT RADIO

Two or more base stations can communicate with each other when permitted by FCC Rules. When used exclusively for point-to-point communication, these base stations are called operational fixed stations.

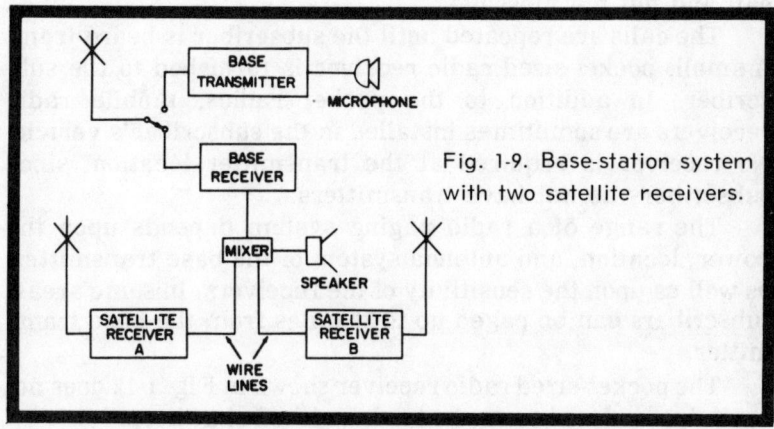

Fig. 1-9. Base-station system with two satellite receivers.

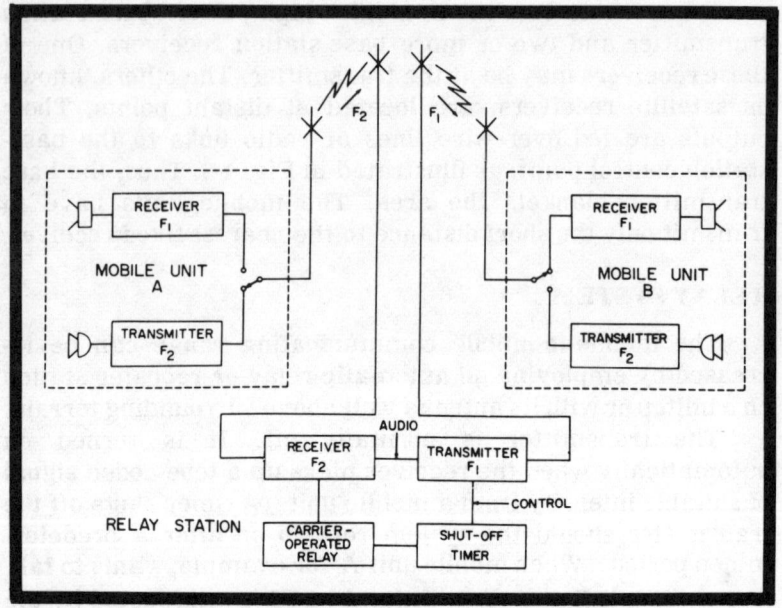

Fig. 1-10. Relay system for mobile-to-mobile communication.

RADIO PAGING

A radio paging system consists of a base transmitter and any number of mobile receivers. A subscriber to a radio paging service is alerted by a beep tone or a radio voice transmission from a central office (see Fig. 1-11), often a telephone answering service. The subscriber then goes to a telephone and calls the office, to acknowledge receipt of the call and get the message.

The calls are repeated until the subscriber is heard from. A small, pocket-sized radio receiver is furnished to the subscriber. In addition to the pocket radios, mobile radio receivers are sometimes installed in the subscriber's vehicle. No receiver is required at the transmitter location, since subscribers do not have transmitters.

The range of a radio paging system depends upon the power, location, and antenna system of the base transmitter, as well as upon the sensitivity of the receivers. In some areas, subscribers can be paged up to 50 miles from the base transmitter.

The pocket-sized radio receiver shown in Fig. 1-12 does not reproduce voice signals; instead, it gives out a "beep."

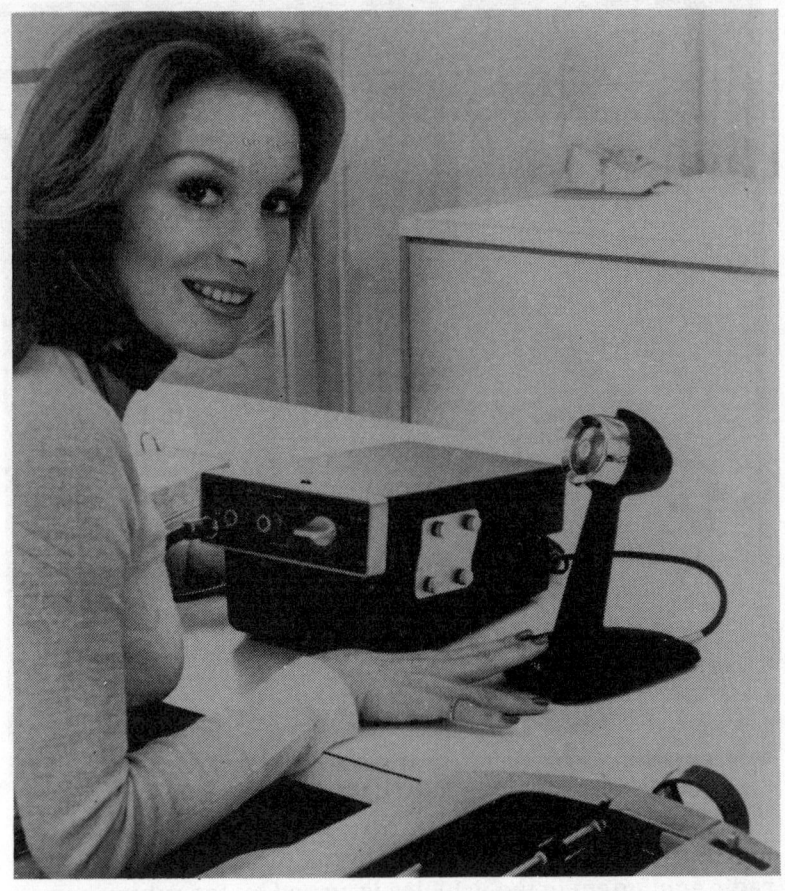

Fig. 1-11. Base station serves as paging system.

The receiver is always on. When the base-station operator wants to signal a certain subscriber, she transmits a coded tone signal to which only that subscriber's receiver will respond. The receiver ignores all signals except the one whose code matches the receiver decoder actuating the alarm. Now the subscriber no longer has to listen frequently to determine whether he has a call.

RADIO DISPATCHING SERVICES

In addition to private communications systems, radio dispatching services also use mobile radio. These Radio Common Carriers (RCC) operate base stations for com-

Fig. 1-12. Selective "beep" receiver that can be easily concealed by strapping it ot the user's leg.

municating with the mobile units of their subscribers. The radio equipment in the vehicles is owned by the subscribers or leased to them by the operator of the radio dispatching service.

These independent common carriers provide dispatching service for a monthly fee or on a per-call basis. In some instances the base station relays messages to subscriber vechicles. Some other operators, however, provide their subscribers' offices with remote-control units connected by wire lines to the base station. This enables the subscribers to talk directly to the drivers of their radio-equipped vehicles.

Some telephone companies also provide radio paging, radio dispatching, and one-way signaling services. The latter consists of actuating by radio a visual or audible signal in a subscriber's vehicle. Each vehicle responds to its own code signal, which is selectively generated at the central office.

MOBILE TELEPHONE SERVICE

Mobile telephone services use essentially the same equipment that private mobile radio systems do, except for the addition of a selective ringing decoder, and sometimes a dial or a Touch-Tone encoder. In a typical mobile installation, a speaker is used. It is kept turned on to enable occupants of the vehicle to intercept all conversations transmitted on the channel to which the radio equipment is tuned. In regular telephone service this practice would be unthinkable, because subscribers demand privacy.

The subscriber listens with a conventional telephone handset instead of a speaker. Ordinarily, nothing is heard when the handset is on the hook. To ring a specific vehicle, the central office operator sends a coded tone signal. This signal is intercepted by all mobile units within range whose receivers are tuned to the central-office transmitter frequency. A decoder is actuated in all vehicles; but only the decoder whose code was transmitted responds. It rings a bell or buzzer momentarily, as well as turning on a call-indicator lamp. The lamp remains lit until the call is answered.

None of the other mobile telephone subscribers are signaled; in fact, they are unaware that the "party-line" telephone channel they share is busy. They can, however, listen in with the telephone handset.

TWO-WAY DIALING

Dial and Touch-Tone telephone service is being extended to vehicles in many areas. A dial control head (Fig. 1-13) or Touch-Tone dialer is provided with a mobile telephone which enables a subscriber to dial calls directly without the aid oof an operator. When the handset is lifted from its cradle, coded tone pulses are automatically transmittted. These pulses identify the mobile unit to the automatic central-office equipment. The subscriber dials the desired number. When the called party answers, ticketing and billing machines are actuated. As soon as the calling mobile telephone is hung up, these machines record the number of the calling mobile telephone and the number of message units or amount of toll charges involved.

Thus, it is possible to dial even long-distance calls directly from a mobile telephone. Similarly, mobile telephones can be dialed directly from regular telephones.

Fig. 1-13. A two-way dialing system.

AM vs FM

Although both AM (amplitude modulation) and FM (frequency modulation) are employed in mobile radio systems, FM is by far the more popular. A system may employ AM or FM, but not both, since they are not compatible.

FM offers certain advantages, the most significant being a reduction of noise. However, noise becomes less of a problem as the operating frequency increases. In the 450-512 MHz band, for example, there is little or no noticeable difference between AM and FM as far as noise is concerned. As far as distance is concerned, tests indicate that for a given carrier power, FM is slightly superior. This is attributable to the fact that AM spends much of its power on the carrier, which bears none of the transmitted intelligence.

Trans-mitters

Both FM and AM transmitters are used in the land mobile radio services. Most transmitters of modern manufacture employ solid-state circuitry throughout, though some employ hybrid circuitry (both tubes and transistors). Since there are many tube-type transmitters in service which require repair and adjustment, tube circuits will be discussed first.

TUBE-TYPE TRANSMITTERS

A simplified block diagram of an FM transmitter is given in Fig. 2-1. The carrier frequency signal, generated by the

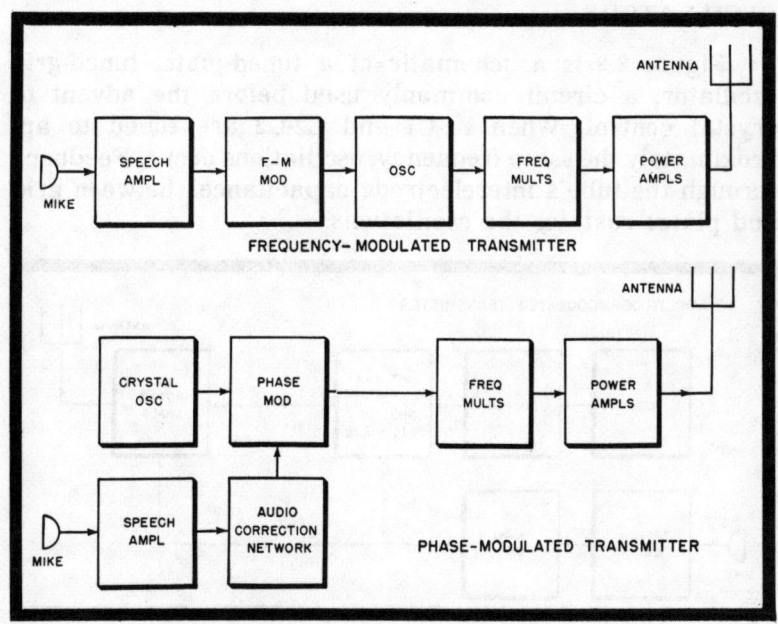

Fig. 2-1. Block diagrams of FM transmitters.

oscillator, is fed through a phase modulator to a string of frequency multipliers and then directly or through a driver amplifier to the rf power amplifier.

The phase modulator converts the unmodulated signal from the oscillator into an FM signal. Interestingly, the signal is not actually FM at all; rather, it is **phase-modulated**, which does differ from true FM in subtle ways. Since the two are indiscernible as far as the receiver is concerned, the difference is academic rather than pragmatic. The frequency of this signal is multiplied to the desired channel frequency. For example, if the oscillator operates at 14 MHz and this frequency is multiplied 12 times, the transmitter output frequency will be 168 MHz.

As can be seen in Fig. 2-2, modulation is applied to the rf power amplifier stage in a typical AM transmitter. The oscillator frequency is usually multiplied as in an FM transmitter, but remains unmodulated until it reaches the rf power amplifier.

In both Figs. 2-1 and 2-2, the harmonic filter attenuates spurious emissions at frequencies higher than the radiated carrier frequency.

OSCILLATORS

Figure 2-3 is a schematic of a tuned-plate, tuned-grid oscillator, a circuit commonly used before the advent of crystal control. When L1-C1 and L2-C2 are tuned to approximately the same frequency, oscillations occur. Feedback through the tube's interelectrode capacitance (between grid and plate) sustains the oscillations.

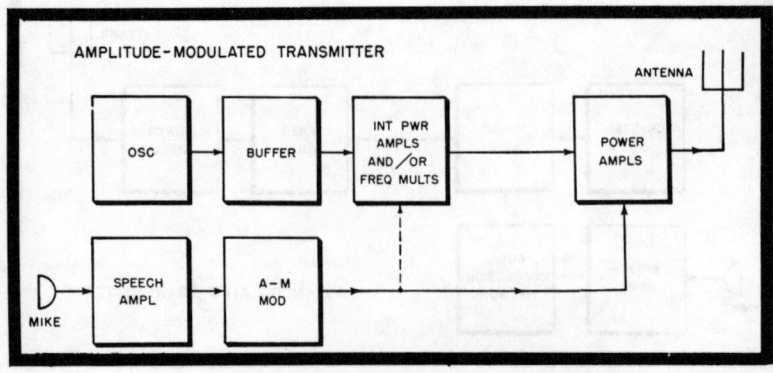

Fig. 2-2. AM transmitter block diagram.

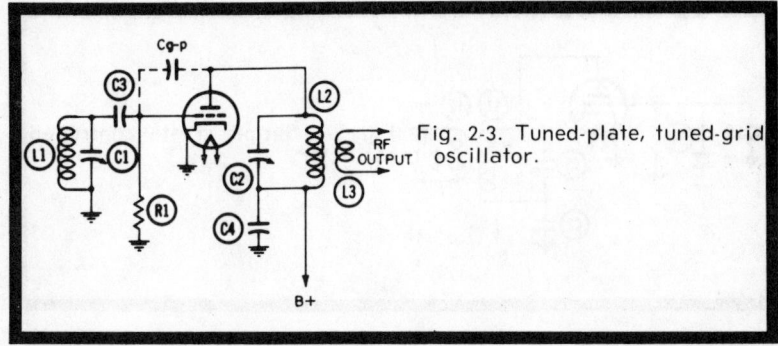

Fig. 2-3. Tuned-plate, tuned-grid oscillator.

When a crystal is substituted for L1-C1, the circuit will oscillate when L2-C2 is tuned to a frequency slightly higher than the one at which the crystal is resonant. The crystal appears as a tuned circuit at its resonant frequency. It remains constant at this frequency only, not varying except when temperature changes distort it physically.

A crystal provides adequate frequency stability for most applications. When greater stability is required, the crystal is enclosed in an oven, the temperature of which is held constant by a thermostat.

The frequency of a crystal-controlled oscillator can be changed slightly by adding a capacitor (Fig. 2-4) across the crystal. Increasing the capacitance lowers the frequency; decreasing it raises the frequency.

Crystals are ordinarily ground to resonate at a lower frequency than the operating frequency of the transmitter. The frequency is increased by means of multiplier stages. For example, when a crystal is ground to resonate at 6.75 MHz and the operating frequency is 27 MHz, the crystal frequency must be quadrupled. This can be done by using two doubler stages after the crystal oscillator stage. The first doubler changes the frequency to 13.5 MHz, and the second, to 27 MHz. A frequency-multiplier stage is an amplifier whose input is tuned to the incoming frequency and whose output is tuned to the desired output frequency, a multiple of the input frequency. The amplifier is operated class C so that nonlinearity will result. The incoming frequency and its harmonics appear in the output.

In most commercial transmitters, the crystal frequency must be multiplied many times before the desired output frequency can be obtained. The amount of multiplication can

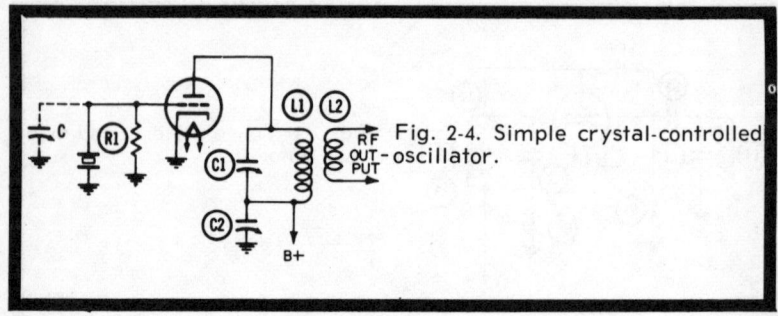

Fig. 2-4. Simple crystal-controlled oscillator.

be reduced, however, by using the **overtone** operation of the crystal. When harmonic operation is employed, the crystal vibrates at its fundamental frequency. In overtone operation, the crystal oscillates at one of its overtones, rather than at the fundamental frequency to which it is cut.

Figure 2-5 shows the circuit of a tri-tet oscillator. L1-C1 is tuned to a frequency higher than that of the crystal, and L2-C2 is tuned to a harmonic.

In Fig. 2-6, the crystal acts as a series-resonant circuit at its fundamental or at an overtone frequency, depending upon the crystal and the tuning of L1-C1. The tuned circuit, L1-C1, is tuned to the desired overtone of the crystal.

For operation on two frequencies, a second crystal may be connected in place of the first crystal by a switch-controlled relay, as shown in Fig. 2-7. The two frequencies must be fairly close together so that optimum tuning of the oscillator circuits and succeeding stages can be obtained for both channels. Obviously, it is impractical to retune these circuits while switching from one channel to another.

Many transmitters, however, employ a separate oscillator for each channel, with means for choosing any one of them. Figure 2-8 shows an oscillator circuit used for dual-channel operation.

An electron-coupled oscillator circuit is used. When switch S1 is set to position 1, only V1 is activated. When S1 is set to position 2, V1 is disabled and V2 (operating on a different frequency) becomes operative. For 25-54 MHz operation, the crystal frequency is multiplied twelve times in the succeeding stages of the transmitter.

For single-channel operation, the circuitry of V2 is omitted, and the cathode circuit of V1 is grounded instead of being routed through the switch (in the control unit).

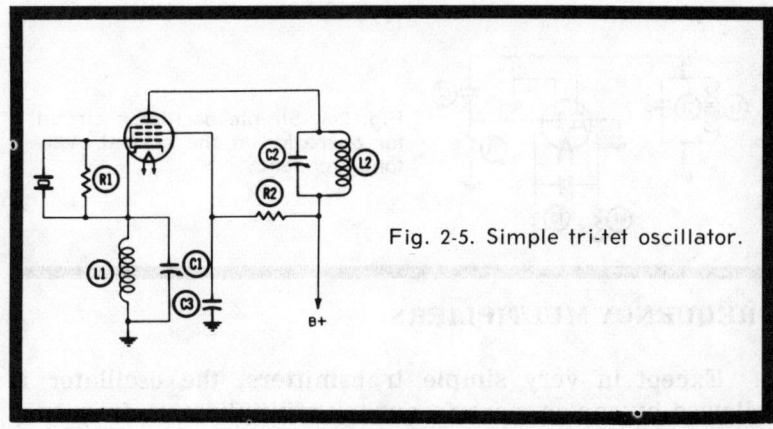

Fig. 2-5. Simple tri-tet oscillator.

Figure 2-9 shows the oscillator circuit of a 450-512 MHz transmitter. The crystal frequency, multiplied 36 times in the succeeding stages, can be varied slightly by adjustment of C1 (shunted across crystal). C5 is pretuned at the factory, but may require field adjustment after a new oscillator tube is installed.

For two-frequency operation, a second, identical oscillator is used. It is connected to the first oscillator and to the channel selector, as shown in Fig. 2-8.

PHASE MODULATOR

In a tube-type FM transmitter, the oscillator output is fed to the phase modulator, which converts the basic signal into an FM signal. An example of a phase modulator circuit is given in Fig. 2-10. The basic signal is fed to the grid of the triode through C1 and also to the plate through C2. The signal applied to the grid is shifted in phase by 180 degrees. Therefore, there are two rf signals flowing through plate load L.

The audio modulating signal is also fed to the grid through R1. When an audio signal is applied, the plate current is modulated, and those causing a variation in the phase of the basic signal that corresponds with the applied audio.

The amount of deviation is controlled with R2 across which a limited audio signal is applied. The amplitude of the signal must be limited so that excessive FM deviation will not result. The frequency range of the audio signal is also limited to the voice band by a rolloff filter to minimize generation of unwanted sidebands.

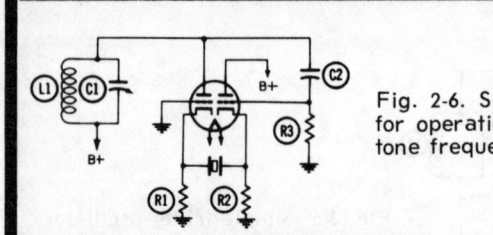

Fig. 2-6. Simple oscillator circuit for operation at the crystal overtone frequency.

FREQUENCY MULTIPLIERS

Except in very simple transmitters, the oscillator is followed by one or more frequency multipliers. A frequency multiplier is an amplifier stage biased to distort as well as amplify the signal. The distortion is used to advantage. If no distortion were present, the output would be a clean replica of the input, both of the same frequency.

Because of the distortion, the output signal contains the input frequency as well as harmonics. By putting a tuned circuit in the output circuit, it is possible to derive the desired harmonic while suppressing the fundamental (input frequency) and the unwanted harmonics.

Figure 2-11 shows a typical frequency multiplier. The grid leak, R2, is of much higher value than required for normal operation of the stage as an amplifier. Since the tube is thus biased for cutoff, it conducts during the positive half of the input cycle only, which causes the output to be rich in harmonics. The desired one is captured by appropriate tuning of C6-L2.

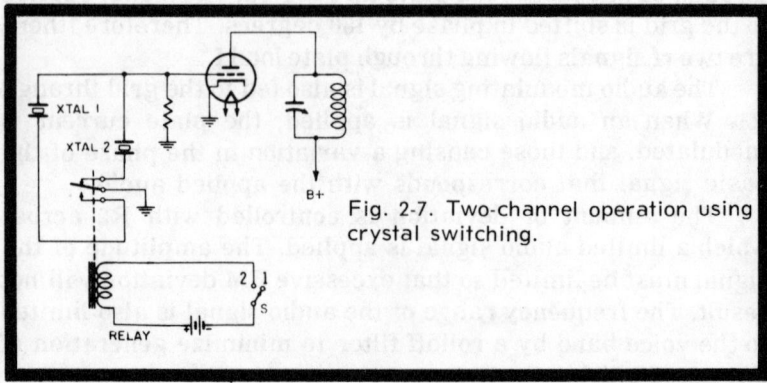

Fig. 2-7. Two-channel operation using crystal switching.

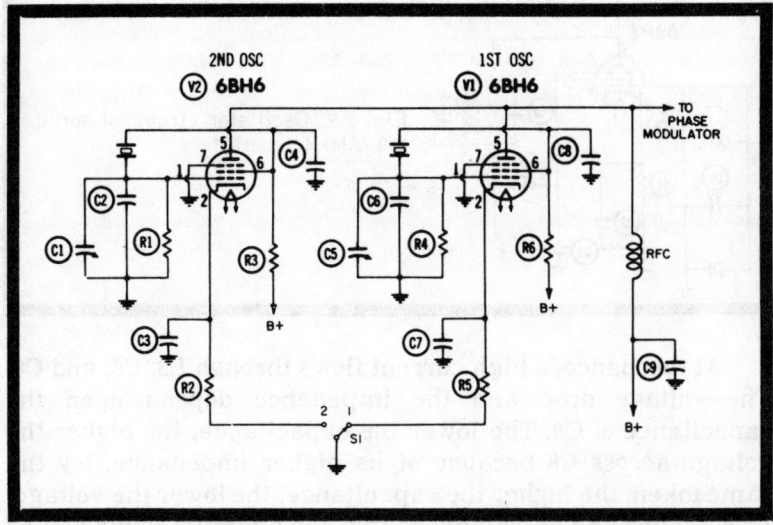

Fig. 2-8. Two oscillators, switch-operated, for two-channel operation.

The test point (TP) at the junction of R2-R3 may be available at a pin jack or metering socket. Grid current is measured between the test point and ground with a dc voltmeter or microammeter. L1 and C1, which tune the plate circuit of the preceding stage to the input frequency, are adjusted for maximum indication at the test point.

Various types of frequency multipliers are in use. Push-pull stages are utilized where even harmonics are to be suppressed; single-ended stages can produce even and odd harmonics; and push-push stages are found where even harmonics are to be favored.

RF POWER AMPLIFIERS

In some transmitters the final rf power amplifier also acts as a frequency multiplier. However, this is often avoided to prevent spurious radiation of unwanted harmonics.

Figure 2-12 shows the rf amplifier circuit of a 25-50 MHz band transmitter. L1-C1 and L3-C6 are tuned to the operating frequency. Although the output circuit looks more complex because of refinements, it is basically a pi-type circuit. C6 tunes L3 to resonance at the operating frequency, while C8 controls antenna loading.

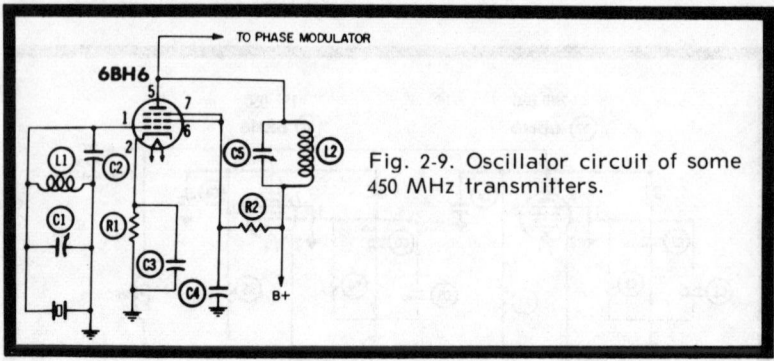

Fig. 2-9. Oscillator circuit of some 450 MHz transmitters.

At resonance, a high current flows through L3, C6, and C8. The voltage drop and the impedance depend upon the capacitance of C8. The lower the capacitance, the higher the voltage across C8 because of its higher impedance. By the same token, the higher the capacitance, the lower the voltage. L3 is tapped and adjustable so that the optimum value can be obtained for the operating frequency.

Two tubes are often paralleled in the final amplifier stage of a 25-50 MHz transmitter to increase the power output. In Fig. 2-13, two 6146 tubes are paralleled. L3 is shunted by R8 in series with the plate of V1; L4 is shunted by R9 in series with the plate of V2; R5 is in series with the grid of V1; and R6 is in series with the grid of V2. Together they suppress parasitic oscillations, which might otherwise occur within this stage.

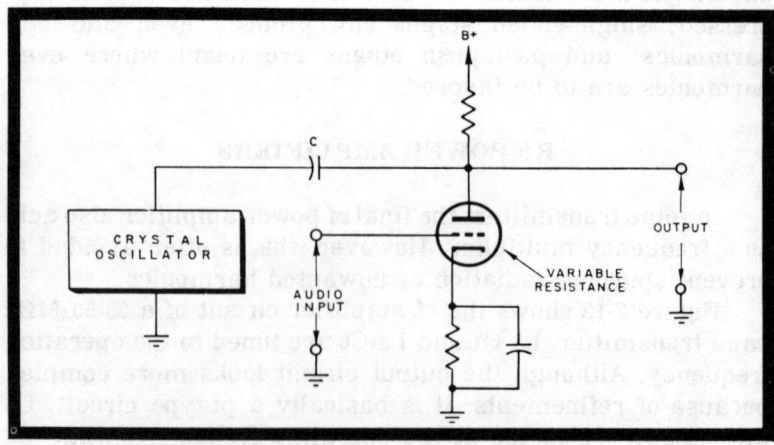

Fig. 2-10. Phase modulator circuit.

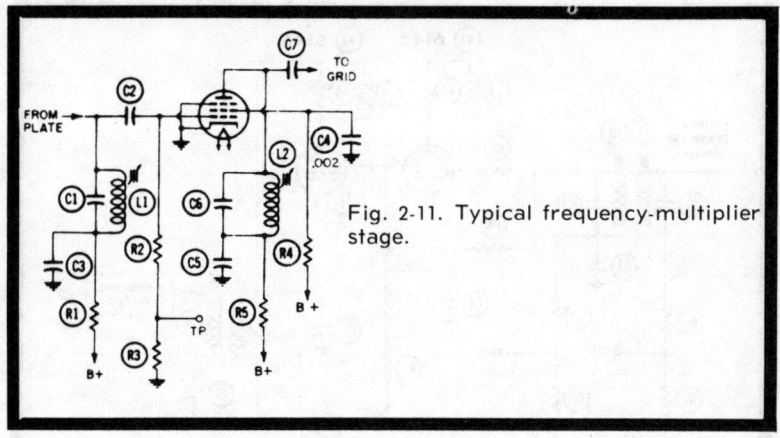

Fig. 2-11. Typical frequency-multiplier stage.

L1-C1, L2-C2, and L5-C5 are tuned to the operating frequency. Plate current for the driver stage is measured at TP1, and grid current for the power amplifier is measured at TP2. C7 is used to adjust antenna loading. A low-pass harmonic filter between the rf amplifier and the antenna suppresses the transmission of harmonics.

A single 6146 tube is employed in the rf amplifier circuit of Fig. 2-14. The output power depends upon the applied plate voltage, which can range from 350 to 400 volts. C2-L2, C3-L3, and C7-L4 (series-resonant circuits) are tuned to the

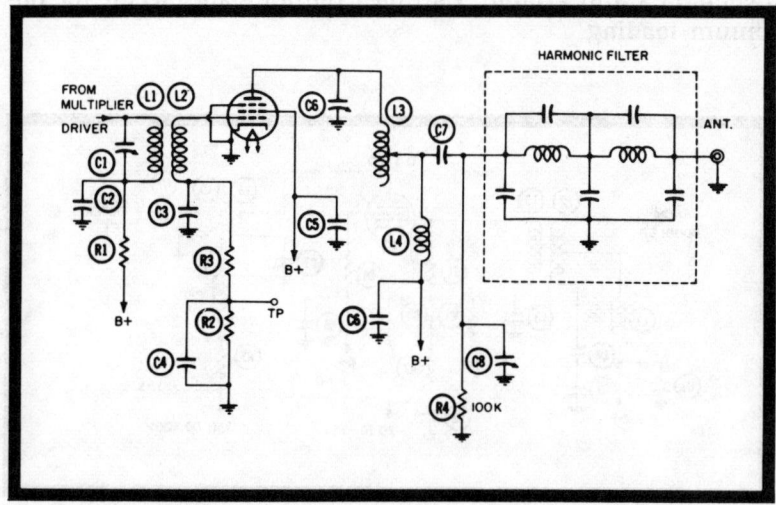

Fig. 2-12. Typical power amplifier in 25-50 MHz band transmitter.

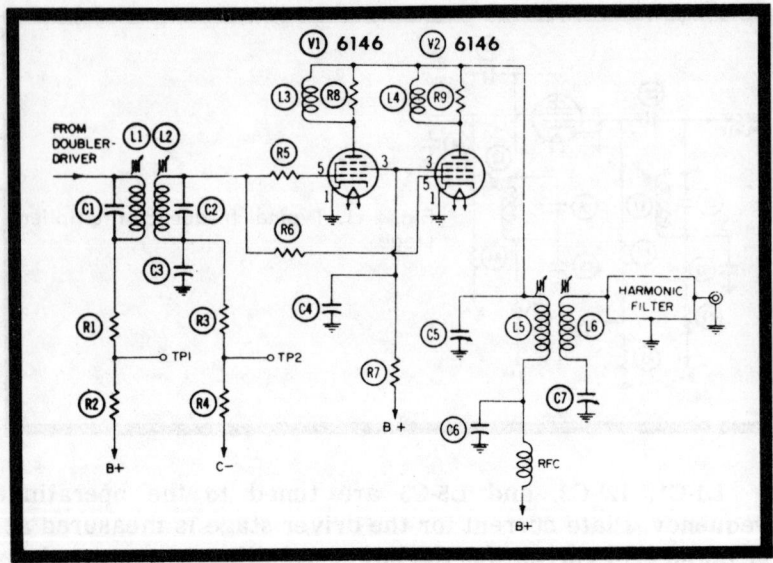

Fig. 2-13. Two 6146 tubes are paralleled to provide a higher power output.

operating frequency. Grid current, monitored at TP1, is measured to determine optimum tuning of C2-L2 and C3-L3. The plate current is determined by measuring the drop between TP2 and TP3, and the B-plus voltage is measured between TP3 and ground. C9 tunes the antenna circuit for optimum loading.

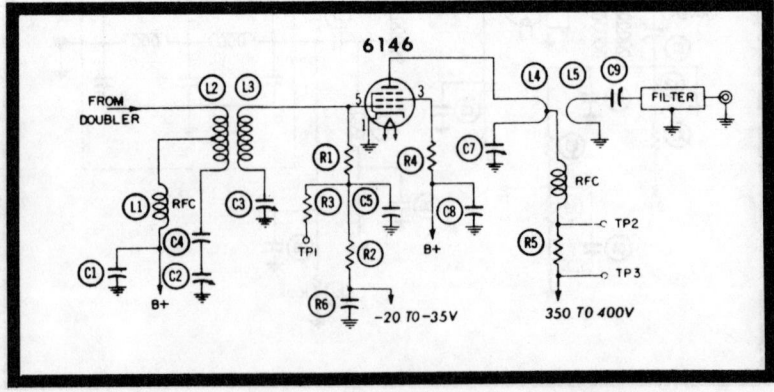

Fig. 2-14. Single-ended power amplifier for the 152-174 MHz band.

Figure 2-15 shows the circuit of a push-pull UHF amplifier. Note that the tuned circuits consist of lines, the resonant points of which are adjusted by capacitors. The input, fed inductively from the preceding stage, is tuned by C1; the output is tuned by C2; antenna loading is adjusted by C3; and the antenna circuit is tuned by C4.

Grid-leak bias is developed across R1 and R2 for each half of the dual tube. In addition, the amount of bias—and hence, the grid drive—can be adjusted with R3. Grid current can be metered between TP1 and ground. Plate current for the power amplifier is measured across TP2 and TP3, and B-plus is measured between TP2 and ground.

BOOSTER AMPLIFIERS

Nearly all mobile transmitters and most low and medium power base transmitters have a self-contained rf power amplifier. A booster power amplifier may be added at base stations when higher power is required. Figure 2-16 is a schematic of a 250-watt amplifier which may be driven by a lower-powered transmitter.

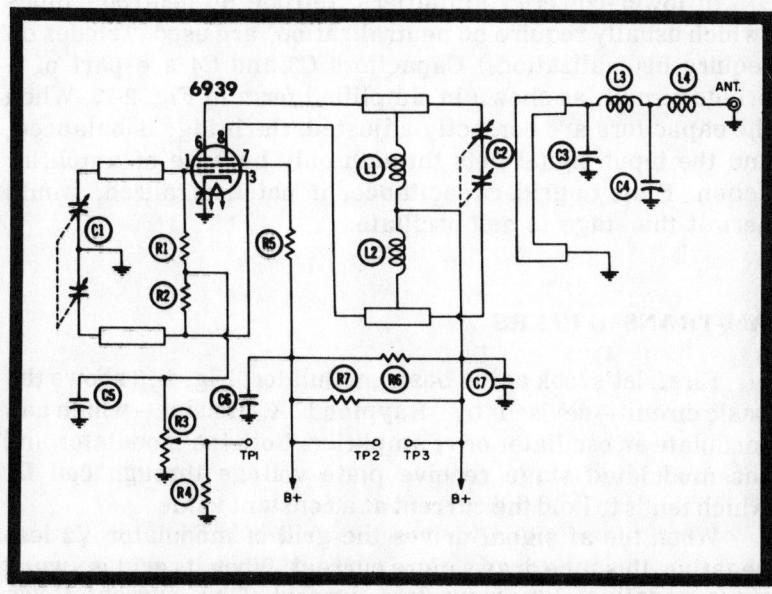

Fig. 2-15. The push-pull amplifier in a 450-470 MHz band transmitter.

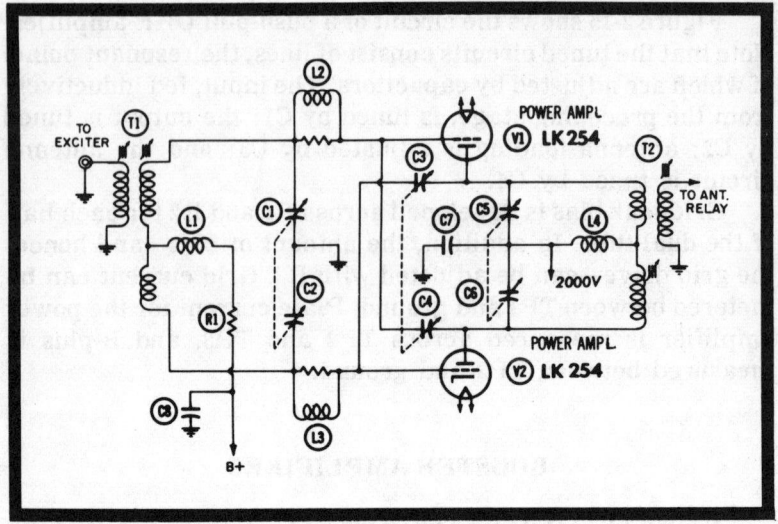

Fig. 2-16. A typical 250-watt booster amplifier.

Input is applied through a coaxial cable which drives the pair of LK254 tubes connected in push-pull. Since 2000 volts dc is required as the plate voltage, a separate power supply is employed.

In lower-powered amplifiers, tetrode or pentrode tubes (which usually require no neutralization) are used. Triodes do require neutralization.) Capacitors C3 and C4 are part of a bridge circuit, as shown in simplified form in Fig. 2-17. When the capacitors are correctly adjusted, the bridge is balanced, and the input signal gets through only because of amplifier action. Plate-to-grid capacitance, if not neutralized, would permit the stage to self-oscillate.

AM-TRANSMITTERS

First, let's look at the basic modulator; Fig. 2-18 shows the basic circuit—devised by Raymond A. Heising—which can modulate an oscillator or rf amplifier. Both the modulator and the modulated stage receive plate voltage through coil L1 which tends to hold the current at a constant value.

When the af signal drives the grid of modulator V2 less negative, this tube draws more current. When its grid is swung more negative, V2 draws less current. This current flows

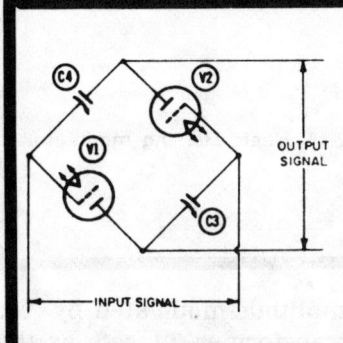

Fig. 2-17. Neutralizing capacitors and tubes of Fig. 2-16 rearranged to show bridge network.

through the reactor. The varying current causes the reactor to build up across it a voltage in series with the dc plate voltage.

Without modulation, the plate current of V1 remains constant. When modulated, it varies because its plate voltage is being modulated (the voltage developed across the reactor alternately adds to and subtracts from the dc plate voltage).

Fig. 2-19 is a simplification of a commercial modulator system. Here the primary of transformer T1 acts as an autotransformer. When the plate current of V2 varies with modulation, an ac voltage is developed between points X and Y. The same ac voltage is developed between points Y and Z because of transformer action. The ac voltage between points Y and Z is added to and subtracted from the dc plate and screen voltages of V1, thus varying rf output.

Fig. 2-20 shows an example of an AM transmitter circuit. It can be used in any land mobile service in the 25-50 MHz band. The AM transmitter has three stages (V1, V2, and V3). V1 is the crystal oscillator, V2 is a frequency doubler and V3 is an rf power amplifier and doubler.

The values of all capacitors except C5, C12, and C14 are shown in Fig. 2-20. The values of the latter depend upon the exact operating frequency. Test points TP1, TP2, TP3, and TP4 actually run to a socket into which a special test meter is connected when the transmitter is being tuned. TP1 provides an indication of oscillator tuning, which is controlled by adjusting the slug of L1. At TP2, the adjustment of L1 indicates the amount of drive to V2. At TP3, the amount of grid drive to V3 is measured when L3 is adjusted. At TP4, a microammeter is connected for measuring the plate current to V3 when L5 is tuned for minimum current and C15 for antenna loading.

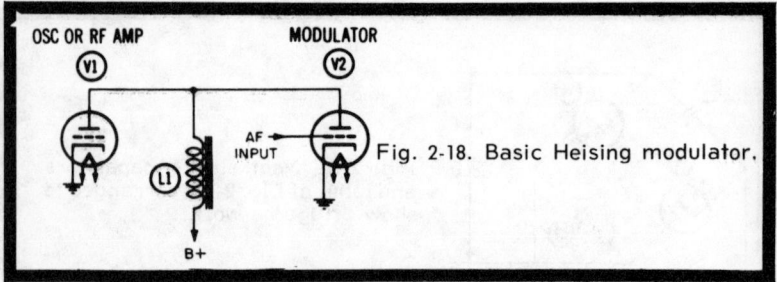

Fig. 2-18. Basic Heising modulator.

The final amplifier, V3, is amplitude-modulated by V4. The primary of receiver output transformer T1 acts as the reactor in a Heising modulator circuit. R16 lowers the plate voltage to V3, so that the audio voltage at V4 will be greater than the dc plate voltage on V3 to allow a higher percentage of modulation.

V5, one triode section of a 12AX7 tube, serves as the speech amplifier when transmitting, as well as the af voltage amplifier when receiving. When the unit is set for receiving, this tube is controlled by the squelch circuit (not shown). In Fig. 2-20, note the clever way of hooking in the carbon microphone. Its excitation voltage is obtained from the junction of R19 and R20, through which the cathode current of V4 flows. The speech amplifier receives its input signal from the common point of R20 and R21, where the current flow is varied by the microphone current.

The simple basic Heising circuit in Fig. 2-18 is not used in a modern high-powered AM transmitter. Instead, the circuit is similar to the one in Fig. 2-21. V1 and V2 are the modulator tubes (shown here in a push-pull circuit). Plate current to V3 flows through modulation coil L1.

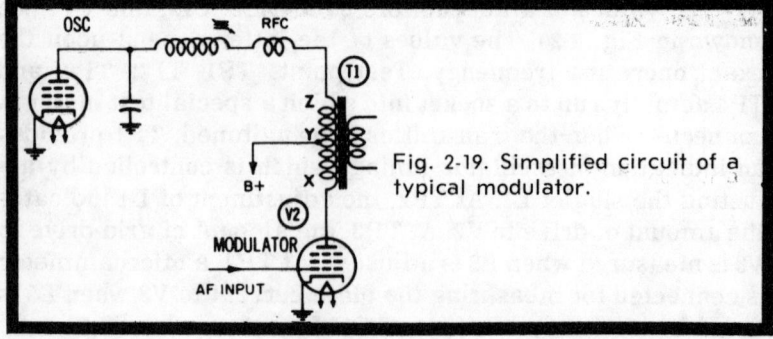

Fig. 2-19. Simplified circuit of a typical modulator.

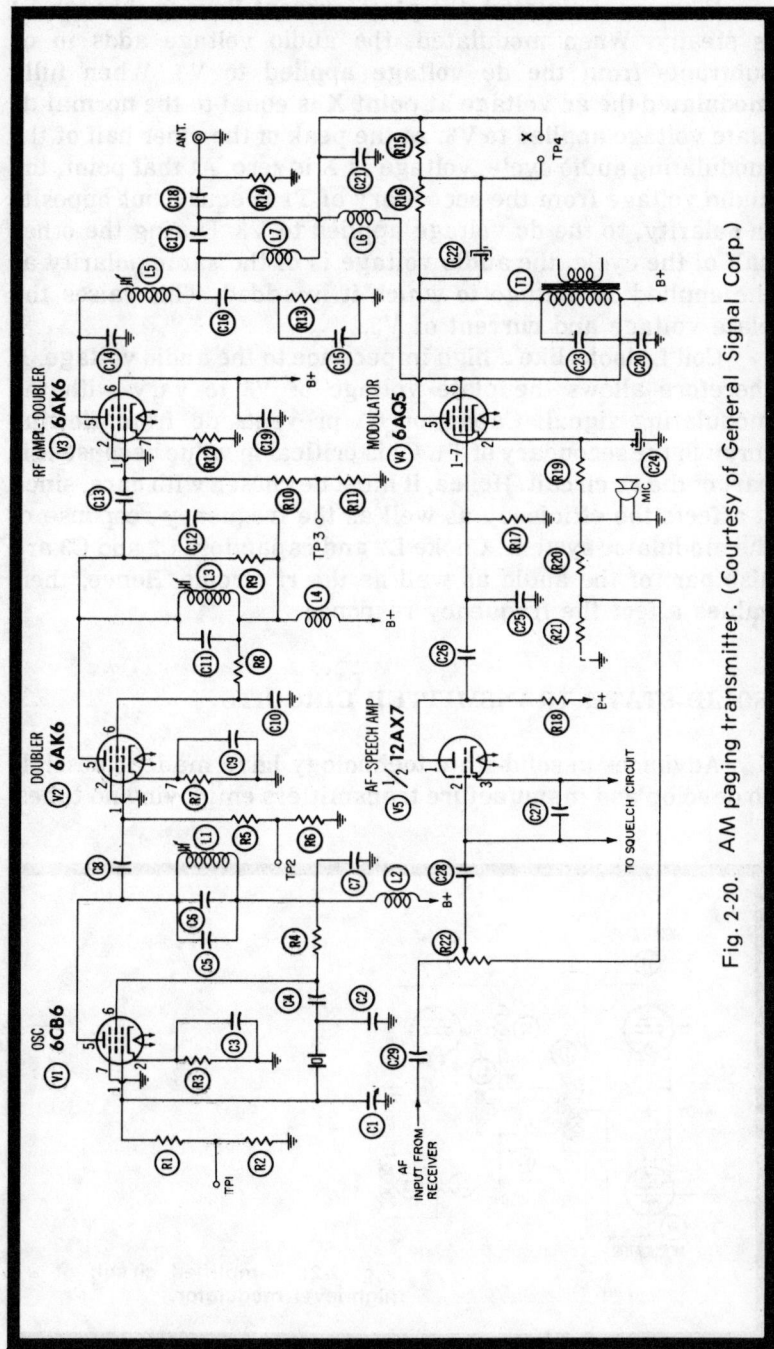

Fig. 2-20. AM paging transmitter. (Courtesy of General Signal Corp.)

When unmodulated, the plate current flowing through L1 is steady. When modulated, the audio voltage adds to or subtracts from the dc voltage applied to V3. When fully modulated the ac voltage at point X is equal to the normal dc plate voltage applied to V3. At the peak of the other half of the modulating audio cycle, voltage at X is zero. At that point, the audio voltage from the secondary of T1 is equal, but opposite in polarity, to the dc voltage applied to V3. During the other half of the cycle, the audio voltage is of the same polarity as the applied dc voltage to which it is added. This raises the plate voltage and current of V3.

Coil L1 looks like a high impedance to the audio voltage. It therefore allows the plate voltage of V3 to vary with the modulating signal. Capacitor C1 prevents dc from flowing through the secondary of T1. C1 is critical in value because it is part of the ac circuit. Hence, it must be chosen with care, since it affects the efficiency as well as the frequency response of the modulator system. Choke L2 and capacitors C2 and C3 are also part of the audio as well as the rf circuit. Hence, their values affect the frequency response.

SOLID-STATE TRANSMITTER CIRCUITS

Advances in solid-state technology have made it possible to develop and manufacture transmitters employing no tubes,

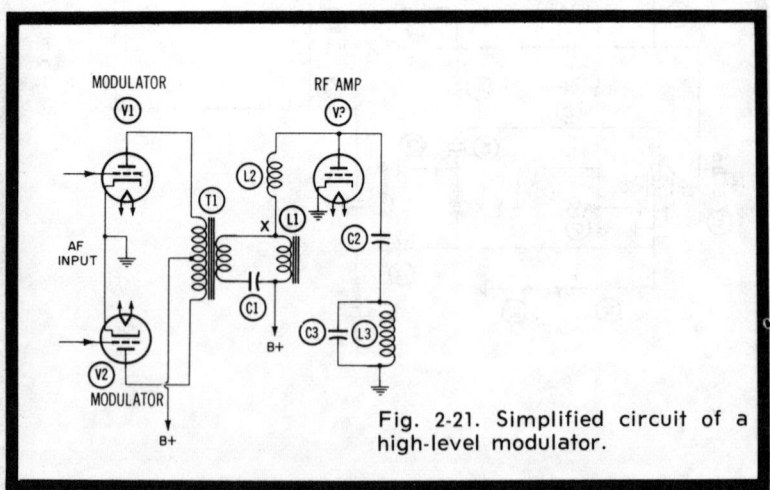

Fig. 2-21. Simplified circuit of a high-level modulator.

not even in the output rf amplifier stage. Most of the circuits described here are applicable to both hybrid and fully solid-state transmitters.

Oscillators

An FM transmitter employs at least one crystal-controlled oscillator. A multichannel transmitter may employ a single oscillator and utilize a switch for selecting the crystal required for a particular channel. Many transmitters employ a separate oscillator for each channel. These oscillators may be permanently wired into the transmitter or they may be plug-in modules.

Figure 2-22 is an example of a transmitter oscillator circuit which employs two transistors. Q1 functions as the oscillator and Q2 as a buffer which isolates the oscillator from the other circuits. The frequency of the oscillator is determined by crystal Y and the inductances and capacitances of the associated circuitry. The oscillator frequency can be varied over a narrow range by adjusting C2.

The oscillator signal is fed from the emitter of Q1 through R4 to the base of Q2. The signal from the collector of Q2 is fed through C6 to a tap on L which can be tuned without affecting

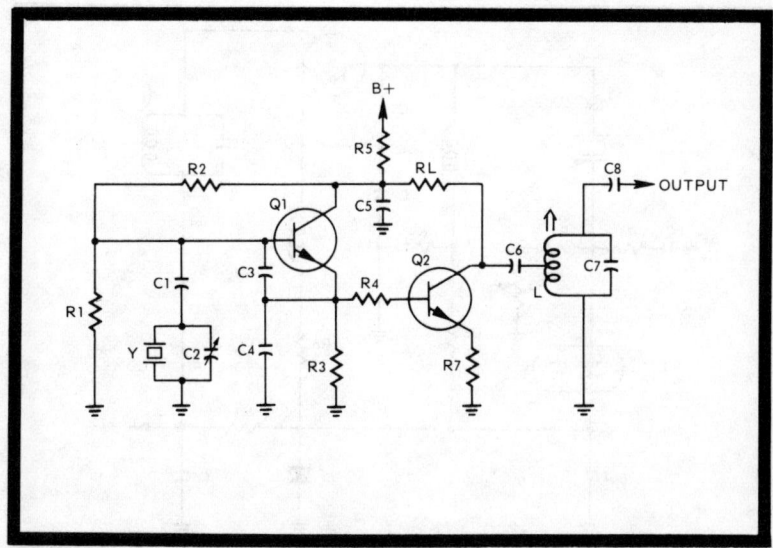

Fig. 2-22. Two-transistor oscillator circuit.

the oscillator frequency. Q1 is connected in the common-collector configuration, whereas Q2 operates as a common-emitter amplifier.

Modulated Oscillator

In most FM transmitters, phase modulation is introduced between the oscillator and the first frequency multiplier. However, as shown in Fig. 2-23, the oscillator can be frequency-modulated by using a varactor. The oscillator frequency is determined by crystal Y and the series capacitance of varactor. The varactor is reverse-biased by dc voltage, and regulated by the zener diode. The oscillator frequency can be trimmed by adjusting R3, which sets the level of normal bias on the varactor.

The modulating signal is fed to the junction of Y and the zener through C1 and R1 and alternately bucks and boosts the bias on the varactor, causing the oscillator frequency to deviate at the af rate. The effective capacitance of the varactor is determined by the bias across it.

The output tank circuit, C5-L3, can be tuned to a harmonic of the crystal frequency. This circuit, therefore, can function as an oscillator, frequency modulator, and frequency multiplier.

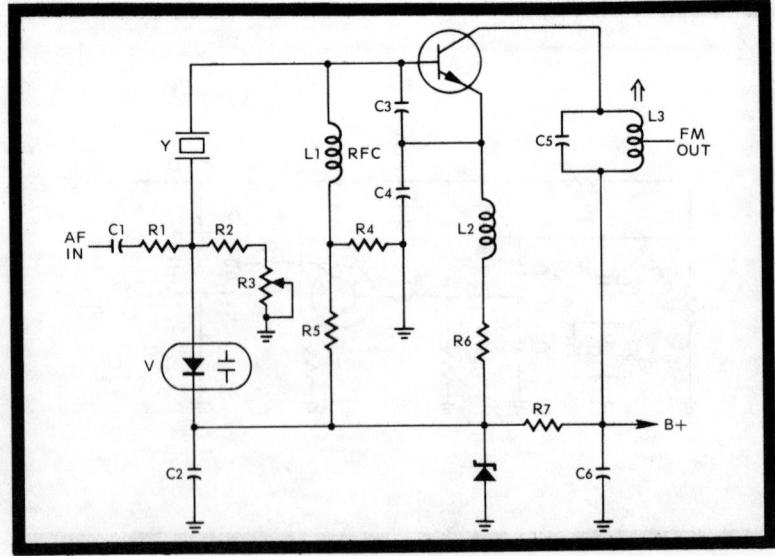

Fig. 2-23. Using a varactor to frequency-modulate an rf stage.

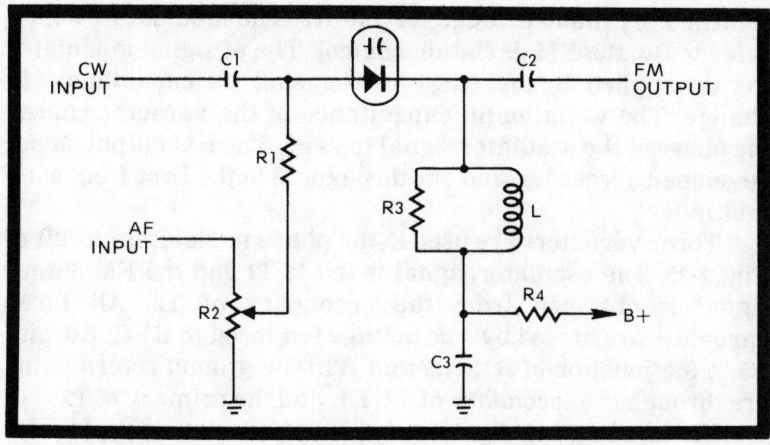

Fig. 2-24. Using one varactor for phase modulation.

Phase Modulators

The phase modulator circuit shown in Fig. 2-24 employs a single varactor and is connected between the oscillator (or buffer) and the first frequency multiplier. The basic oscillator signal is fed to output load L through C1 and the varactor. Normal bias is fed through R4 and L (shunted by R3 to broaden frequency response) to the varactor, whose anode is

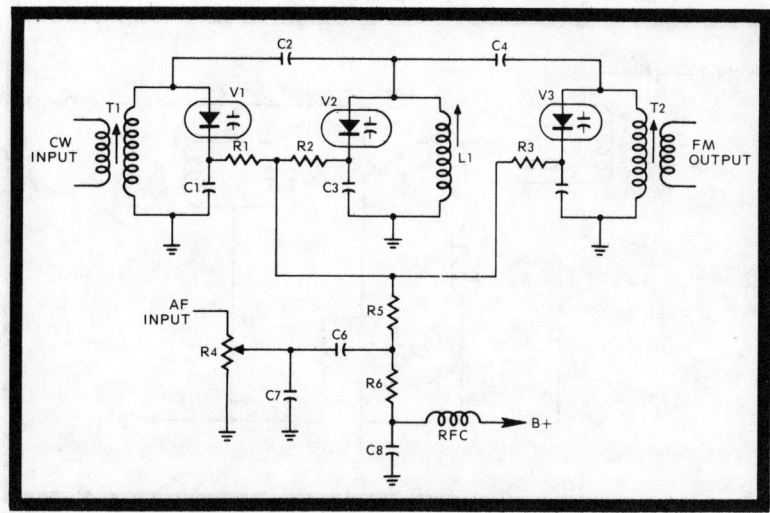

Fig. 2-25. Typical FM transmitter's varactor modulation circuitry.

returned to ground through R1 and R2. The modulating signal is fed to R2, the FM deviation control. The af signal modulates the dc applied to the varactor, causing its capacitance to change. The variation in capacitance of the varactor causes the phase of the oscillator signal to vary. The FM output signal developed across L is fed out through C3 to the first frequency multiplier.

Three varactors are used in the phase modulator circuit of Fig. 2-25. The oscillator signal is fed to T1 and the FM output signal is obtained from the secondary of T2. All three varactors are biased by a dc voltage fed through RFC, R6, and R5 to the junction of R1, R2, and R3. The ground return paths are through the secondary of T1, L1, and the primary of T2.

The modulating signal is fed to FM deviation control R4 and then through C6 and R5 to the varactors through the junction of R1, R2, and R3. The af signal varies the capacitances of the three varactors simultaneously, causing the resonant frequencies of T1, L1, and T2 to vary at the af rate.

Frequency Multipliers

A frequency multiplier may employ a single diode as a nonlinear device in order to produce harmonics of the input signal. Nearly all FM transmitters, however, employ a

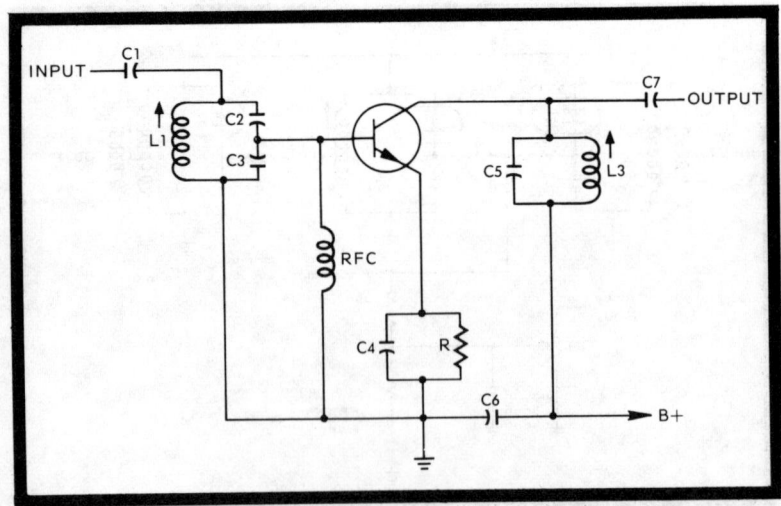

Fig. 2-26. Transistor frequency multiplier stage.

transistor in each multiplier stage. The multiplier circuit of Fig. 2-26 employs tuned input and output tank circuits. L1 is tuned to the frequency of the input signal and L3 is tuned to the second or third harmonic of the input signal.

The transistor is operated class C. Since its base is grounded for dc through the rf choke and since it has an emitter bias resistor (R), the amplifier is reverse-biased when no input signal is present. The input signal is fed to the base from the junction of capacitive voltage divider C2-C3, which also functions as an impedance matcher.

When the input signal swings positive, the transistor is forward-biased and collector current flows through L3. When the input signal swings negative, it is reverse-biased and collector current is cut off. However, because of the **flywheel** effect developed in the output tank circuit (C5-L3), the output signal is a sine wave whose frequency is a multiple of the input signal frequency.

Another frequency multiplier circuit is shown in Fig. 2-27. The input tank circuit is not shown since it is the output tank circuit of the previous stage. A small amount of forward bias is applied to the base of the transistor by voltage divider R1-R2. Emitter bias is provided by R3. Positive-going input signals increase the forward bias and collector current. Negative-going input signals reduce the forward bias and

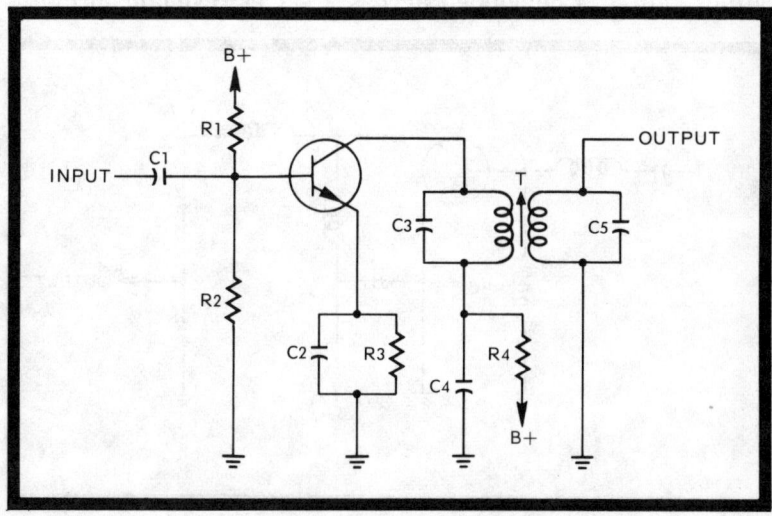

Fig. 2-27. Simplified multiplier circuit.

collector current. However, the transistor is biased by dc and the rf signal in such a manner as to cause the transistor to operate as a nonlinear amplifier. Harmonics of the input signal are generated in the collector circuit. The tuned circuit is resonant at the frequency of the desired harmonic of the input signal.

Driver Amplifier

Except in some low-power transmitters, the output of the last frequency multiplier stage is fed to a driver amplifier which in turn drives the rf amplifier. The driver may or may not also function as a frequency multiplier.

In the simplified schematic of Fig. 2-28, the input signal is fed to the base through a series-resonant circuit. The base is grounded for dc through an rf choke. Since there is no emitter resistor, there is no dc bias on the base. Positive-going input signals cause a large increase in collector current through the collector rf choke and negative-going input signals reduce collector current to zero. The output tank circuit is series-resonant. The two output capacitors form a variable capacitive voltage divider and impedance matcher.

Another driver amplifier circuit is shown in Fig. 2-29. The input signal is fed to the base through a capacitor adjusted to set input level and impedance. The base is grounded for dc through the rf choke and no emitter bias is provided. The output signal is developed across a series-resonant circuit.

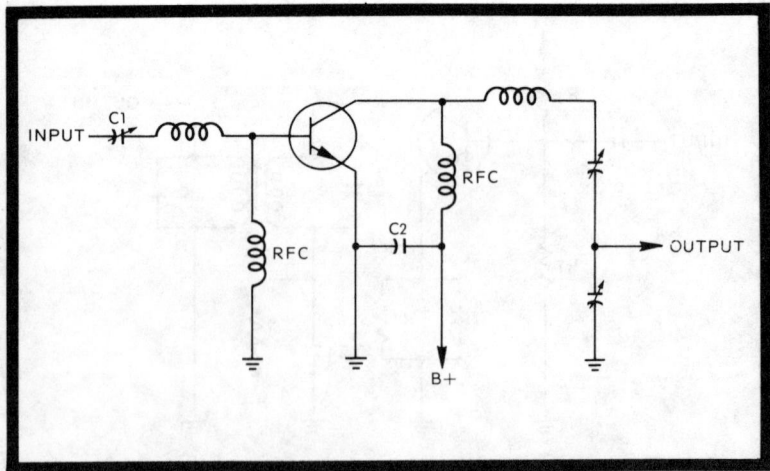

Fig. 2-28. Simplified driver-stage circuit.

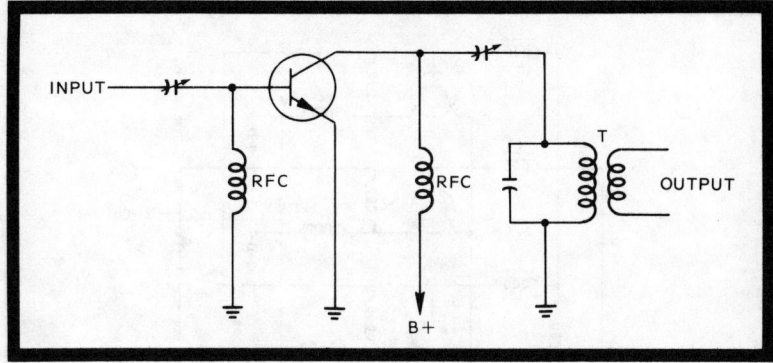

Fig. 2-29. Practical rf driver stage.

RF Power Amplifiers

Two power transistors are used in the rf power amplifier circuit of Fig. 2-30. No forward bias is provided. The input signal is fed through the input transformer to the transistor bases.

Three paralleled transistors are used in the high-power rf amplifier shown in Fig. 2-31. The input signal is fed to the impedance matcher C1-C2 and through C2 to the junction of L1, L2, and L3, which are adjusted to equalize the collector currents of Q1, Q2, and Q3. The bases of all three transistors are grounded for dc through rf choke of L4.

The output signals of all three transistors are combined across C6-C7, which are adjusted to resonate the output circuits at the desired frequency and to obtain the required output impedance.

All of the solid-state phase modulators, frequency multipliers, driver amplifiers, and rf power amplifiers

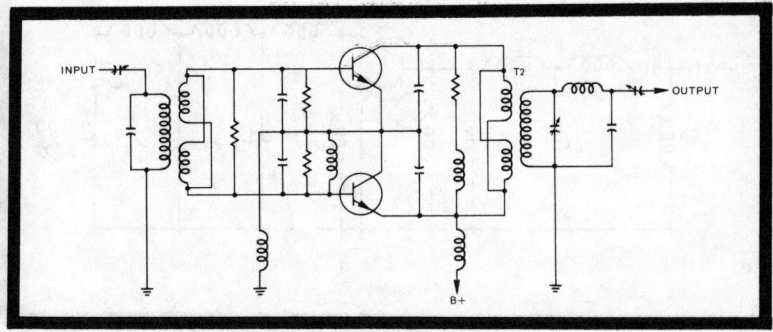

Fig. 2-30. Two-transistor power amplifier.

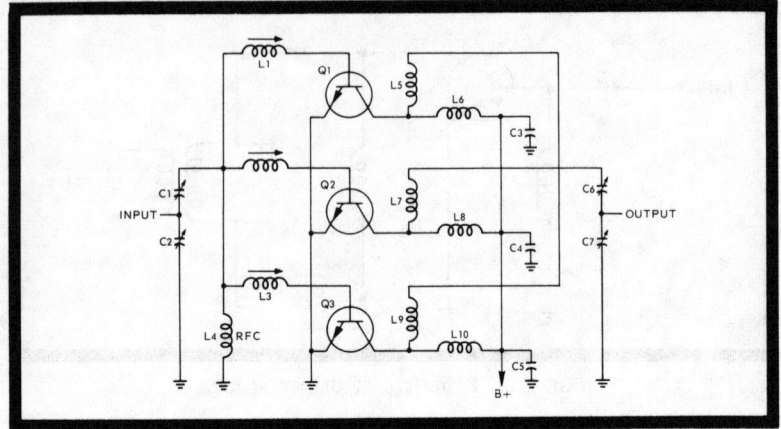

Fig. 2-31. Using paralleled transistors to increase rf output.

discussed so far are intended to be tuned to a specific frequency. In a multichannel transmitter, these circuits are compromise-tuned for equal performance on all channels. The rf amplifier circuit shown in Fig. 2-32, however, is a broadband type that can be used over a wide range of frequencies without returning. Both the input and output networks are low-pass filters adjusted to match the input signal source impedance to the transistor input resistance and the transistor output resistance to the load impedance.

Linear Amplifiers

The solid-state rf amplifier and frequency multiplier circuits discussed here operate as nonlinear amplifiers and

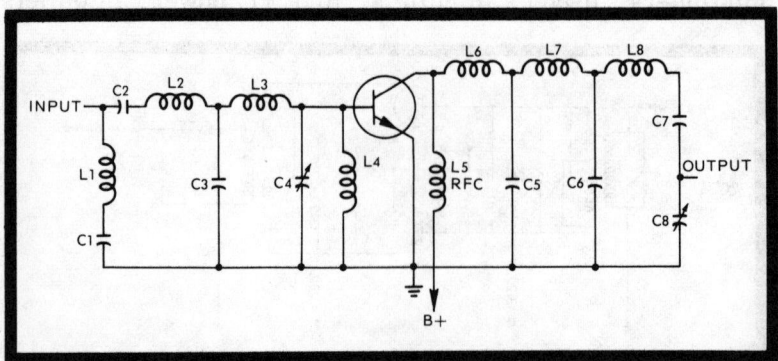

Fig. 2-32. Wideband rf amplifier.

are not used in AM transmitters beyond the point where amplitude modulation is introduced. In most low-power AM transmitters, the rf power amplifier stage is modulated and it can operate class C, as can all of the rf stages preceding it.

An amplifier used for amplifying an AM or SSB signal must be linear—which rules out class C. "Linear" means that it must react equally to both positive- and negative-going rf input signals. When a single transistor is used, it is biased for class A operation. When two transistors are used in a push-pull circuit, they may be biased for class B operation so that neither transistor conducts at all times. When the collector current of one transistor is rising, the collector current of the other transistor is falling, in see-saw fashion.

3 Receivers

All radio units used in the land mobile radio services employ crystal-controlled superheterodyne receivers. Most common is the single-conversion superheterodyne receiver, illustrated in block-diagram form in Fig. 3-1.

Assume that the receiver is to be used for receiving on 151.925 MHz and that the receiver intermediate frequency (i-f) amplifiers, limiters, and detector are tuned to 10.7 MHz. The local oscillator must operate at 10.7 MHz above or below 151.925 MHz. If the oscillator operates at 162.625 MHz, a 10.7 MHz i-f signal will be produced when a 151.925 MHz signal is intercepted.

TUBE-TYPE RECEIVERS

In an FM receiver, the i-f signal is amplified and fed through limiter stages to the FM detector. The limiters cause a constant-amplitude signal to be fed to the detector. Only the

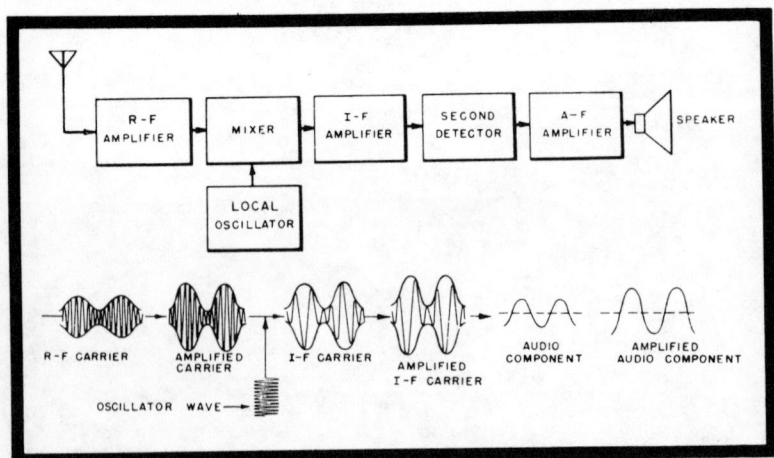

Fig. 3-1. Block diagram of a single-conversion FM superheterodyne receiver.

46

frequency of the i-f signal seen by the detector, should vary.

The squelch circuit senses the signal-to-noise ratio (SNR) at the output of the detector. If the SNR is too low (too much noise), the squelch circuit mutes the loudspeaker automatically by disabling the af amplifier. When a signal is intercepted which adequately quiets the noise, the squelch automatically reactivates the af amplifier.

Many receivers employ a dual-conversion superheterodyne circuit. (Some early models employ triple conversion.) Figure 3-2 is a partial block diagram of a dual-conversion receiver. It has two mixers and two local oscillators.

Assume that the first local oscillator operates at 162.625 MHz and the output of the first mixer and the input of the second mixer are tuned to 10.7 MHz (the high i-f). Interception of a 151.925 MHz signal will cause a 10.7 MHz signal to be produced.

If the second local oscillator operates at 10.245 MHz or 11.155 MHz, the 10.7-MHz signal will cause a 455 kHz signal to be produced at the output of the second mixer. This 455 kHz low i-f signal is fed through the i-f amplifiers and limiters to the detector.

An AM receiver differs from an FM receiver in the type of detector used and in that it does not employ limiter stages. As shown in Fig. 3-3, the output of the last i-f amplifier stage is fed directly to the detector. The demodulated AM signal is fed through a noise limiter to the af amplifier.

Front Ends

Most receivers are designed for connection to the antenna through an unbalanced (one side grounded) 50-ohm trans-

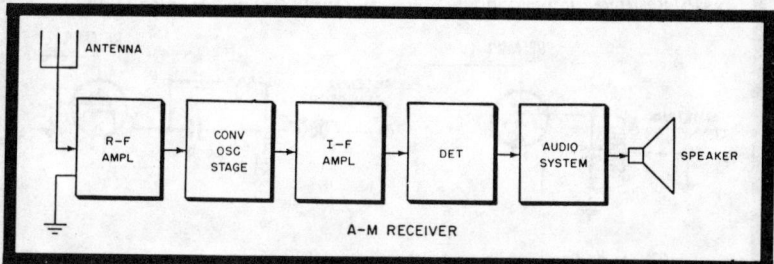

Fig. 3-2. Partial block diagram of a dual-conversion superheterodyne receiver.

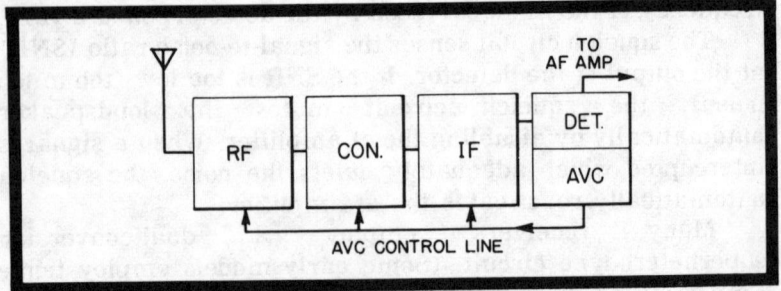

Fig. 3-3. Partial block diagram of an AM receiver.

mission line. In mobile units and at base stations arranged for simplex operation, the antenna transmission line is fed to a relay which normally connects the antenna to the receiver. When energized, this relay connects the antenna to the transmitter.

Input circuit designs vary as to the requirements of the low, high, and UHF bands, which are, respectively, 25 MHz, 150 MHz, and 450 MHz. Fig. 3-4 shows some typical input circuits, all of which accomplish the same purpose—transfer of energy from antenna to receiver. The input may match a 50-ohm line, although the match is not critical.

The antenna relay is part of the receiver input circuit, even though not always installed on the same chassis. This

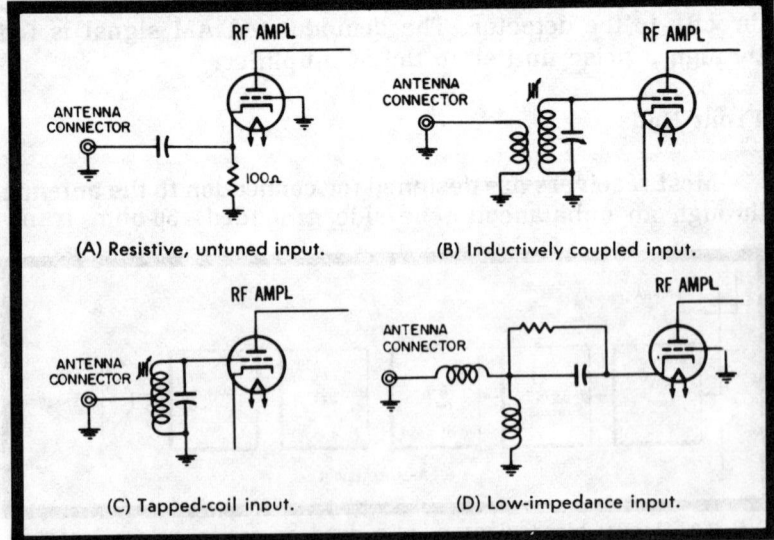

Fig. 3-4. Typical receiver input circuits.

relay is a possible source of trouble, since it has moving parts which can fail to make proper contact. Many relays have enclosed contacts to protect them from coarse dust and mechanical damage. However, as long as air, moisture, and gases can reach the contacts, they can become contaminated.

Contact contamination may cause the equivalent of inserting a resistor in series with the antenna. Although this may not impair reception, it can greatly deteriorate transmitter performance. More harmful to reception is erratic contact, which can cause noise and varying sensitivity. A quick check can be made by tapping the relay assembly when a signal is being received, and noting whether any noise is produced in the receiver output.

When the relay coil is not energized, a continuity check with an ohmmeter should indicate zero resistance between the center contacts of the relay antenna connector and the receiver connector. When the relay is energized, the circuit between the transmitter connector and the antenna connector should be closed, and the one between the antenna and receiver connectors should be open.

Although the resistance is not really zero under any circumstances, it should be low enough that it will measure zero with a conventional ohmmeter. Even if such a continuity check does show that the relay contacts make and break properly, there still may be contact trouble.

The moving contact, or armature, and the stationary contact make and break what is known as a "dry" circuit. This is one in which voltages and currents are in the "**micro**" and "**pico**" range. Doing this successfully is more difficult than handling heavy currents, which cause relay sparking. Relay sparking, in turn, burns off the dust film. Thus, the contacts must be very clean, and contact pressure must be adequate.

"Dry" circuit switching problems can be avoided by using relays whose contacts are in a vacuum.

Although persons skilled in the repair of delicate mechanisms can clean and adjust relays, it is often faster and less expensive to replace a doubtful relay with a new one. The replacement relay must match the impedance of the original to coaxial cables, to avoid increasing the voltage standing-wave ratio. Such an increase can affect the transmitter performance, even if the receiver performance does not seem to be adversely affected. Inaccessible relay contacts within an enclosure which has some openings can be cleaned by immersing the entire relay into a suitable detergent in the cleaning tank of an ultrasonic cleaner. The ultrasonic cleaning treatment will generally remove all accumulated dirt and film. The relay should be dried with forced air or other means before being placed back in service.

Component failures can also occur in the antenna circuit. Trimmer capacitors, tuning slugs, ceramic fixed capacitors and coils, and cavities or tuning lines should be checked visually. However, these components have such a range of electrical values that most conventional test equipment is inadequate for checking their electrical characteristics, except for continuity. Moisture, dirt, and temperature can alter the electrical characteristics of input-circuit components enough to degrade the receiver performance.

RF Amplifiers

The rf amplifier performs several functions. By adding to the overall selectivity of the receiver, its tuned circuits reduce the intensity of unwanted signals which reach the first mixer. The rf amplifier also minimizes radiation of the signal generated by the first heterodyne oscillator and fed into the first mixer. In addition, it provides gain, amplifying the input signal before it is fed to the first mixer. Most receivers have either one or two rf stages ahead of the first mixer. Various tube types and tuned circuits are used, depending upon the frequency band and design choice.

When a receiver is used for reception on one channel only, the rf amplifier is tuned for best performance at the frequency of that channel. When reception on two or more channels is required, tuning is optimized for all channels.

Low Band. Since the frequency span on low band is two to one, it becomes impractical to provide trimmers which will tune through the entire range. This requirement is met by connecting various combinations of capacitors across the slug-tuned coils to divide the band into four sections. Figure 3-5 is a schematic of a two-stage rf-amplifier section (shunting capacitors not shown). Figure 3-6 shows how the capacitors are connected to provide coverage of the band in four different sections. (The example shows coupling between the first and second rf stages.)

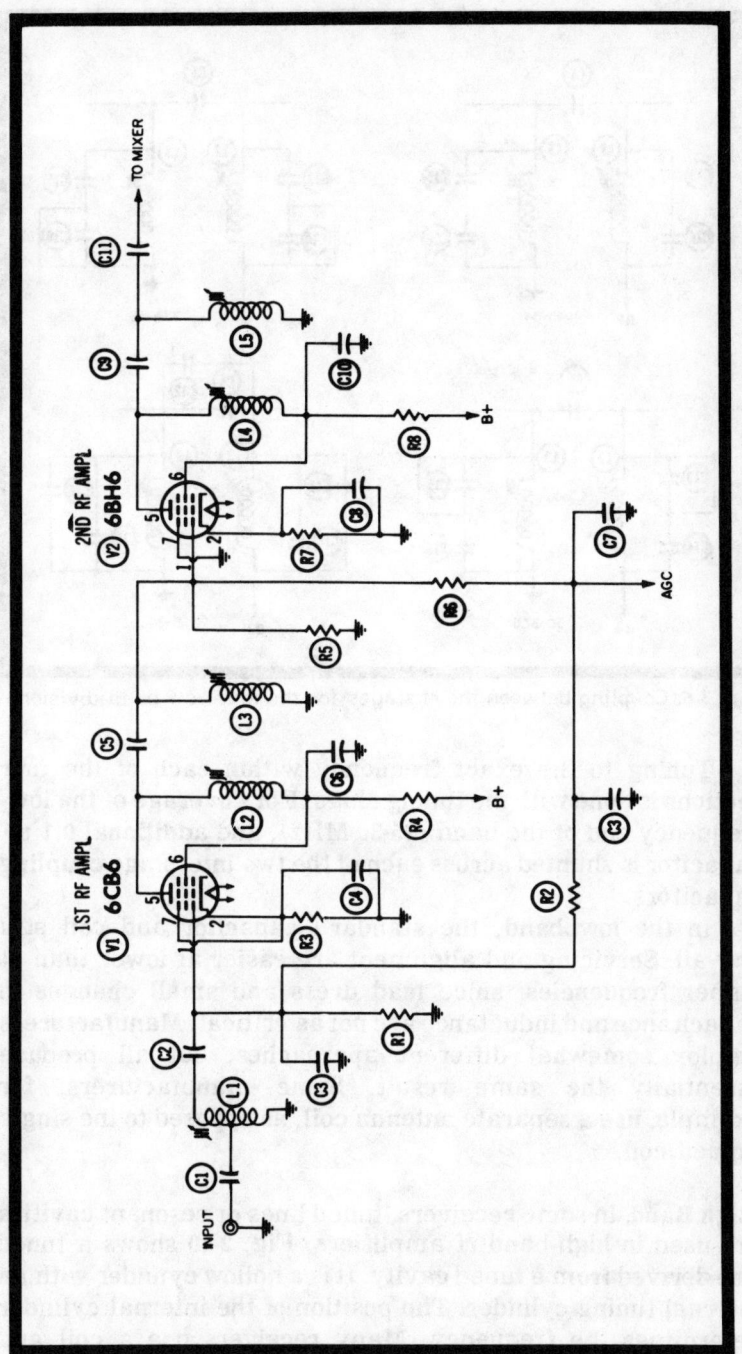

Fig. 3-5. A two-stage low-band amplifier circuit.

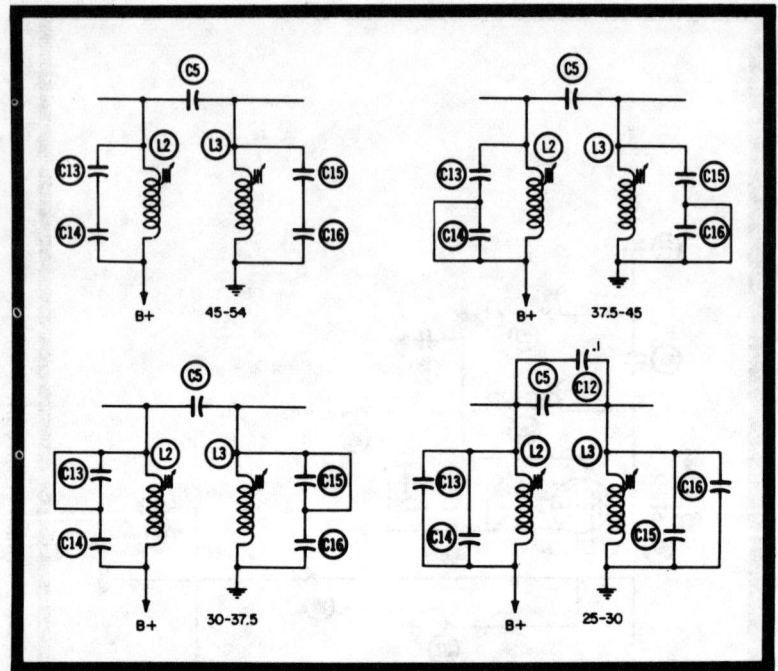

Fig. 3-6. Coupling between the rf stages for the four low-band divisions.

Tuning to the exact frequency within each of the four sections is done with the tuning slugs. For coverage of the low-frequency end of the band (25-30 MHz), and additional 0.1 uF capacitor is shunted across each of the two interstage coupling capacitors.

In the low band, the standard capacitor and coil still prevail. Servicing and alignment are easier at lower than at higher frequencies, since lead dress and small changes in capacitance and inductance are not as critical. Manufacturers employ somewhat different approaches, but all produce essentially the same result. Some manufacturers, for example, use a separate antenna coil, as opposed to the single tapped coil.

High Band. In some receivers, tuned lines or resonant cavities are used in high-band rf amplifiers. Fig. 2-10 shows a tuned line derived from a tuned cavity. It is a hollow cylinder with an internal tuning cylinder. The position of the internal cylinder determines the frequency. Many receivers use a coil and

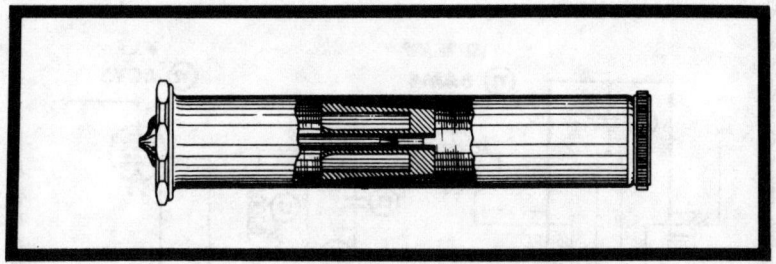

Fig. 3-7. X-ray view of the Iso-Q cavity.

capacitor. The LC circuits of the rf stages and mixer in Fig. 3-8 are tuned with trimmer capacitors. The cathode of the first grounded-grid amplifier is fed from a tap on antenna coil L1. The low-impedance antenna is fed to the cold end of the coil. This coil and capacitors C1 and C3 form a tee network.

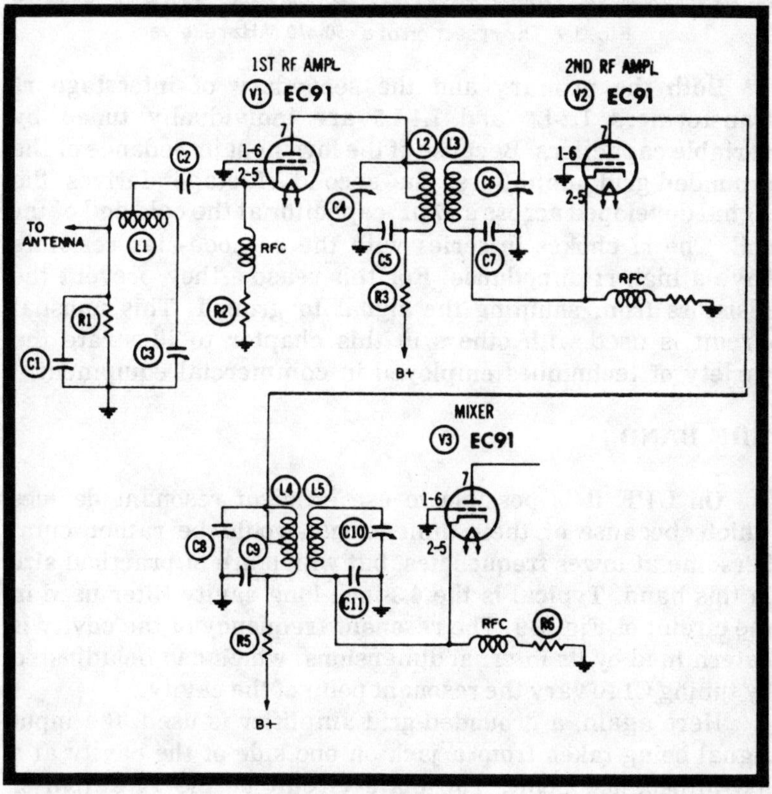

Fig. 3-8. A two-stage grounded grid amplifier for a high-band receiver.

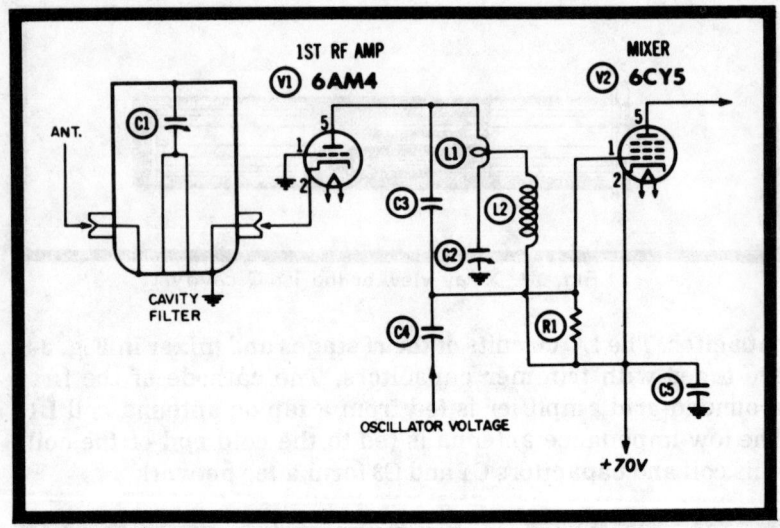

Fig. 3-9. The rf section of a 450-470 MHz receiver.

Both the primary and the secondary of interstage rf transformers L2-L3 and L4-L5 are individually tuned by variable capacitors. Because of the low input impedance of the grounded-grid amplifiers, the second rf stage derives the signal developed across a 47 pF capacitor at the cold end of the coil. The rf chokes in series with the cathode-bias resistors have a high rf impedance. For this reason, they prevent the resistors from shunting the signal to ground. This unusual circuit is used with others in this chapter to illustrate the variety of techniques employed in commercial equipment.

UHF BAND

On UHF it is possible to use efficient resonant devices which, because of their dimensions, would be rather cumbersome at lower frequencies, but which are of practical size in this band. Typical is the 4.3-inch-long cavity filter used in the circuit of Fig. 3-9. The resonant frequency of the cavity is determined by its internal dimensions, which can be adjusted by tuning C1 to vary the resonant point of the cavity.

Here again, a grounded-grid amplifier is used, the input signal being taken from a jack on one side of the cavity at a low-impedance point. The plate circuit of the rf amplifier employs a small wire loop tuned by trimmer capacitor C2.

Mixers

In the first mixer, the signal from the rf amplifier is mixed with a signal from the first heterodyne oscillator. Here these two signals are converted to form the i-f signal, which is fed to the i-f amplifier (second mixer in some receivers). To convert these signals to produce beats (the sum and difference of these two frequencies), the mixer must function as a nonlinear device, or detector. Hence, this stage of a superheterodyne receiver originally was called the first detector, later the converter, and now is known as the mixer.

If a 30 and a 20 MHz signal are fed to a mixer, the output will contain a 50 MHz signal (30 + 20) and a 10 MHz signal (30 - 20). The choice can be made by tuning the output to one of these signals; the tuned circuit will reject the unwanted signals.

The mixer stage of a receiver for the low band in Fig. 3-10 uses a 6AK5 tube. This tube has cathode as well as grid-leak bias developed across R2. The local-oscillator signal is fed to the screen of the mixer tube. Capacitor C8 is of such low value that it does not function as a bypass; instead, it forms a voltage divider with C9. Input tuning at the operating frequency is provided by L1 and L2, shunted by C2 and C3. Coupling from L1 and L2 is via the voltage divider formed by

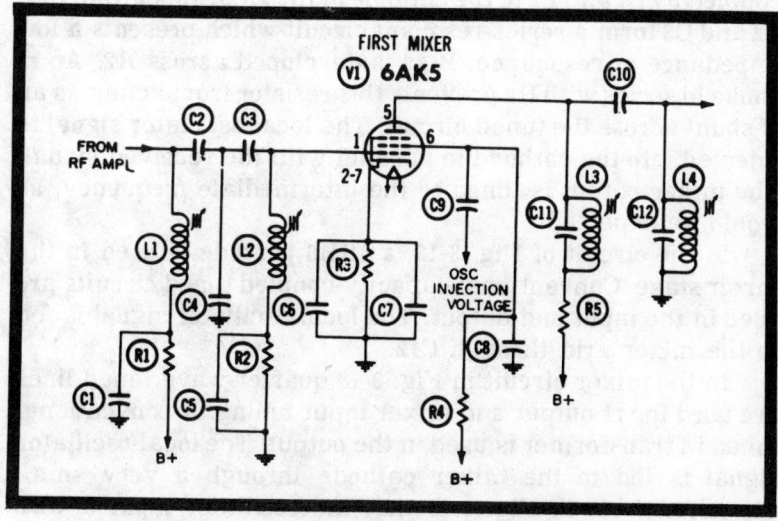

Fig. 3-10. The first mixer circuit of a 25-50 MHz band receiver.

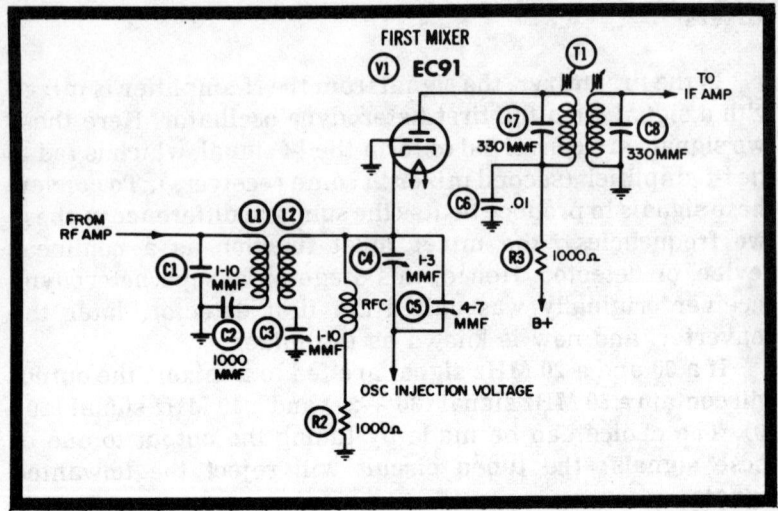

Fig. 3-11. A first mixer circuit which employs a grounded-grid triode.

C2 and C4. Since C4 is of relatively high capacitance only the small rf voltage developed across it is fed to the grid of the mixer through C3. L3 and L4 are tuned to the first intermediate frequency.

A grounded-grid circuit is used in the mixer stage shown in Fig. 3-11. The signal from the rf stages is inductively coupled by L1 and L2 to the cathode of the EC91 tube. Note that L2 and C3 form a series-resonant circuit which presents a low impedance at resonance. Bias is developed across R2. An rf choke in series with R2 prevents this resistor from acting as an rf shunt across the tuned circuit. The local-oscillator signal is injected into the cathode in parallel with the received signal. The mixer output is tuned to the intermediate frequency, as would be expected.

In the circuit of Fig. 3-12, a 6BH6 pentode is used in the mixer stage. Conventional capacity-coupled tuned circuits are used in the input and output. The local-oscillator signal is fed to the mixer grid through C12.

In the mixer circuit in Fig. 3-13 quarter-wave tuned lines are used for rf output and mixer input tuning. A conventional tuned i-f transformer is used in the output. The local-oscillator signal is fed to the mixer cathode through a very small capacitor. Note in Fig. 3-13 that the oscillator input is also tuned by a quarter-wave line.

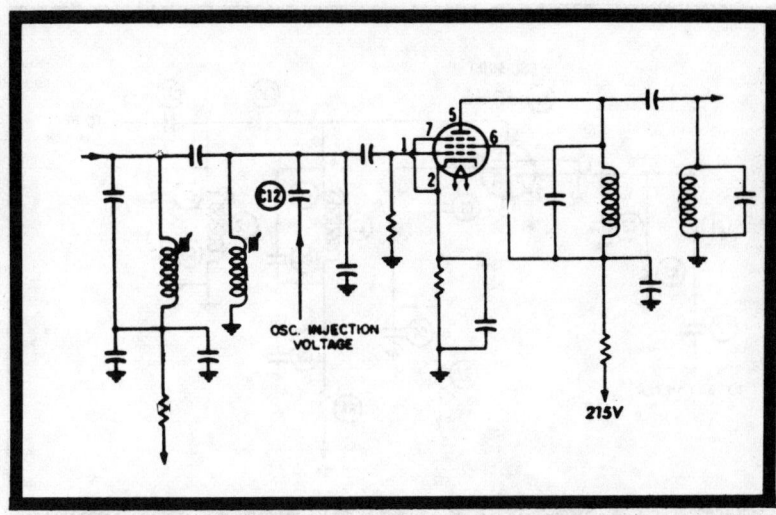

Fig. 3-12. A first mixer circuit which employs a pentode tube.

First Heterodyne Oscillator

The local oscillator for the first mixer produces an unmodulated rf signal which beats with the received signal to form the first i-f signal. It is important that the local-oscillator signal be stable in frequency. Any frequency variation can cause loss of sensitivity as well as unwanted reception of

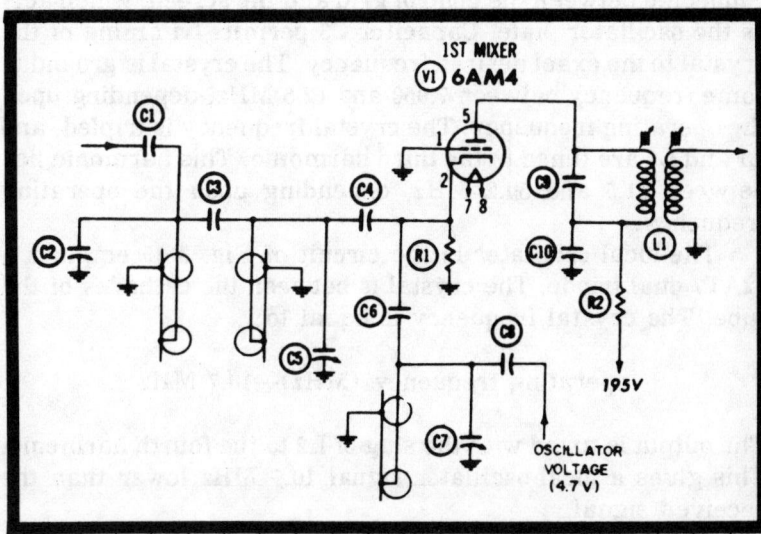

Fig. 3-13. A first mixer circuit for the 450-470 MHz band receiver which employs quarter-wave resonant lines.

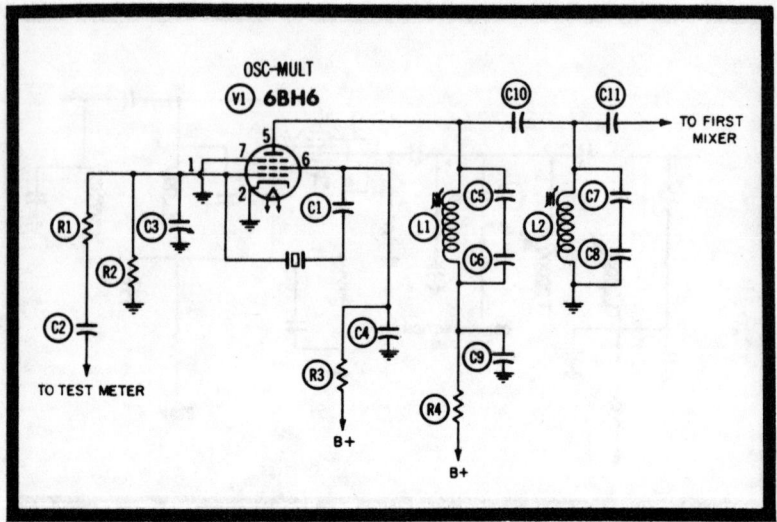

Fig. 3-14. A single-tube oscillator-multiplier for the 25-50 MHz range.

signals on an adjacent channel. Because of the frequency stability requirement, the local oscillator is always crystal-controlled.

A single 6BH6 tube functions as both the oscillator and the frequency multiplier in the circuit of Fig. 3-14. The crystal is connected between the control grid and the screen, which acts as the oscillator plate. Capacitor C3 permits trimming of the crystal to the exact desired frequency. The crystal is ground to some frequency between 7.050 and 12.5 MHz, depending upon the operating frequency. The crystal frequency is tripled, and L1 and L2 are tuned to the third harmonic. This harmonic lies between 21.5 and 50.2 MHz, depending upon the operating frequency.

The local oscillator in the circuit of Fig. 3-15 employs a 12AT7 dual triode. The crystal is between the cathodes of the tube. The crystal frequency is equal to:

operating frequency (MHz)—10.7 MHz

The output is tuned with the slug of L2 to the fourth harmonic. This gives a local-oscillator signal 10.7 MHz lower than the received signal.

In the circuit of Fig. 3-16, only one crystal is required for both the first and the second mixer oscillator functions. The

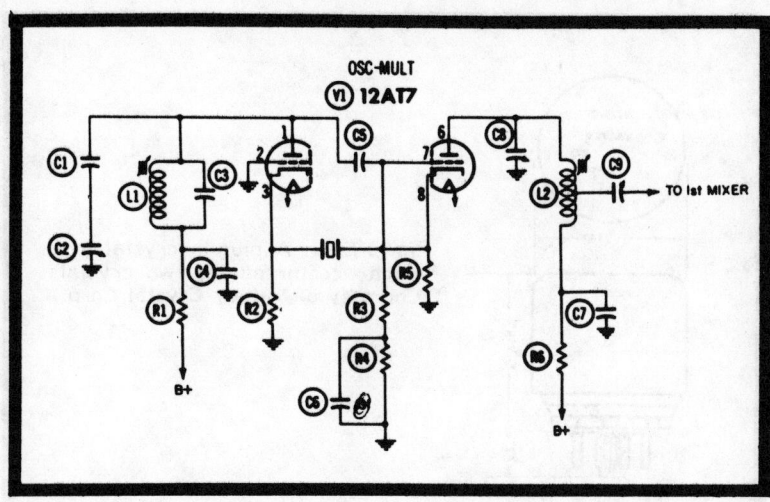

Fig. 3-15. A dual-triode oscillator-multiplier for the 132-174 MHz range.

crystal is in the grid circuit of the oscillator stage, V1. The output is cathode-coupled to the other half of the oscillator stage. Three tripler stages follow. The signal from the plate of the first tripler is fed to the second mixer. The first mixer, however, is fed from the third tripler. Thus, only one crystal is required for the first two mixers.

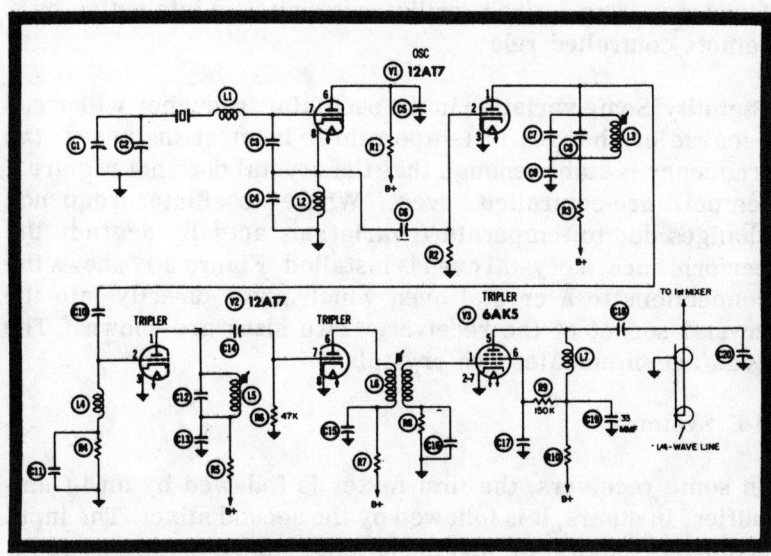

Fig. 3-16. Oscillator-multiplier stages.

59

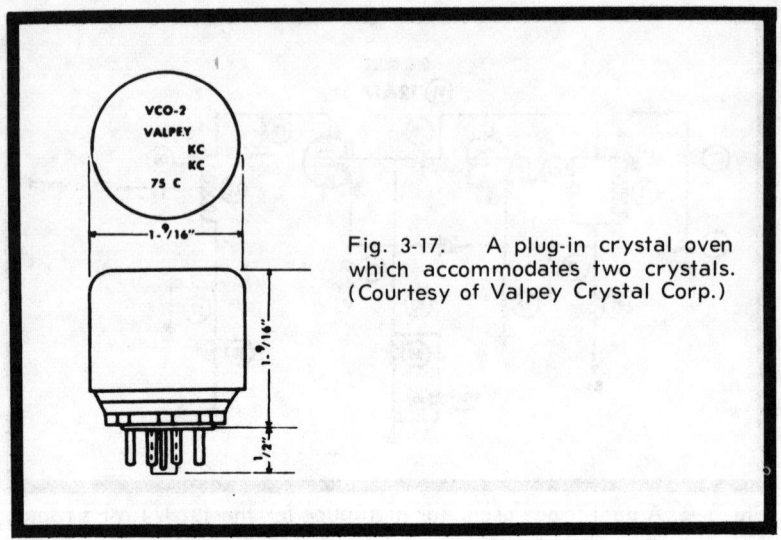

Fig. 3-17. A plug-in crystal oven which accommodates two crystals. (Courtesy of Valpey Crystal Corp.)

Multiple-Frequency Operation. The same receiver can be used for reception on two or more frequencies by employing a separate crystal for each frequency and selecting the desired one with a switch. Many receivers, however, employ individual first heterodyne oscillators for each receiving frequency. The desired oscillator is switched into action by a remote-controlled relay.

Stability. Some variation in the oscillator frequency will occur because of changes in temperature. In most instances, the frequency is stable enough that the crystal does not require a temperature-controlled oven. Where oscillator-frequency changes due to temperature variations actually degrade the performance, a crystal oven is installed. Figure 3-17 shows the connections to a crystal oven which plugs directly into the crystal socket of the receiver. (Two sizes are shown). The oven accommodates two crystals.

I-F Systems

In some receivers, the first mixer is followed by an i-f amplifier. In others, it is followed by the second mixer. The input is tuned to the first i-f, and the output is tuned to the second i-f. The local-oscillator signal for the second mixer is sometimes derived from the same oscillator-multiplier as the first, but more often a separate oscillator is used.

Second Mixer-Oscillator. In the circuit of Fig. 3-18. one triode section of a 12AT7 tube is used as the second mixer and the other as the crystal-controlled local oscillator. The 5.5375 MHz crystal signal, when heterodyned at the second mixer input against the 5.8 MHz i-f signal from the first mixer, results in a 262.5 kHz (5800-5537.5=262.5) signal at the output. A packaged bandpass filter is interjected between the cathode-follower output of the second mixer and the cathode input of the grounded-grid i-f amplifier stage. The same crystals is used in the local oscillator of the second mixer, regardless of the operating frequency. However, a different crystal is used in the local oscillator of the first mixer whenever the operating frequency is changed.

I-F Amplifiers. A single-conversion superheterodyne receiver employs only one i-f amplifier, which may consist of two or more stages. A dual-conversion receiver may or may not employ a high i-f amplifier between the first and second

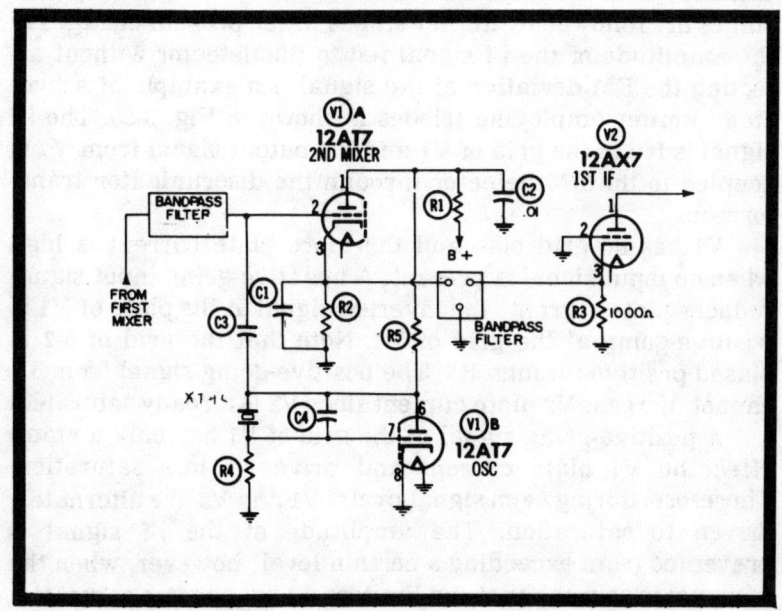

Fig. 3-18. A second mixer-oscillator circuit for the 25-50 MHz range which employs triodes.

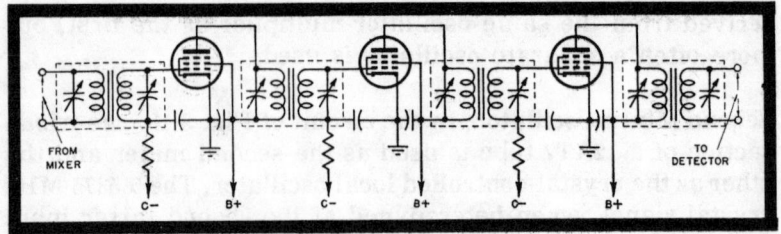

Fig. 3-19. Typical i-f amplifier.

mixers. The output of the first mixer is often fed through a selectivity filter to the second mixer or high i-f amplifier (when one is used).

The output of the second mixer (or the output of the first mixer of a single-conversion receiver) is fed to the input of an i-f amplifier chain through an i-f transformer or filter. Figure 3-19 shows the circuit of a typical input i-f amplifier stage employing a pentode tube and a selectivity filter at its input. Its output is coupled to the next stage through an i-f transformer.

Limiters. In an FM communications receiver, the i-f amplifier stages are followed by limiter stages which prevent changes in the amplitude of the i-f signal fed to the detector without affecting the FM deviation of the signal. An example of a two-stage limiter employing triodes is shown in Fig. 3-20. The i-f signal is fed to the grid of V1 and the output signal from V2 is coupled to the FM detector through the discriminator transformer.

V1 has no grid bias and therefore plate current is high when no input signal is present. A negative-going input signal reduces plate current; the inverted signal at the plate of V1 is positive-going at the grid of V2. Note that the grid of V2 is biased positive through R3. The positive-going signal from V1 cannot increase V2 plate current since V2 is already saturated.

A positive-going signal at the grid of V1 has only a small effect on V1 plate current and drives it into saturation. Therefore, during each signal cycle, V1 and V2 are alternately driven to saturation. The amplitude of the i-f signal is prevented from exceeding a certain level; however, when the i-f signal is so weak that the limiters do not become saturated, they do provide some gain and the output signal voltage does vary.

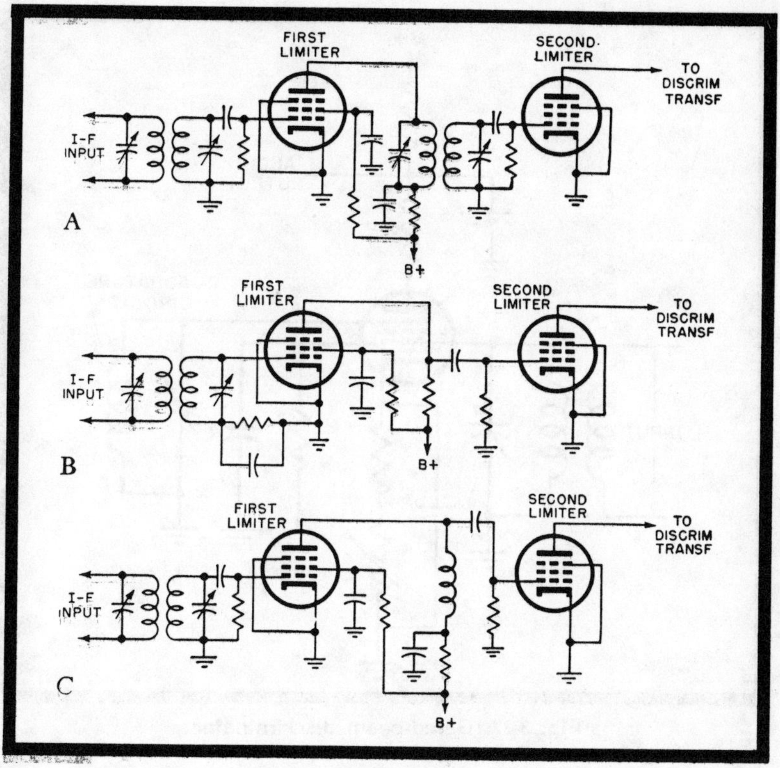

Fig. 3-20. Cascaded limiter.

FM Detectors

The most widely used FM detector is the Foster-Seeley phase discriminator, of which one version is shown

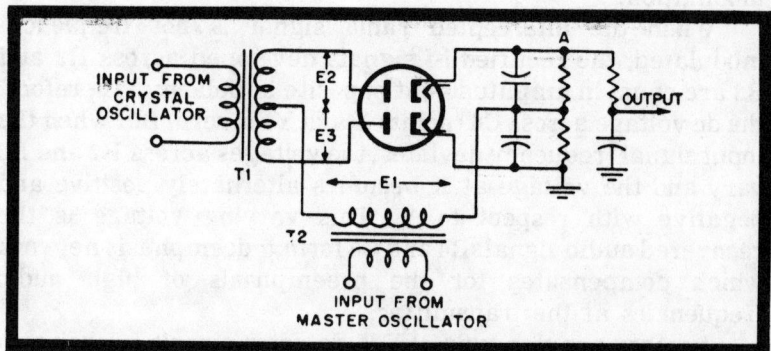

Fig. 3-21. Typical discriminator circuit.

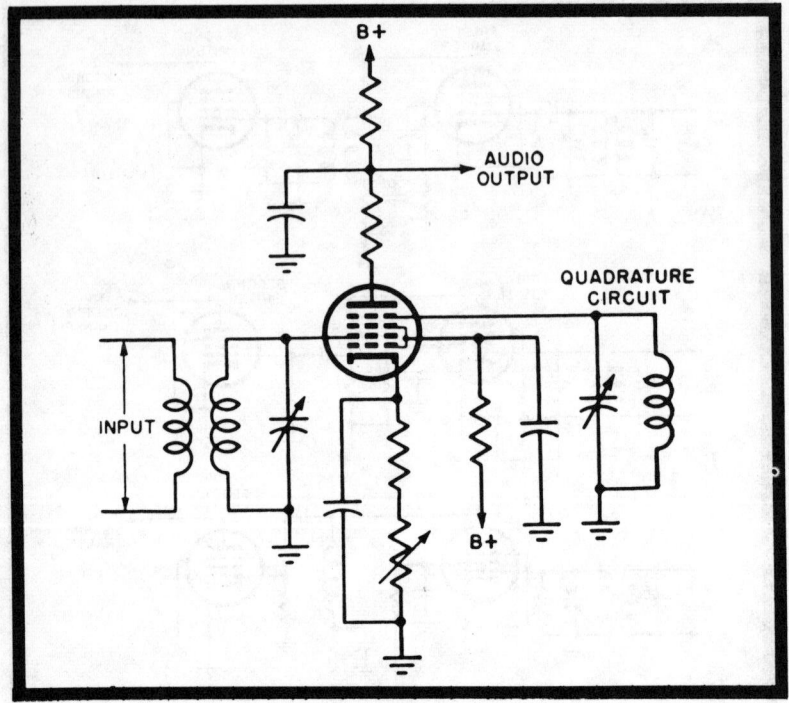

Fig. 3-22. Gated-beam discriminator.

schematically in Fig. 3-21. The i-f signal is inductively coupled to diodes V1 and V2 through the discriminator transformer and capacitively coupled through C1 to the junction of C2 and C3. The phase relationship of the signals fed to the plates of V1 and V2 varies as the frequency of the i-f signal deviates due to modulation.

When the intercepted radio signal is not frequency-modulated, the rectified i-f signals developed across R2 and R3 are equal in amplitude but opposite in polarity. Therefore, the dc voltage across C6 (points X and Y) is zero. But when the input signal frequency deviates, the voltages across R2 and R3 vary and the voltage at X becomes alternately positive and negative with respect to Y. This varying voltage is the recovered audio signal. R4 and C6 form a deemphasis network which compensates for the preemphasis of high audio frequencies at the transmitter.

Another popular type of FM detector circuit is shown in Fig. 3-22. This is known as the **gated-beam** discriminator.

Although the symbol of the tube is the same as that of a conventional pentode, the gated-beam tube is quite different. In a conventional pentode, grid G3 is the suppressor grid, which has very little effect on plate current. In the gated-beam tube, G3 is the quadrature grid, which exercises very great control of plate current.

If either G1 (the control grid) or G3 is made about 2 volts negative, plate current will be cut off completely. And if both G1 and G3 are made about 2 volts positive, the tube will become saturated (plate current reaches maximum).

The FM i-f signal is fed through the i-f transformer to G1 and through C1 to G3. The parallel-resonant circuit L2-C2 is tuned to the center frequency of the i-f signal. The i-f signal excites this high-Q circuit so that it oscillates at its resonant frequency. The frequency of the i-f signal fed to G1 varies in frequency when modulation is present. But the frequency of the signal at G3 tends to remain steady. Therefore, the phase relationship of the signals at G1 and G3 varies and plate current is varied at the applied af rate. The audio output signal is developed across R3 and is fed to the af amplifier through C6. Since the plate current variations consist of a train of rounded pulses, they are smoothed by the filter.

The gated-beam tube also acts as a limiter, since it is easily driven to cutoff and saturation. Its audio recovery is excellent and adjustment of L2 does not require the use of a meter.

Squelch Circuits

In AM receivers, the squelch is usually controlled by the automatic gain control (agc) voltage. In most FM receivers, the squelch is controlled by the quieting of the noise at the output of the detector when a signal is present. When no radio signal is present, the output of the detector consists of noise generated within the receiver itself. When a weak radio signal is intercepted, the noise level is reduced. And when a strong radio signal is intercepted, the noise disappears.

An example of a noise-controlled squelch circuit is shown in Fig. 3-23. The output of the detector is fed through a low-pass filter to volume control R3 and then to af amplifier V4. The output of the detector is also fed through a high-pass filter to the grid of noise amplifier V1. The noise is further amplified

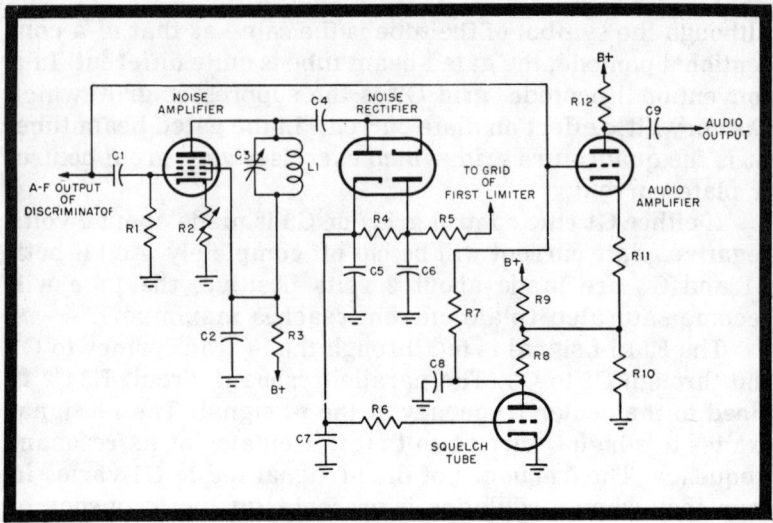

Fig. 3-23. Noise-operated squelch circuit.

by V2 and is then rectified by diode V3. The dc voltage across C10 is negative with respect to ground and varies in level with the SNR at the output of the detector.

With no i-f signal present, the dc voltage across C10 is at its maximum level and biases V4 to cutoff. Since V4 is cutoff, the af signal (noise, in this case) does not get through to the next af amplifier stage and the loudspeaker is silent. When a radio signal is intercepted and the noise at the output of the detector is quieted, the dc voltage across C10 drops and the bias on the grid of V4 is reduced. V4 now functions and allows the af signal to be fed to the next af amplifier stage and the loudspeaker is now operational. The squelch awakening threshold is adjusted with squelch control R9.

AM Detectors

An AM receiver does not contain limiter stages but does contain an agc circuit which varies the gain of one or more rf or i-f amplifier stages as the level of the intercepted radio signal varies.

Figure 3-24 shows a combination AM detector, agc rectifier and af amplifier circuit employing a multielement tube. The AM i-f signal is fed through the i-f transformer to one of the diode plates and the audio signal is recovered across volume control R3. R2, C2, and C3 form a filter which removes any remaining rf from the af signal. The i-f signal is also fed through C6 to the other diode plate. This plate and the cathode function as a shunt rectifier. A dc voltage is developed across C5 which is fed to the control grid of one or more stages to control their gain. This voltage rises, and vice versa. When voltage rises, the controlled stages are biased so they will produce less gain.

The triode section of the tube functions as an audio amplifier. The value of grid leak R4 is several megohms and allows space charge bias to be developed.

Impulse Noise Silencers

Most AM communications receivers contain a noise limiter (Fig. 3-25) which momentarily opens the audio path between the detector and the af amplifier whenever a noise pulse is intercepted. Noise pulses reverse-bias V2, and momentarily open the audio path. This actually chops holes in the audio signal, but they are of such short duration that they have but a negligible effect on audio quality.

In FM receivers noise limiters are not employed. When a signal strong enough to saturate the limiters is being received,

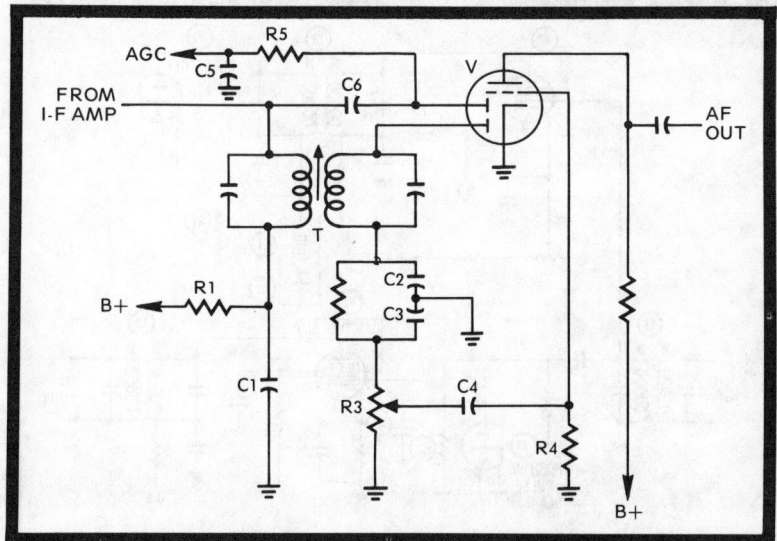

Fig. 3-24. A single tube serves as detector, agc source, and audio amplifier.

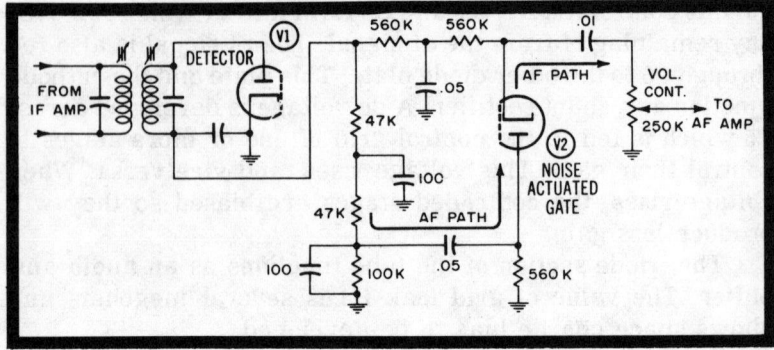

Fig. 3-25. A typical noise limiter used between the detector and amplifier.

most of the impulse noise is removed by the i-f limiters. Noise, even if inaudible, can limit the effective sensitivity of an FM receiver; it saturates the limiters and makes the receiver insensitive to weaker radio signals. To increase the effective sensitivity, a noise blanker is sometimes used. It may be built into the receiver or be an outboard accessory.

The circuit for one type of noise blanker is given in Fig. 3-26. It has an extra i-f stage (V1) which is inserted in parallel with the normal i-f amplifier. The i-f signal path is from the i-f

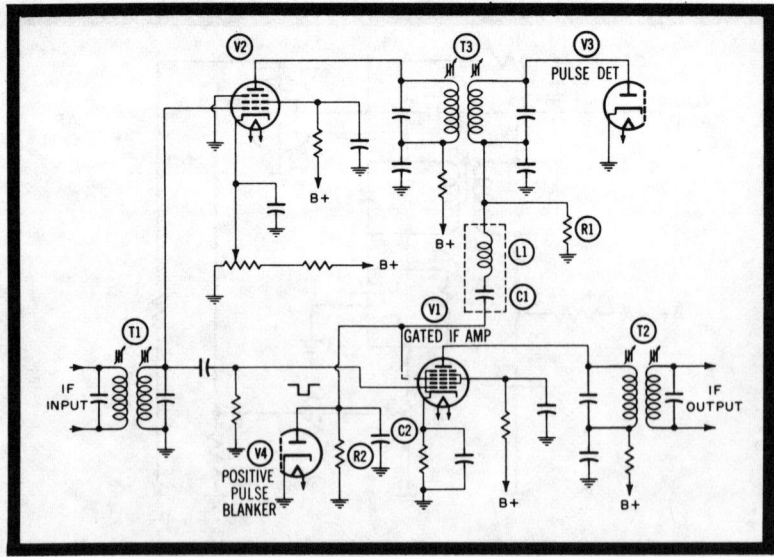

Fig. 3-26. A gated noise-blanker circuit.

input transformer, through V1, and i-f output transformer. The tube used for the i-f amplifier is of the same type as ordinarily used in pentagrid converter applications (6BE6, etc.).

V1 is normally operative; however, when a noise pulse is received, V1 is momentarily cut off and the passage of the i-f signal is blocked. This action chops the i-f signal, but the no-signal places are of such short duration that the desired signal is not significantly affected, while the noise pulses are removed. Thus, V1 is essentially a **gated** amplifier.

The amplifier is controlled by another circuit consisting of an i-f amplifier (V2) and a conventional AM detector (V3). The i-f input signal is fed to the grids of V2 and V1 simultaneously, so V2 amplifies the IF signal and feeds it to AM detector V3. The AM components of the signal (including the noise pulses) appear across R1 as a result of the demodulation by V3. The filter, consisting of L1 and C1, blocks passage of any i-f signal remaining and allows the noise pulses to be coupled to the third grid of V1. These pulses control the conductivity of V1. When the pulses are negative, V1 is cut off and the i-f signal is prevented from passing through the tube. Positive pulses, which would increase the gain of V1, are removed by V4, which short-circuits them to ground. Hence, noise pulses are applied as negative gating pulses to grid 3 of V1 and chop holes in the i-f signal. The time constant of C2-R2 must be very short to prevent making the holes unnecessarily long. The action of the noise blanker is controlled by R3, which varies the bias on V2.

Automatic Frequency Control

Some receivers are equipped with afc (automatic frequency control), which automatically varies the frequency of the first heterodyne oscillator so as to maintain the desired i-f signal frequency and thus compensate for variations and drift.

For instance, if the received signal drifts 5 kHz from its intended frequency, the resultant i-f signal will also shift 5 kHz. However, afc action will shift the local oscillator frequency of the receiver 5 kHz to restore the correct i-f.

When the incoming signal or the oscillator drifts in frequency, a dc voltage is developed at the output of the detector. Its polarity depends upon the direction of the

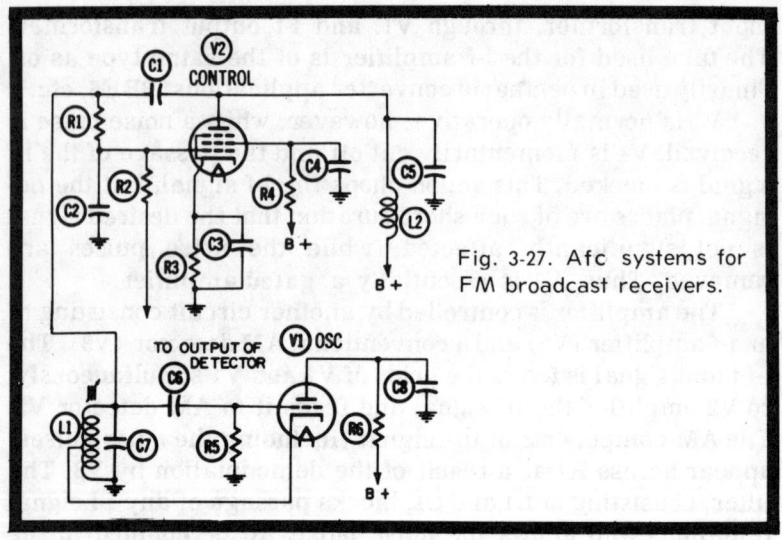

Fig. 3-27. Afc systems for FM broadcast receivers.

frequency shift, and its voltage depends upon the magnitude.

This dc voltage can be used to control the plate current of a reactance tube. When the dc voltage is negative, it adds to the normal bias on the reactance tube, reducing its plate current. When the control voltage is positive, the bias is reduced and the plate current is increased. The magnitude of the control voltage thus determines the amount of frequency correction, and its polarity determines whether the shunted reactance increases or decreases.

Figure 3-27 is a basic afc circuit for FM broadcast receivers employing a tunable heterodyne oscillator. The tuned circuit L1-C7 is shunted by control tube V2 and by a phase splitter consisting of R1 and C2.

The rf voltage developed across L1-C7 is applied across the phase splitter (R1-C2), which applies an rf signal voltage to the grid of V2. This voltage lags the current in R1 by 90 degrees because the resistance is much greater than the reactance of C2.

The plate current of reactance tube V2 is in phase with the voltage applied to its grid, but lags the voltage across the tuned circuit (L1-C7) by 90 degrees. Since this lagging current through the tuned circuit decreases the inductive reactance of L1, the frequency of the oscillator is increased.

When the oscillator tuning and the frequency of the incoming signal are such that the correct i-f signal is provided, the afc voltage is zero. Under this condition, no frequency correction is required; but since the reactance tube and phase splitter are permanently shunted across the oscillator tuning circuit, allowance is made in the design for their effect.

In Fig. 3-28, a reactance tube (V1) is shunted across the crystal, which is the tuned element of the receiver heterodyne oscillator. The afc voltage varies the plate current of control tube V1. This affects the amount of reactance shunted across the crystal. R1 isolates the discriminator from the control tube, while C1 bypasses any audio component. The two jointly provide the desired afc time constant. Capacitor C2, a very small value, provides the desired phase shift.

SOLID-STATE RECEIVER CIRCUITS

A solid-state receiver may employ discrete transistors and diodes or a combination of discrete active components and integrated circuits. As in solid-state transmitters and other electronic devices, these components are usually mounted on printed circuit boards.

RF Amplifiers

One or more rf amplifiers are used in some solid-state communications receivers ahead of the mixer of a single-conversion superheterodyne receiver, or the first mixer of a dual-conversion superheterodyne receiver. However, many solid-state receivers do not have an rf amplifier because, in many cases, the added gain is not required and because an rf

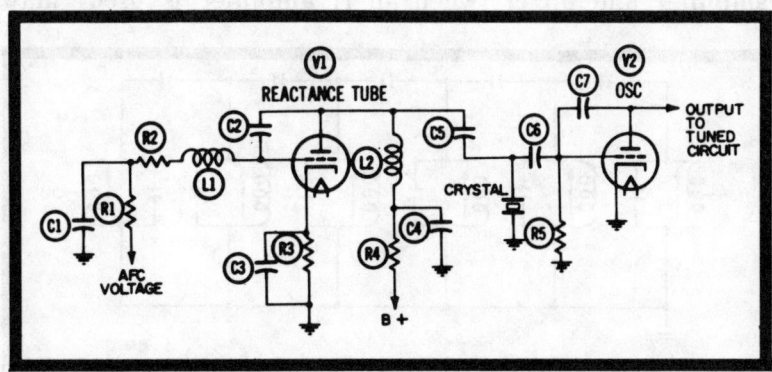

Fig. 3-28. Circuit for controlling a crystal oscillator.

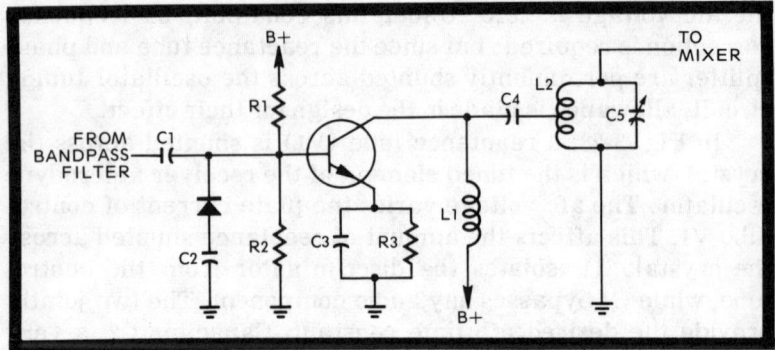

Fig. 3-29. Solid-state rf amplifier.

amplifier can compound intermoduation problems. In such receivers, the signal from the antenna is fed directly to the mixer input through a bandpass filter.

A simplified schematic of an rf amplifier stage is shown in Fig. 3-29. The input signal is fed through a bandpass filter (not shown) and C1 to the base of the transistor. The transistor is protected from damage by overly strong signals by a diode, which shunts negative-going signals to ground through C2. The amplified output signal is fed through C4 to a tap on coil L3 of the output tank circuit, which functions as a bandpass filter and impedance matcher.

RF Bandpass Filters

The bandpass filter between the antenna transmission line and the input stage of the receiver (as well as between the rf amplifier and mixer, when an rf amplifier is used) may

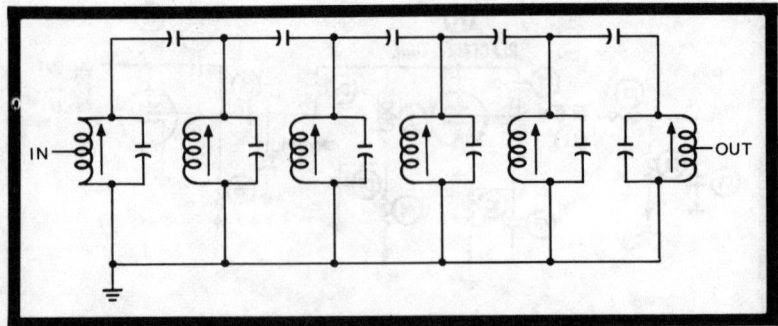

Fig. 3-30. LC bandpass filtering circuits.

consist of a number of resonant LC circuits or of resonant lines or cavity resonators. An example of a bandpass filter circuit employing LC circuits is given in Fig. 3-30.

The signal from the antenna is fed to a tap on the first coil and through the filter. The filter consists of six capacitively coupled parallel-resonant circuits. For optimum single-channel reception, all coils are tuned to the channel frequency. In a multichannel receiver, they are tuned so that the filter will pass all of the frequencies to be received.

Mixer Circuits

The mixer may employ a diode but would then provide no gain. Most receivers employ a bipolar transistor, FET, or MOSFET in the first mixer stage.

An example of a transistor mixer circuit is shown in Fig. 3-31. The intercepted radio signal is fed to the base of the transistor through C1, and the local oscillator signal is fed to the base through C2. The resulting i-f signal is developed across the output tank (L-C5) and is fed through C6 to the i-f amplifier (or second mixer, when used).

Figure 3-32 shows a typical FET mixer circuit. The intercepted radio signal is fed to a tuned-circuit tap which steps up the impedance. The signal is then fed to the gate of the FET. The local oscillator signal is fed through a capacitor to the source of the FET. The resulting i-f signal from the drain is developed across the output tank.

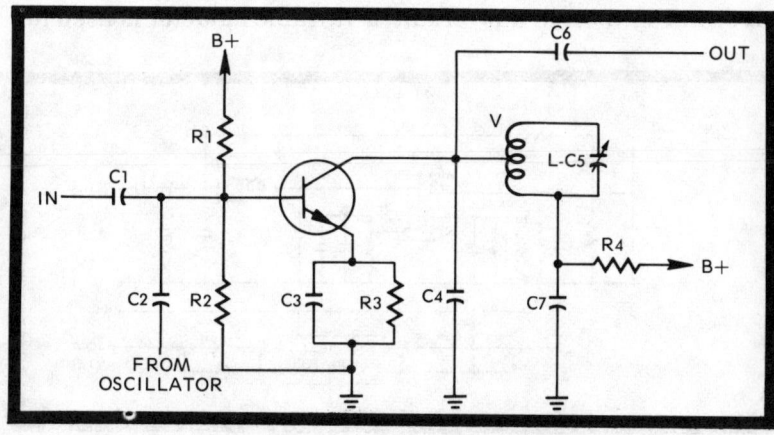

Fig. 3-31. Bipolar transistor mixer.

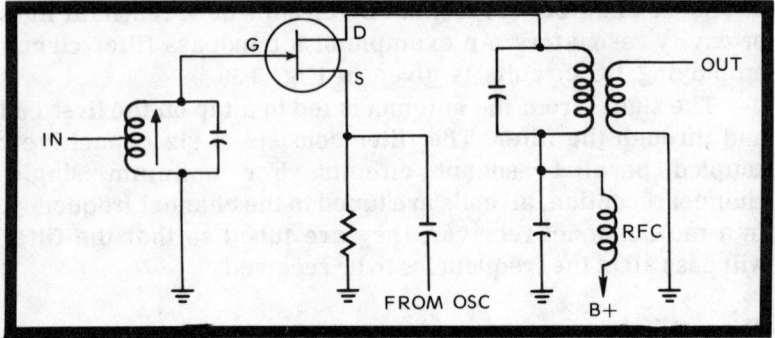

Fig. 3-32. FET mixer.

A dual-gate MOSFET is used in the mixer circuit shown in Fig. 3-33. The intercepted radio signal is fed to one gate and the local oscillator signal to the other. Both signals modulate drain current. The diodes within the MOSFET protect it from damage by excessively strong signals.

Local Oscillators

The circuits of receiver local oscillators are essentially the same as those of transmitter oscillators. A multichannel receiver may employ a separate oscillator for each channel or a single oscillator with crystal switching. As in a transmitter, the local oscillator output is usually fed to one or more frequency multipliers.

A schematic of a local oscillator employing an FET is given in Fig. 3-34. In this circuit, a variable inductor is used for

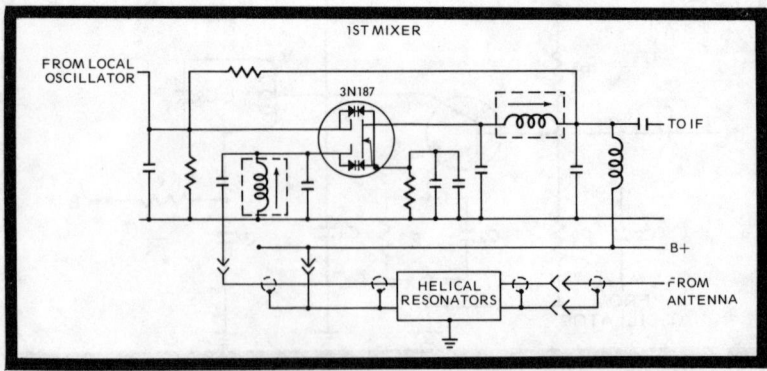

Fig. 3-33. A dual-gate MOSFET.

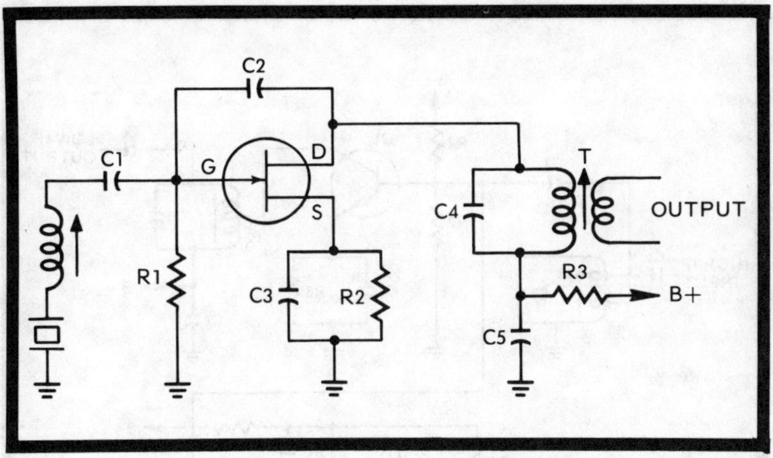

Fig. 3-34. Local oscillator.

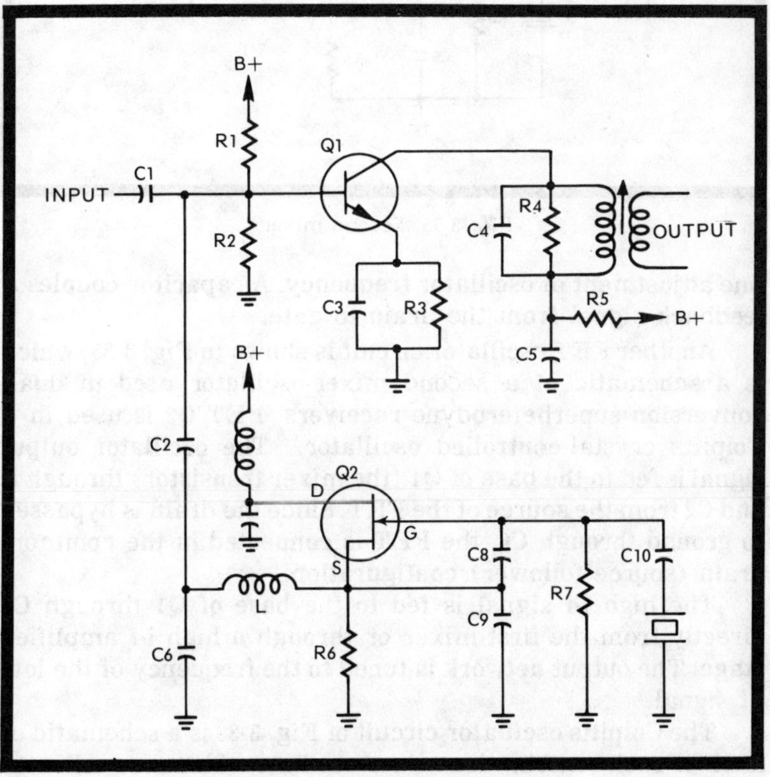

Fig. 3-35. Second mixer-oscillator.

75

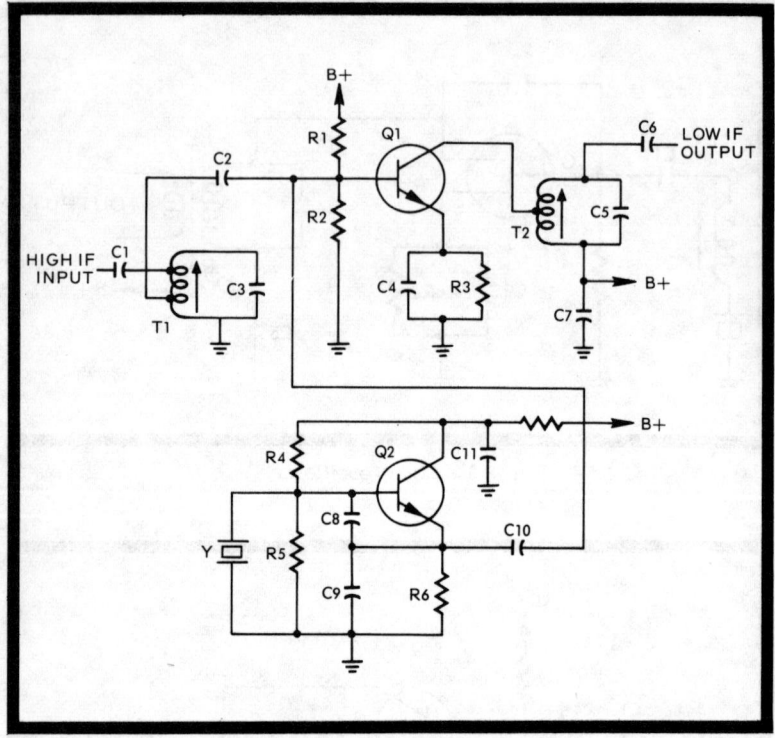

Fig. 3-36. Second mixer.

fine adjustment of oscillator frequency. A capacitor couples a feedback signal from the drain to gate.

Another FET oscillator circuit is shown in Fig. 3-35, which is a schematic of a second mixer-oscillator used in dual-conversion superheterodyne receivers. FET Q2 is used in a Colpitts crystal-controlled oscillator. The oscillator output signal is fed to the base of Q1 (the mixer transistor) through L and C2 from the source of the FET. Since the drain is bypassed to ground through C6, the FET is connected in the common-drain (source follower) configuration.

The high i-f signal is fed to the base of Q1 through C1 directly from the first mixer or through a high i-f amplifier stage. The output network is tuned to the frequency of the low i-f signal.

The Colpitts oscillator circuit of Fig. 3-36 is a schematic of another such combination mixer-oscillator. Since the collector of Q2 is bypassed to ground through C11, the transistor is connected in the common-collector (emitter-follower) configuration. The local oscillator signal is fed from the emitter of Q2 through C10 to the base of mixer transistor Q1.

I-F Amplifiers

Many receivers employ a single-conversion superheterodyne circuit in which the output of the mixer is fed through a mechanical, ceramic, or crystal-lattice bandpass filter to a multistage i-f amplifier. It is this filter that determines the selectivity of the receiver.

In dual-conversion superheterodyne receivers, the output (high i-f) of the first mixer is fed directly or through a selectivity filter to the input of the second mixer. In some receivers, an i-f amplifier stage is used between the two mixers.

Figure 3-37 shows the circuit of a transistor i-f amplifier. Since the collector is grounded for dc through the primary of the output transformer, the collector is made negative with respect to the emitter by applying positive voltage to the emitter as shown.

The i-f amplifier circuit shown in Fig. 3-38 employs a common-gate FET configuration. The input signal is fed to the source, and the output signal from the drain is coupled to the second mixer input through a transformer.

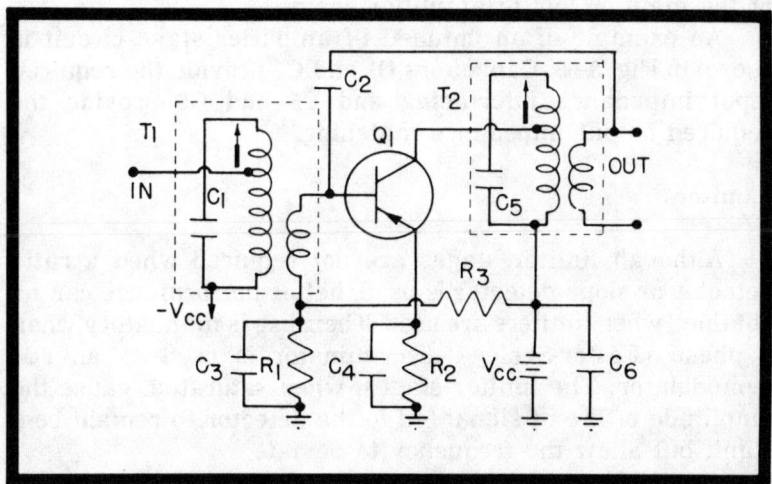

Fig. 3-37. High i-f amplifier stage employing a bipolar transistor.

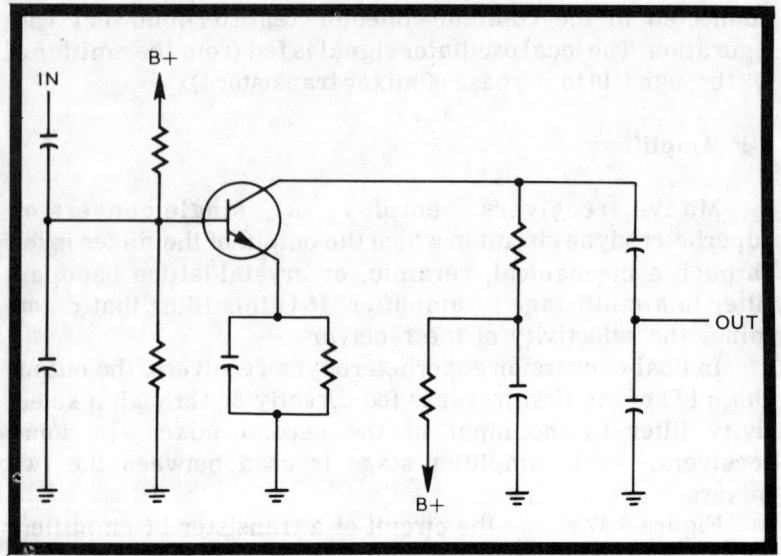

Fig. 3-38. High i-f amplifier stage employing FET.

Although it has been customary to employ tuned i-f amplifier stages in single-conversion superheterodyne receivers and tuned low i-f amplifier stages in dual-conversion receivers, untuned i-f amplifier stages are commonly used. The selectivity provided by interstage i-f transformers is often not as good as that provided by a selectivity filter at the input of the main or low i-f amplifier chain.

An example of an untuned i-f amplifier stage circuit is shown in Fig. 3-39. Capacitors C1 and C2 provide the required input impedance interfacing and C5 and C6 provide the required output impedance matching.

Limiters

Although limiter stages are not required when a ratio detector or slope detector is used, better performance can be obtained when limiters are used. Their use is mandatory when a phase (Foster-Seeley) discriminator is used as an FM demodulator. The limiter stages, when saturated, cause the amplitude of the i-f signal fed to the detector to remain constant, but allow the frequency to deviate.

A pair of butted diodes can be used as a limiter, but most receivers employ a pair of cascaded transistors. An example of a two-stage limiter circuit is shown in Fig. 3-40. The transistors are biased so that, when saturated, they prevent the output signal from exceeding a specific level, regardless of the amplitude of the input signal.

FM Detectors

The circuitry of a solid-state discriminator is essentially the same as that of the tube-type discriminator. Instead of a pair of vacuum-tube diodes, semiconductors are used. Quadrature FM detectors are incorporated in ICs (integrated circuits) in some receivers.

Squelch Circuits

The squelch circuit can be controlled by the amplitude of the processed i-f signal or by the SNR at the output of the detector, or both. Figure 3-41 is a simplified schematic of a noise-operated squelch circuit. The base of noise amplifier transistor Q1 is connected to the output of the detector through a high-pass filter (C1, C2, R1, R3). When no radio signal is being received (or SNR is too low), Q1 amplifies the background noise. The amplified noise is rectified by diodes D1 and D2. The dc voltage across C6 forward-biases squelch gate transistor Q2, causing it to conduct heavily and the voltage at point X to be very low.

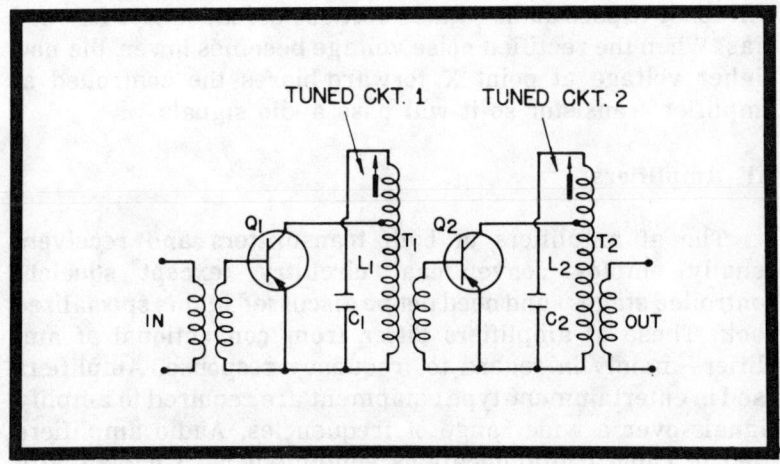

Fig. 3-39. Untuned i-f amplifier stage.

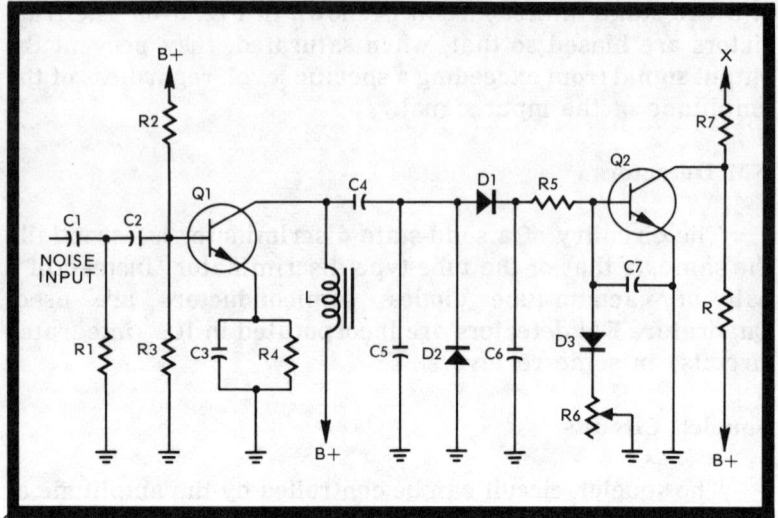

Fig. 3-40. Cascaded limiter.

When a radio signal is intercepted and the noise voltage at the base of Q1 approaches zero, the dc voltage across C6 will also be very low. Q2 is no longer forward biased and its collector current (through R8) will fall and the voltage at point X will rise. The voltage at point X is fed to the base of an af amplifier transistor to control its conduction. Thus, when the rectified noise causes Q2 to conduct heavily, the dc voltage at X will drop so low that the controlled af amplifier transistor will cease to pass audio signals because of inadequate forward bias. When the rectified noise voltage becomes lower, the now higher voltage at point X forward-biases the controlled af amplifier transistor so it will pass audio signals.

AF Amplifiers

The af amplifiers of both transmitters and receivers usually employ conventional circuitry (except squelch-controlled stages) and need not be discussed in this specialized book. These af amplifiers differ from conventional af amplifiers mainly in regard to frequency response. Amplifiers used in entertainment-type equipment are required to amplify signals over a wide range of frequencies. Audio amplifiers used in radio communications equipment need not amplify frequencies higher than 3 kHz.

Control Systems

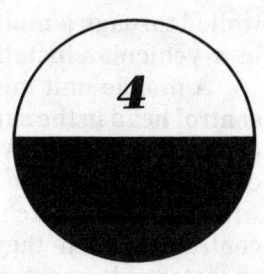

A mobile unit or base station may have its controls built in. This is true in the case of under-dash mobile units and consolette-type base-station assemblies. A trunk-mounted mobile unit is usually remotely controlled. With the latter arrangement, a control head with speaker (Fig. 4-1) and microphone is installed in the driver compartment. The microphone, speaker, and control leads are extended to the control head through a multiconductor cable. Power from the battery is usually run directly to the set through a separate power cable.

A mobile unit equipped with an appropriate power supply is sometimes used as a base station. The unit may be con-

Fig. 4-1. A typical remote-control head with built-in speaker.

trolled through a multiconductor cable, in the same manner as in a vehicular installation.

A mobile unit mounted in the trunk and operated from a control head in the same vehicle is legally considered a locally controlled station. A base station is also considered locally controlled when the transmitter and the control point are within sight of each other. It is considered to be remote-controlled when they are in different rooms, or when the operator at the control point cannot see the transmitter.

The operator must have indicators which show when the power is on or off, as well as when the transmitter control circuits have been set to "transmit." Pilot lamps are customary for this purpose.

The remote control point may be in the same building as the transmitter, or it may be many miles away. Although a station may have more than one control point, only one is called the **remote control point**. The others are called **dispatch** points. The person at the remote control point is in charge of the station. He must have means for cutting off the transmitter at all times to prevent improper use of the station by persons at dispatch points. As shown in Fig. 4-2, a cutoff switch is provided to disable the dispatch units.

A base station is most often connected to its control points through a two-wire telephone circuit. Audio is fed via the line to the transmitter from a remote-control unit. Audio from the remote receiver is also fed via the line to the control units.

Figure 4-3 shows various methods for transmitting audio in both directions over a two-wire line sequentially but not

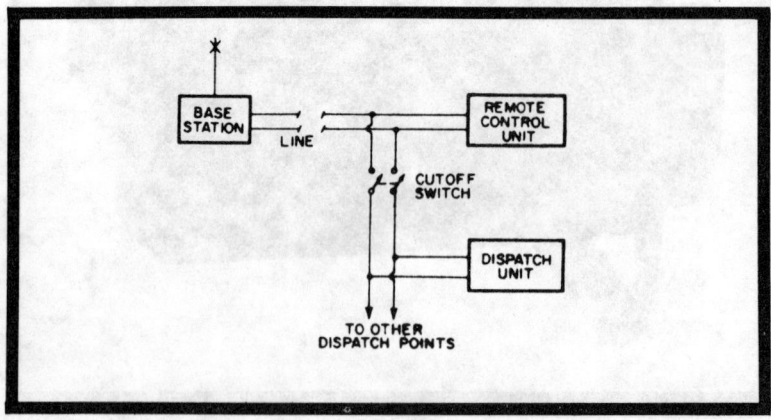

Fig. 4-2. Cutoff switch can be used to disable dispatch units.

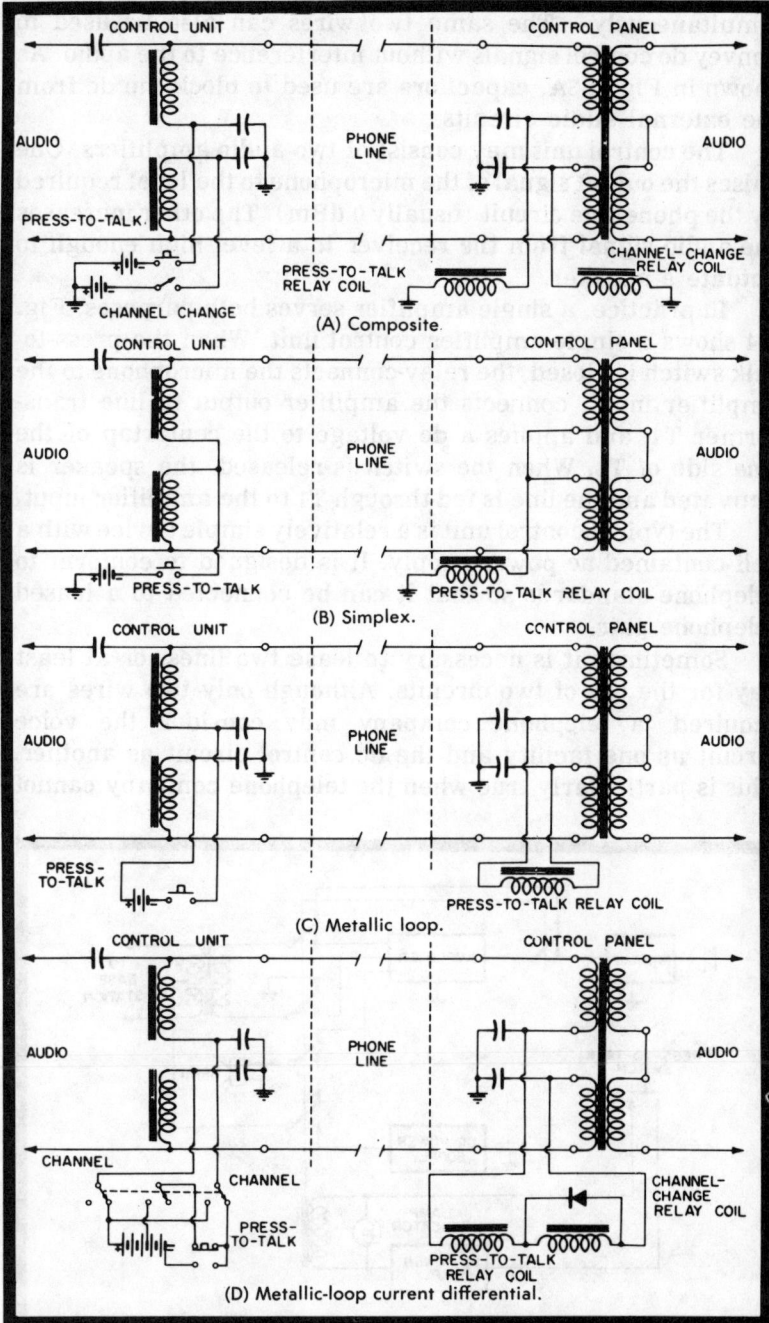

Fig. 4-3. Base-station control circuitry.

simultaneously. The same two wires can also be used to convey dc control signals without interference to the audio. As shown in Fig. 4-3A, capacitors are used to block the dc from the external audio circuits.

The control unit may consist of two audio amplifiers. One raises the output signal of the microphone to the level required by the phone-line circuit (usually 0 dBm). The other increases the audio signal from the receiver to a level high enough to actuate a speaker.

In practice, a single amplifier serves both purposes. Fig. 4-4 shows a single-amplifier control unit. When the press-to-talk switch is closed, the relay connects the microphone to the amplifier input, connects the amplifier output to line transformer T1, and applies a dc voltage to the centertap of the line side of T1. When the switch is released, the speaker is activated and the line is fed through T1 to the amplifier input.

The typical control unit is a relatively simple device with a self-contained ac power supply. It is designed to conform to telephone standards so that it can be connected to a leased telephone pair.

Sometimes it is necessary to lease two lines, or at least pay for the use of two circuits. Although only two wires are required, a telephone company may consider the voice circuit as one facility and the dc control circuit as another. This is particularly true when the telephone company cannot

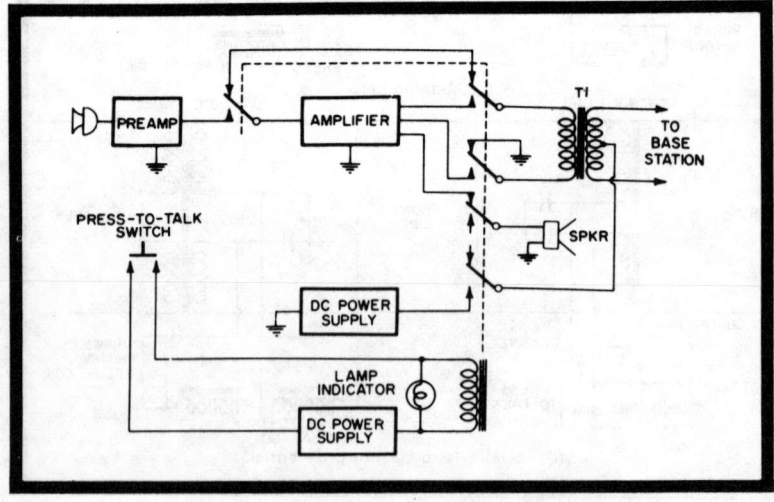

Fig. 4-4. Single-amplifier control unit.

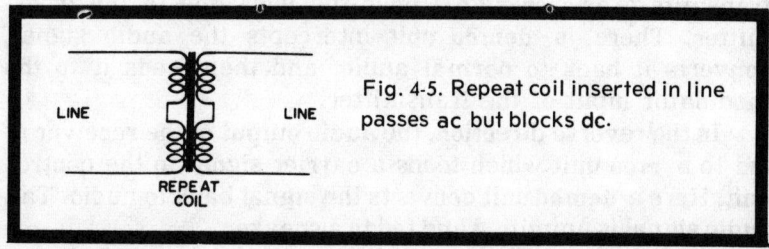

Fig. 4-5. Repeat coil inserted in line passes ac but blocks dc.

supply a true **metallic pair** for the voice-grade circuit. Sometimes a repeat coil (line transformer) is inserted in a line, so that dc cannot be transmitted over the line (see Fig. 4-5). Yet transmission of audio frequencies is not opposed.

Where private wire facilities are available for station control and such lines are already employed for other purposes, telephone carrier equipment can be used for superimposing another two-way voice channel on the line. At the control point, the microphone output, after preamplification, is fed to a carrier **mod** unit. (See Fig. 4-6.) This unit

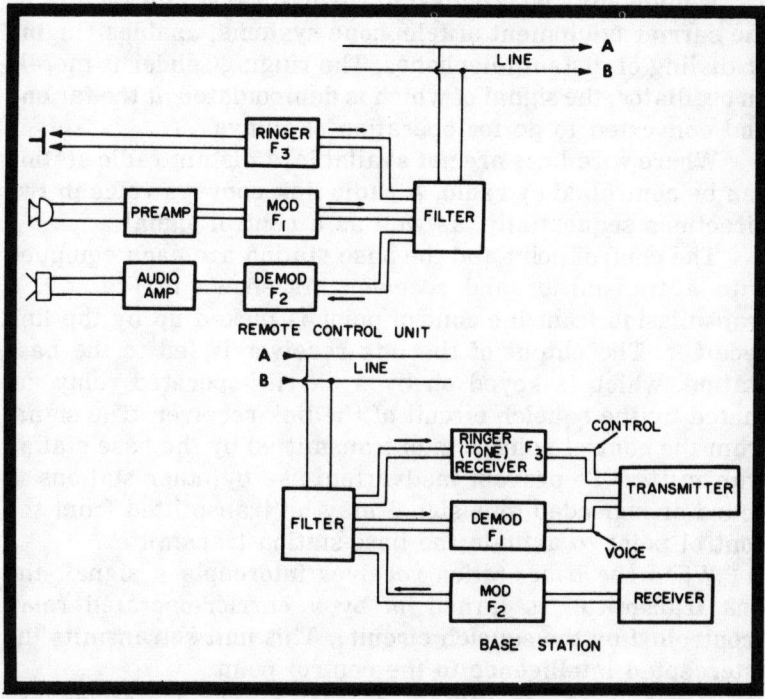

Fig. 4-6. Telephone carrier equipment for controlling a remote base station over a regular telephone line.

transmits a carrier signal over the wire line to the transmitter. There, a **demod** unit intercepts the audio signal, converts it back to normal audio, and then feeds it to the modulator input of the transmitter.

In the reverse direction, the audio output of the receiver is fed to a **mod** unit which feeds a carrier signal to the control unit. Here a **demod** unit converts the signal back to audio. The audio signal is amplified and fed to a speaker.

The "ringing" circuit of the carrier equipment is used for keying the transmitter. When the press-to-talk switch is closed, a tone is transmitted over the line. The tone actuates a relay in the tone receiver at the distant station.

There are several types of carrier equipment. Most popular is the single sideband, suppressed-carrier type. The audio signal modulates a small AM radio transmitter (**mod** unit) operating at a frequency above audibility. The carrier is removed, and only one of the sidebands is transmitted. At the receiving end, the carrier is generated locally, and the radio signal is demodulated (**demod** unit).

Ringing may be provided in various ways. This facility, in the carrier equipment of telephone systems, enables ringing or dialing of distant telephones. The ringing sender is merely an oscillator, the signal of which is demodulated at the far end and converted to dc for operation of relays.

Where wire lines are not available, a distant radio station can be controlled by radio. A radio link conveys voice in two directions sequentially, as well as a control signal.

The control point and the base station are each equipped with a transmitter and receiver. As shown in Fig. 4-7, a transmission from the control point is picked up by the link receiver. The output of the link receiver is fed to the base station, which is keyed on by a carrier-operated relay actuated by the squelch circuit of the link receiver. The signal from the control point is then transmitted by the base-station transmitter. To prevent inadvertent use by other stations, a coded or noncoded tone signal may be transmitted from the control point to actuate the base-station transmitter.

When the base-station receiver intercepts a signal, the link transmitter is turned on by a carrier-operated relay (controlled by the squelch circuit). This unit retransmits the intercepted intelligence to the control point.

Radio links for remote control of radio stations are generally operated in the 952-960 MHz UHF band. Although

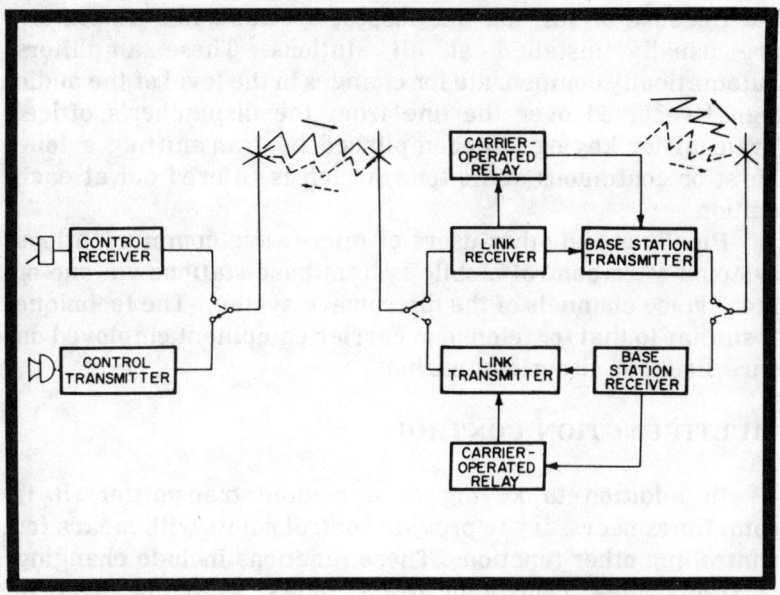

Fig. 4-7. Simplex radio link used to control a remote base station.

operation in the microwave bands might be more desirable under such circumstances, the cost of such an installation could be prohibitive.

RIGHT-OF-WAY SYSTEMS

Railroads in particular operate extensive right-of-way radio communications systems, which consist of numerous base stations along the right of way. These radio stations are sometimes controlled by telegraph operators at wayside towers. Often, however, they are controlled from the dispatcher's office, which may be a hundred or more miles away.

When controlled from a central point, these radio stations are generally connected to a party-line telephone circuit. All stations in the same division are bridged across the same wire line. The dispatcher can usually select any base station individually. A different tone or combination of tones can be used for actuating frequency-selective decoders at each station. Coded tones may also be transmitted which actuate special selectors. The selector at each station is responsive to its own code only.

Because of varying line losses, special audio amplifiers are usually installed at all stations. These amplifiers automatically compensate for changes in the level of the audio signal received over the line from the dispatcher's office. Transmitter keying is accomplished by transmitting a tone burst or continuous audio tone, which is filtered out at each station.

Pipelines and other users of microwave communications systems often control mobile-system base stations via one or more voice channels of the microwave system. The technique is similar to that for telephone carrier equipment employed on wire lines, as described earlier.

MULTIFUNCTION CONTROL

In addition to keying of a remote transmitter, it is sometimes necessary to provide control points with means for controlling other functions. These functions include changing of frequencies, control of tower lights, switching over to standby equipment, etc.

This can be done—over a two-wire line—on a dc basis to a limited extent, and on a tone (ac) basis to a very broad extent. Fig. 4-3 shows how, on a dc basis, the transmitter can be keyed

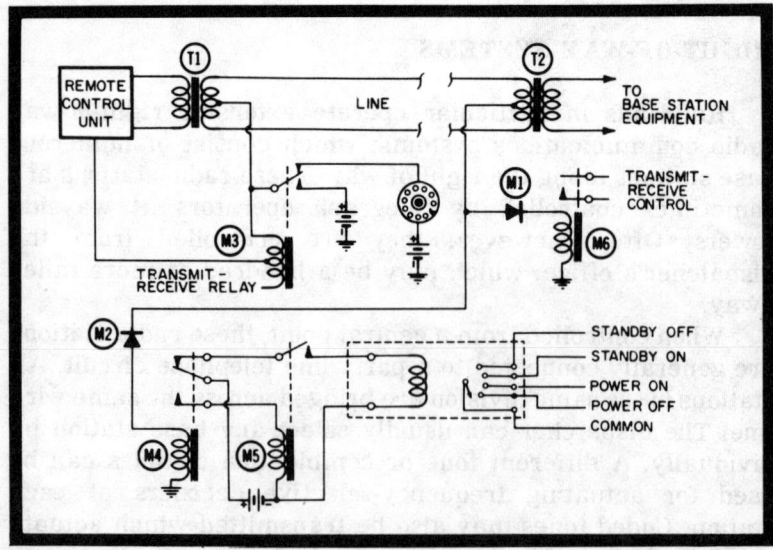

Fig. 4-8. Single pair, simplexed to ground, for controlling several functions.

and the frequency changed. Further functions can be performed by providing a dial at the control point and a selector at the distant station, as shown in Figs. 4-8 and 4-9. In Fig. 4-8, a single pair, simplexed to ground, can be used for remote control of several functions at a base station, as well as control of the transmit-receive function and transmission of audio information. In Fig. 4-9 the operator can select any of four antennas at the base station by dialing the proper number. The same single pair is used for audio transmission, transmit-receive control, and conveyance of dialing pulses.

On an ac basis, multiple functions can be controlled over a wire line, carrier channel, or radio link. Each function requires a different audio tone. A single tone can be coded to permit its use for a very large number of functions; Fig. 4-10 and 4-11 illustrate both techniques.

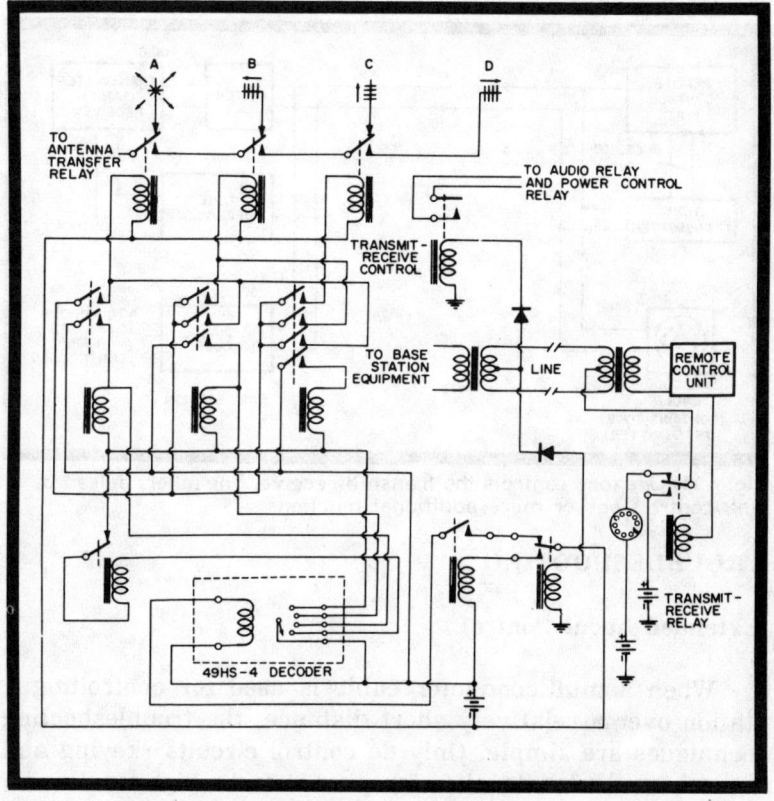

Fig. 4-9. Base-station operator selects antenna by dialing proper number.

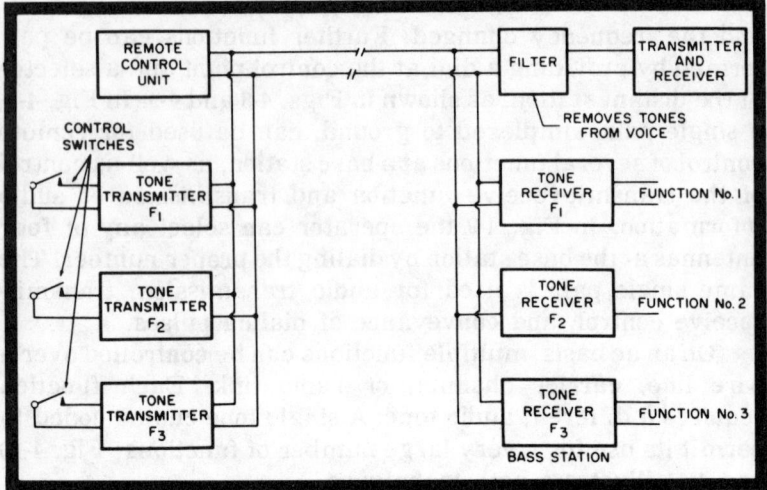

Fig. 4-10. Different tones can be used to control various functions.

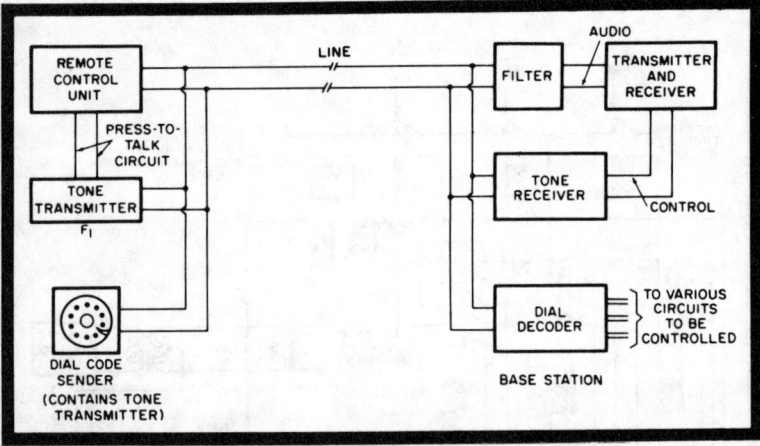

Fig. 4-11. One tone controls the transmit-receive. The other, pulsed by a dial, controls one or more additional functions.

TROUBLESHOOTING

Extended Local Control

When a multiconductor cable is used for controlling a station over a relatively short distance, the troubleshooting techniques are simple. Only dc control circuits (keying and squelch) and a low-level (microphone) and a high-level audio circuit are involved.

The transmitter control circuit may fail because of a poor connection or a defective push-to-talk switch, relay connector, or cable. A small dc voltage should be found across the switch contacts when the switch is open. If the relay at the radio equipment closes but the transmitter does not turn on, the trouble, of course, is not in the control system.

If no sound is heard at the remote speaker, the audio output at the receiver should be checked with a speaker. If there is audio at the receiver output, either the circuit to the control point is shorted or open, the remote volume control is defective, or the speaker itself has an open voice coil.

Hum in the carrier when transmitting can be caused by inadequate shielding of the microphone line. The shield should be grounded at the radio-unit end of the cable only, never at the microphone location. If the shield is grounded at both ends, hum is most likely to result.

Two-Wire Remote Control

When one is speaking into the microphone of a remote-control unit and the push-to-talk switch is closed, an audio signal should be present at the line terminals of the control unit. A reading of around 0.775 volt should be obtained (0 dBm) when the unit is connected to the line or its output is loaded with a 600-ohm resistor.

No audio at this point could be due to a defective microphone or amplifier, a poor connection, or dirty relay contacts. It it turns out to be relay trouble, burnish the contacts with a proper burnishing tool. Never sandpaper relay contacts!

If audio is present but the transmitter does not go on, the fault could be in the remote control unit, the line, or the line relay at the station.

With the push-to-talk relay closed, the dc control voltage should be available between one of the line terminals and the ground terminal if a simplexed-to-ground system is used (see Fig. 4-12). If one of the composite circuits is used, check the schematic to determine where dc should be present when the control unit is set to transmit.

The voltage across the coil of the line relay at the station end of the circuit can be checked. When the remote control unit is set to transmit, a dc voltage should appear across the

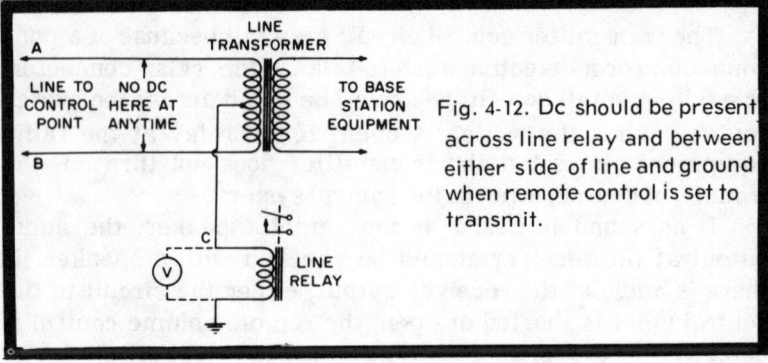

Fig. 4-12. Dc should be present across line relay and between either side of line and ground when remote control is set to transmit.

coil. If this voltage is too low to pull in the relay and at the control unit it is normal, the trouble could be a poor ground at either or both ends of the line or ground currents. Although the voltage at the control unit is adequate and the line is all right, ground currents of opposing polarity can reduce the voltage across the relay coil, and thus make the relay inoperative.

A good ground is absolutely necessary at each end of the system when a simplexed-to-ground circuit is employed. A ground connection can be easily checked. Merely connect one terminal of a 115-volt lamp to the ground connection and the other terminal to one side of the ac line, at a convenient outlet (see Fig. 4-13). If the lamp does not light, try the other side of the line. If it will not light either way, the ground is ineffective. The lamp should light brightly when connected to one side of the ac line (ungrounded side) and ground, but not when connected to the other side of the line (grounded).

If the line is leased from a telephone company and is suspected as being defective, do not make any tests or repairs. Instead, call the telephone company. The continuity of a private line can easily be checked by shorting one end and measuring the resistance at the open end. The normal resistance can be learned by consulting a wire table. Remember that a one-mile line has two miles of wire.

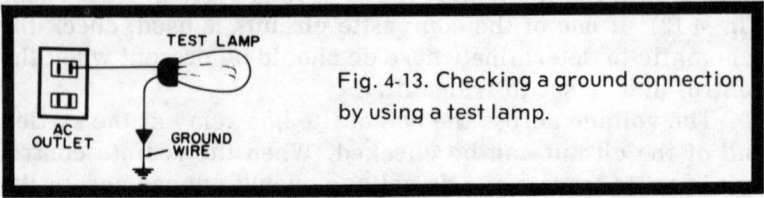

Fig. 4-13. Checking a ground connection by using a test lamp.

MONITORING

A radio station which transmits and receives on the same frequency is provided with means for automatically monitoring on its operating frequency. Many two-frequency radio stations which transmit on one channel and receive on another are not—but should be—equipped for monitoring the transmitter channel to avoid interfering with other systems operating on the same frequency.

A monitor receiver at the main remote control point enables the operator to hear his own signal and thus determine its quality. A meter can be connected to the receiver to indicate the relative field strength so that the operator can note when the power output falls off. The monitor receiver can also serve as the station receiver when the main receiver is not functioning.

Numerous monitor receivers are now on the market, both tunable and fixed-tuned types. Some of the crystal-controlled, fixed-tuned types can be equipped with crystals for operation on from 2 to 10 channels. One channel can be used to monitor the station frequency; another can be used to monitor other channels, such as 162.40 MHz on which the National Weather Service broadcasts weather information.

SELECTIVE CALLING

Ordinarily, mobile radio units and base stations are arranged so that all transmissions within range on the same frequency will be heard. When the base station calls one mobile unit of a system, all other mobiles will also hear the transmission. When two or more systems share the same channel in the same vicinity, they will hear each other's transmissions. The channel is like a party line, with everybody listening in.

As the number of systems that must share a common channel becomes greater, the mutual interference and lack of privacy will become less tolerable. Many systems have already been equipped with tone squelch, and the number of systems equipped with selective calling is increasing rapidly.

In a conventional mobile unit, the speaker is muted except when a signal of sufficient strength is intercepted. The squelch is not selective in regard to the station to which it will respond.

When tone squelch is added, the speaker will be activated only when the incoming radio carrier is accompanied by a tone of a specific frequency. If all mobile units and base stations are equipped with tone squelch, the speakers at these stations will be activated only by transmissions from stations within the same system, not by stations of other systems operating on the same frequency.

A tone-squelch device may be an add-on accessory or a built-in feature. It consists of a tone generator and a frequency-selective tone receiver. The tone is actuated automatically when the transmitter is keyed. Both tone and voice are thus transmitted at the same time. The frequency-selective tone receivers at all stations in the system respond to the tone, which is rectified and used to control the speaker. Thus, whenever a station goes on the air, the transmission is heard by all other stations in the same system. However, signals from other systems are locked out.

The tone may be at any frequency between about 50 to 3300 Hz. Since it is transmitted at the same time as the voice, it

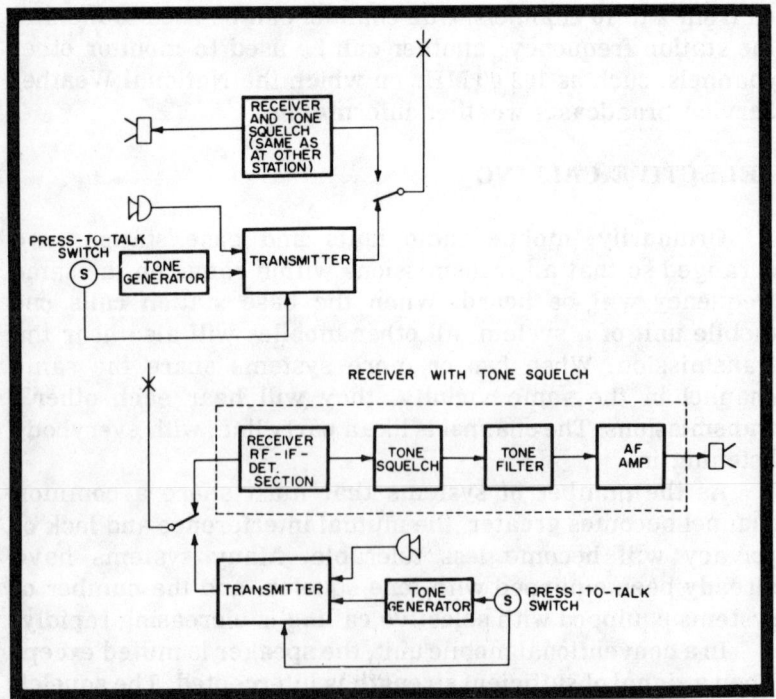

Fig. 4-14. Tone-squelch system.

must be filtered out at the receivers to preclude interference with voice reception. The tone will not be heard by stations within the system because of the filter, but will be heard by all stations not equipped with tone squelch if they are on the same frequency and within range. Fig. 4-14 is a block diagram of a tone-squelch system.

In some tone-squelch systems, the tone is present whenever the transmitter is turned on. In others, a short tone burst is transmitted at the start of a transmission. The tone burst opens the squelch; the radio carrier holds it open, closing it at the end of the transmission. A second tone burst can also be used to disable the squelch.

By using tones of differing frequencies, two or more systems can operate in the same vicinity and on the same radio channel without mutual interference. The stations of system A, for example, will hear transmissions from other system A stations only, and so on.

Tone squelch is a step forward in the right direction. In addition to locking out transmissions from other nearby systems operating on the same frequency, it also locks out long-distance skip interference. The same basic idea has been extended to provide selective calling. In a selective-calling system, the base station is equipped to transmit a different tone to signal each mobile unit. All mobile receivers are equipped with a tone decoder, each responsive to a different tone or tone combination. The base-station operator merely pushes a different button for each mobile to be signaled. The speakers at all mobile units remain silent except when a tone (or the combination) which matches the tone decoder is intercepted. The tone signal may be a burst, a continuous tone, or a combination of tones. Figure 4-15 shows a typical tone-selective signaling system. Tone signaling is fast in response but limited in capacity.

Resonant reeds are widely used in tone generators for frequency control. Vibrating-rred relays and other electromechanical resonators, which react only to tones of the correct frequency, are used in several types of tone decoders.

DIAL SYSTEMS

In a selective-calling dial system, a single tone is pulsed by an ordinary telephone dial. The pulses are transmitted by radio, and are intercepted by all receivers within range that are tuned to the same frequency. Each receiver in a system is

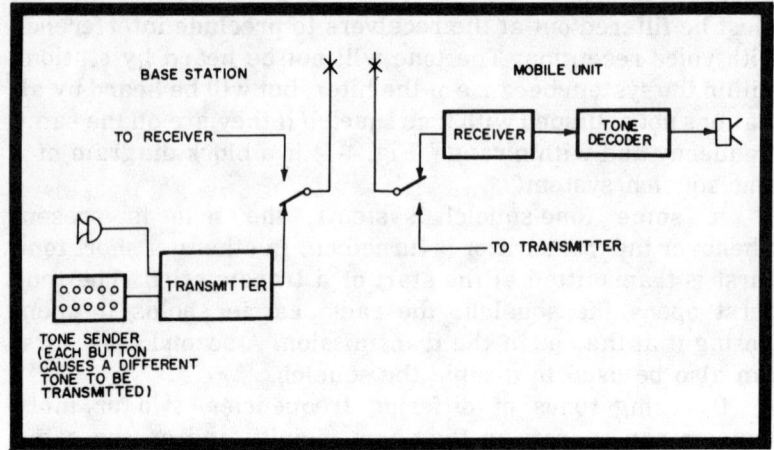

Fig. 4-15. Tone-type selective-calling system.

equipped with a dial pulse decoder. The decoders are set so that each one responds to a different number. The base-station operator dials one number to signal mobile unit **A**, another to signal mobile unit **B**, and so on.

The decoder contains a frequency selective audio amplifier and an electronic control circuit. The latter actuates an electromechanical selector which steps with each pulse. The selector contacts close only when a matching train of pulses is intercepted. Although all of the decoders in a system are actuated by the incoming tone pulses, only the one whose selector setting matches the incoming pulse train closes its contacts. Closure of the contacts momentarily sounds a buzzer and turns on a lamp, which remains lit until turned off by an indicator release switch located on the call head. The lamp serves as a "leave word" indicator. Should a call be intercepted at an unattended mobile station, the lighted lamp warns the driver, upon returning to his vehicle, to check in by radio.

The pulses are generated by a dial code sender, which is connected to the audio input of the base station transmitter. When the dial is spun at the start of a call, its off-normal contacts close a relay circuit. The relay applies voltage to an audio oscillator, connects the oscillator output to the transmitter, and turns on the transmitter. The oscillator now generates a tone. As the dial returns to its normal position, its pulsing springs break (or shift) the tone a number of times (corresponding to the digit dialed). Each time the tone is interrupted or shifted, by a "break" pulse, the selector steps once.

Sometimes the selector is equipped with more than one contact pair. When equipped with five contacts, the same selector can be set to respond to any of five different code combinations. This is advantageous when one number, common to all mobiles, is used for signaling all mobiles at once, another number is used for alerting an individual mobile, another for momentarily turning on the vehicle horn to call the driver back to an unattended vehicle, etc.

In addition to base-to-mobile signaling, selective calling is being used for mobile-to-mobile signaling as well as for mobile-to-base signaling when a system has more than one base station or several remote and dispatch control points, each to be signaled individually.

Solid-state decoders employing transistors and diodes are also available. These units are faster and more reliable than electromechanical decoders.

5 Antenna Systems

A mobile unit or a base station is no more effective than its antenna system. A low-powered transmitter equipped with an effective antenna system will often cover a larger area than a high-powered transmitter with a poor antenna system.

Transmitting range is determined by transmitter power, receiver sensitivity, electrical efficiency of the antenna system, effective antenna elevation, and noise level.

Effective antenna elevation is not the same as **antenna height**. Figure 5-1 illustrates the difference between these often-confused terms. An antenna 200 ft tall in a valley 100 ft deep would have an effective elevation of only 100 ft. On the other hadn, a 20 ft antenna on top of 980 ft Twin Peaks in San Francisco would have an effective elevation of 1000 ft.

A center-fed dipole antenna is often the standard against which antennas are compared for electrical efficiency. It is said to have **unity gain.** An antenna with 10 dB of gain is one which radiates a signal 10 times more powerful than that of a dipole.

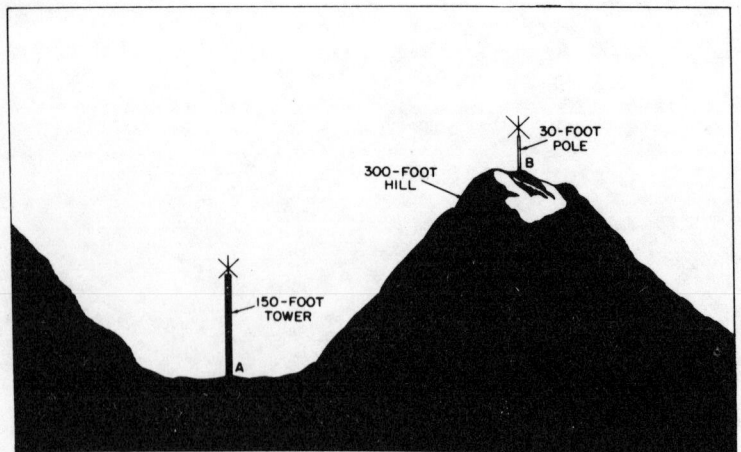

Fig. 5-1. The effective elevation of antenna "A" is less than that of antenna "B", even though "A" is taller than "B". The effective elevation of "B" is 330 feet.

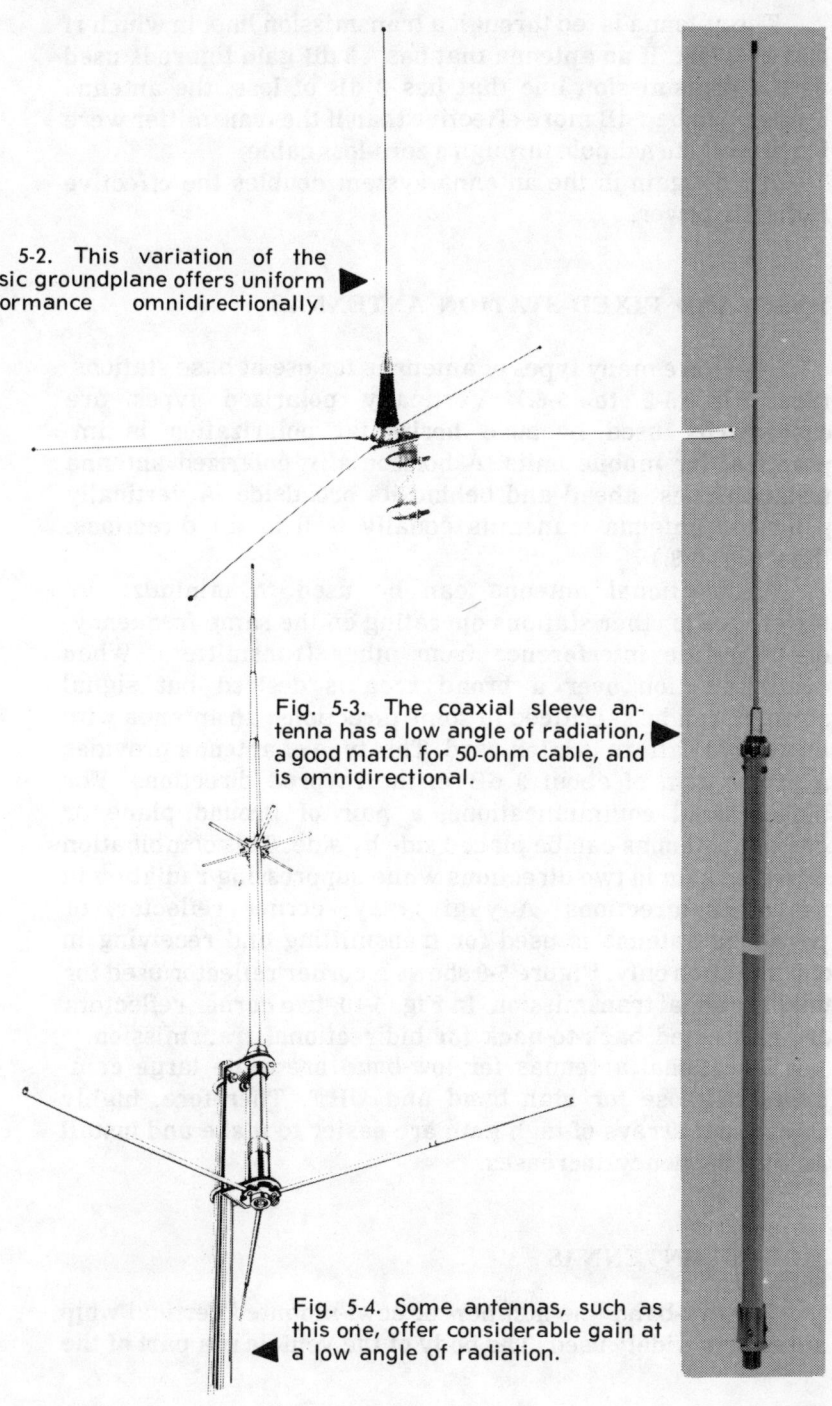

Fig. 5-2. This variation of the classic groundplane offers uniform performance omnidirectionally.

Fig. 5-3. The coaxial sleeve antenna has a low angle of radiation, a good match for 50-ohm cable, and is omnidirectional.

Fig. 5-4. Some antennas, such as this one, offer considerable gain at a low angle of radiation.

The antenna is fed through a transmission line, in which rf power is lost. If an antenna that has a 3 dB gain figure is used with a transmission line that has 2 dB of loss, the antenna system will be 1 dB more effective than if the transmitter were fed directly to a dipole through a zero-loss cable. A 3 dB gain in the antenna system doubles the effective radiated power.

BASE- AND FIXED-STATION ANTENNAS

There are many types of antennas for use at base stations. (See Fig. 5-2 to 5-6.) Vertically polarized types are customarily used because horizontal polarization is impractical for mobile units. A horizontally polarized antenna transmits best ahead and behind its broadside. A vertically polarized antenna transmits equally well in all directions. (See Fig. 5-8.)

A directional antenna can be used to minimize interference to other stations operating on the same frequency, or to reduce interference from other transmitters. When communication over a broad area is desired but signal strength can be sacrificed in some directions, an antenna with a cardioid pattern is often used. This type of antenna provides a power gain of about 3 dB in the favored directions. For bidirectional communications, a pair of ground plane or coaxial antennas can be placed side by side. This combination provides gain in two directions while suppressing radiation in the other directions. A yagi array, corner reflector, or parabolic antenna is used for transmitting and receiving in one direction only. Figure 5-9 shows a corner reflector used for unidirectional transmission. In Fig. 5-10, two corner reflectors are connected back-to-back for bidirectional transmission.

Directional antennas for low-band are quite large compared to those for high band and UHF. Therefore, highly directional arrays of high gain are easier to make and install as the frequency increases.

MOBILE ANTENNAS

For low-band, the bumper- or cowl-mounted vertical whip antenna is widely used. The body of the vehicle is a part of the

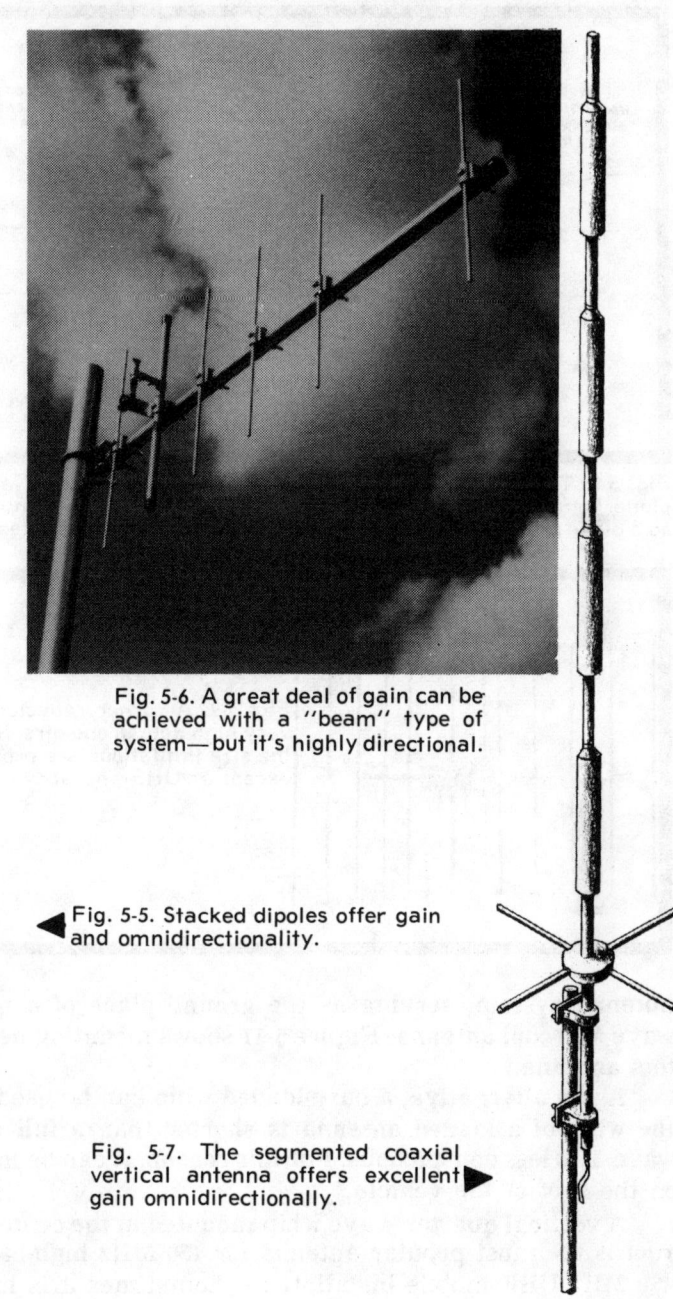

Fig. 5-6. A great deal of gain can be achieved with a "beam" type of system—but it's highly directional.

Fig. 5-5. Stacked dipoles offer gain and omnidirectionality.

Fig. 5-7. The segmented coaxial vertical antenna offers excellent gain omnidirectionally.

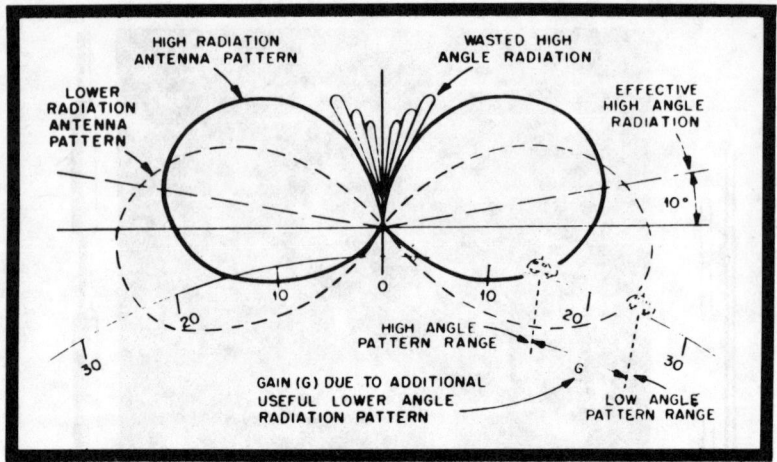

Fig. 5-8. The solid line shows the vertical pattern typical of a ground-plane. Some antennas, however, are built to radiate the maximum signal on a plane precisely perpendicular to the upright axis of the antenna.

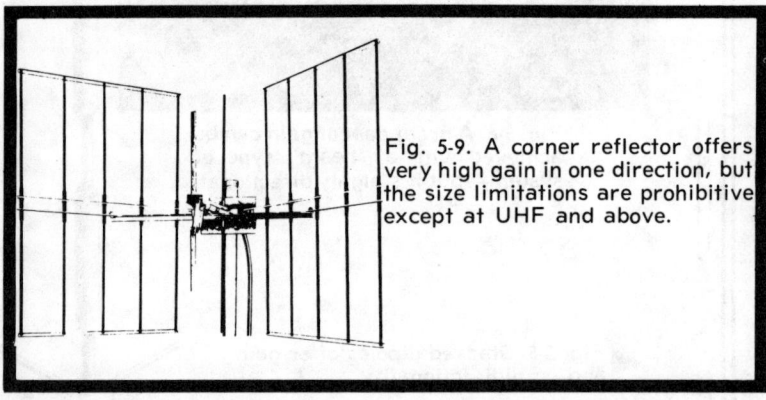

Fig. 5-9. A corner reflector offers very high gain in one direction, but the size limitations are prohibitive except at UHF and above.

antenna system, serving as the ground plane of a quarter-wave Marconi antenna. Figure 5-11 shows mounting details of this antenna.

As an alternative, a base-loaded whip can be used. Since the whip of a loaded antenna is shorter than a full quarter wave, it is less conspicuous. For this reason, it can be installed on the roof of the vehicle.

A vertical quarter-wave whip mounted in the center of the roof is the most popular antenna for 150 MHz high-band and 450 MHz UHF mobile installations. Sometimes it is mounted on the cowl, but reception and transmission are definitely inferior because of the inferior propagation pattern.

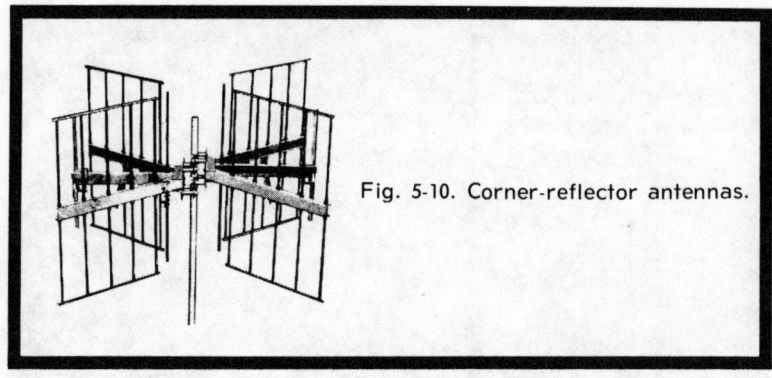

Fig. 5-10. Corner-reflector antennas.

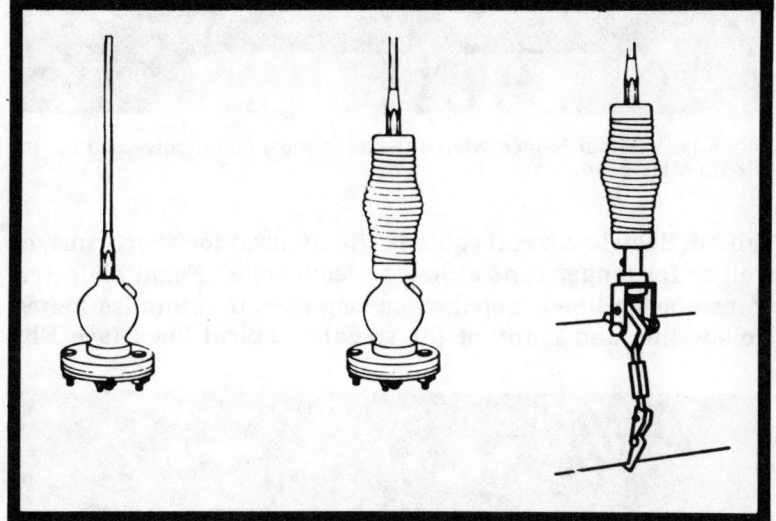

Fig. 5-11. Typical vehicular antennas and their mountings.

A coaxial antenna mounted on a piece of pipe or tubing and supported by a bumper is sometimes used when the owner does not want a hole drilled in the roof of his car. Since an auto body mechanic can easily fill in the small hole, there is little excuse for using a coaxial antenna here, except on convertibles.

TRANSMISSION LINES

Most commercial antennas are designed to match a 50-ohm transmission line, although some match a 72-ohm line.

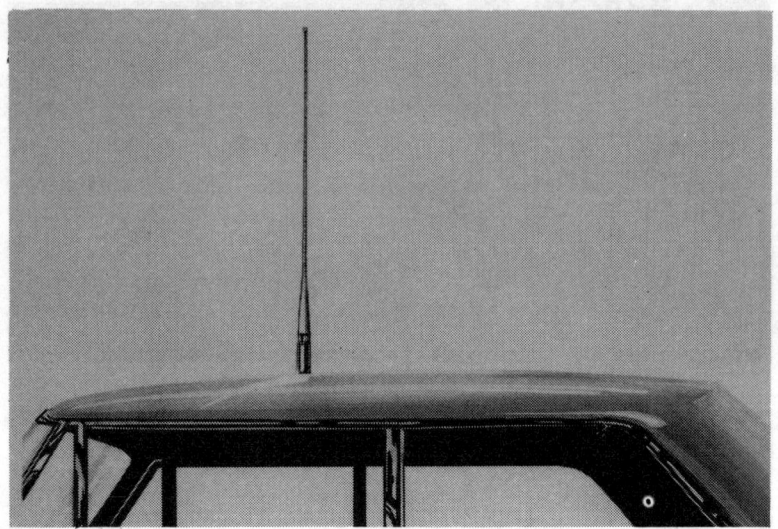

Fig. 5-13. Vertical 18-inch whip antenna is most commonly used for the 152-174 MHz band.

Solid-dielectric coaxial cable is widely used for short runs, as well as for longer runs at lower frequencies. Foam-dielectric transmission line is popular for long runs to minimize losses. Hollow line and many of the so-called spiral lines (see Fig.

Fig. 5-13. A spiral-wound foam dielectric in the coaxial line minimizes losses.

5-13) are filled with a gas or dry air, which is kept within the line under pressure to prevent moisture from entering.

The center conductor of these transmission lines is connected to the radiating element of the antenna and to the antenna terminal of the radio unit. The shield is connected to the ground radials, ground plane, car body, or ground sheath of the antenna (depending upon the type), and to the radio ground terminal.

Figure 5-14 shows the important characteristics of various antenna transmission lines at mobile-system frequencies.

FIXED-ANTENNA SUPPORTS

A wooden telephone or power pole is a convenient base- or fixed-station antenna support. Arrangements for installing the pole can usually be made with a local telephone or power company. Since guy wires are seldom needed, a minimum of ground area is required. Steps should be provided so that the antenna can be easily serviced.

Metal towers are also widely used as antenna supports (Fig. 5-15). Available in great heights, they are excellent where high antennas are required, because they can withstand high winds and heavy ice loading. (The antenna should be no higher than necessary to provide the required range. Other-

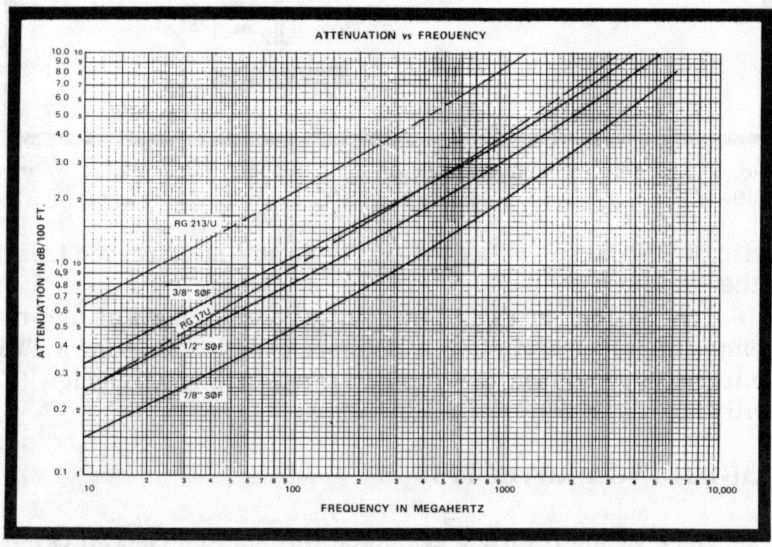

Fig. 5-14. The type of coaxial line has a great deal to do with rf losses.

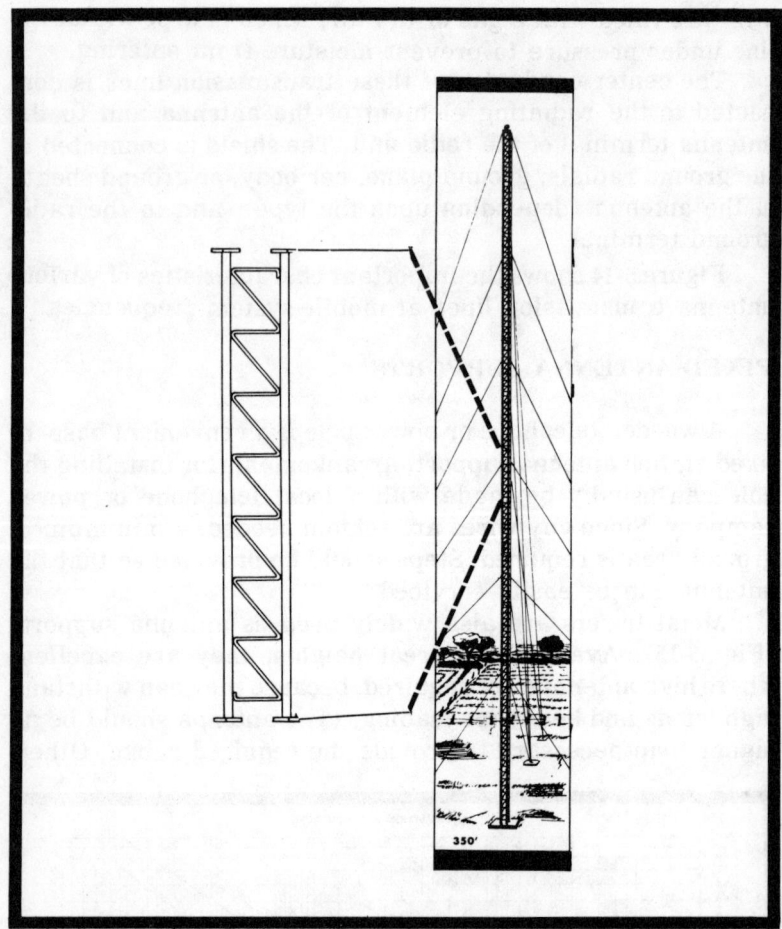

Fig. 5-15. Metal tower used as an antenna support. (Courtesy of Rohn Mfg. Co.)

wise, it will cause—as well as suffer from—interference from other stations.)

A water tank or roof of a building is often used as an antenna support. Installation is no more complex than for a TV antenna, except that the support must be strong enough to withstand high winds and ice loading.

LIGHTNING PROTECTION

The antenna return is grounded through the coaxial cable if the radio unit is grounded. For maximum lightning protection, however, a separate ground should be provided. A short wire, 10-gage or larger, should be run from the base of the antenna to a ground rod. The ground wire should have no kinks or sharp bends, which offer a high impedance to the sharp leading edge of a static discharge.

FIXED-ANTENNA INSTALLATION

Although it is generally true that the higher the antenna, the greater the range, it has sometimes been found that maximum range is obtained by installing the antenna at a critical height. This is often attributed to the role the earth's surface plays in determining antenna impedance. Notice in Fig. 5-16 the increase in useful range obtained with a 300 ft antenna compared with a 125 ft antenna. For example, when a 125 ft antenna is used, a 10 uV signal at 50 MHz can be received at a distance of 23 miles. With a 300 ft antenna, the same signal can be received 32 miles from the base station.

For obvious reasons, the antenna should be kept away from sources of electrical interference. Noise is a problem in the 25-50 MHz band, but is of much less significance in the 450-512 MHz band.

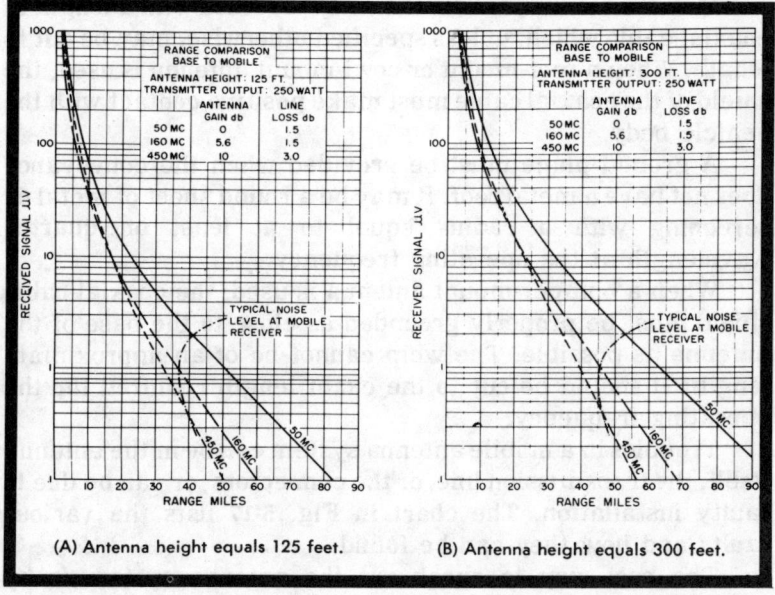

(A) Antenna height equals 125 feet.   (B) Antenna height equals 300 feet.

Fig. 5-16. Performance comparisons with two antenna heights.

Although the transmission line is sometimes connected directly to the antenna, a coaxial connector is usually employed. A connector is always used at the radio end. Only connectors should be used which were specifically designed for the particular transmission line. If not, losses can be introduced because of impedance mismatches.

Whenever possible, the antenna transmission line should be one continuous length: splices should be avoided. When necessary to join two pieces of cable, suitable splicing connectors should be utilized. If hollow transmission line or RG-17—U coaxial cable is used, suitable adaptors and connectors must be used to interface with the antenna and radio unit.

The transmission line must be suspended and not allowed to hang. Care must be exercised, when the cable is fastened, to avoid damaging the line. Changes in the shape of the line can cause impedance variations, which will result in undesirable losses.

MOBILE-ANTENNA INSTALLATIONS

Mobile antennas are customarily provided with a length of coaxial cable which, unless specified otherwise, may be cut to length. When a roof-mount or cowl-mount antenna is used, the shield of the coaxial cable must make positive contact with the vehicle body.

A ground plane must be provided when the conveyance does not have a metal roof. It may be a round sheet of metal or screening with a radius equal to at least one-quarter wavelength at the operating frequency.

When a bumper-mount antenna is used, the coaxial-cable shield must be properly grounded as close to the base of the antenna as possible. The whip cannot be of an approximate length: it should be cut to the exact length required for the operating frequency.

Troubles in a mobile antenna system can be in the antenna itself, the transmission line, or the connectors, or can be due to faulty installation. The chart in Fig. 5-17 lists the various faults and how they can be found.

The best way to check out the antenna system is by measuring the signal strength at a distant receiver, and comparing it with the signal from another mobile unit at the

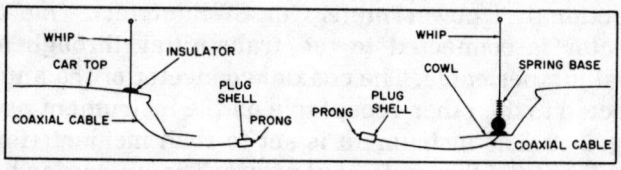

Ohmmeter Connections	Indication	Condition
Prong and shell of coaxial connector.	Open circuit.	OK.
	Low resistance.	Short circuit in cable or plug, or at antenna insulator.
	High resistance.	Leaky cable insulation; dirty plug or antenna insulator.
Shell of coaxial connector and vehicle body.	Short circuit.	OK.
	Open circuit.	Defective ground connection at antenna base, or broken connection to cable shield at antenna base or plug.
Prong at coaxial connector and vehicle body, but with antenna whip temporarily grounded through a test lead to vehicle body.	Short circuit.	OK.
	Open circuit.	Open cable or broken connection.

Fig. 5-17. Trouble chart for mobile quarter-wave antennas. (Does not apply to antennas with shunt-fed loading coils or shorted matching stubs.)

same location. The comparative signal strengths can be measured by metering the limiter voltage in an FM receiver or the agc voltage in an AM receiver. This check requires three people, one at each mobile unit and the third at the distant receiver.

A one-man check can be made with a fluorescent lamp. One end of the lamp is touched to the antenna (near the top) while the transmitter is on. If power is reaching the antenna, the lamp should glow. Another one-man check is with a bidirectional rf power meter (or SWR meter). One coaxial connector is connected to the transmitter through a short coaxial jumper cable. The coaxial connector of the antenna is connected to the other receptacle on the instrument as shown in Fig. 5-18. The instrument is set to read incident (forward) power first, and then reflected power. The difference between the two is theoretically the amount of power absorbed by the antenna, but it doesn't work quite that way. When return power is more than 20 percent of outgoing power, the standing waves are severe enough to cause readings higher than actual power levels. When return power is less than 15 percent of outgoing power, you can safely calculate output power by subtracting the return power from the outgoing power. For example, if the first reading is 40 watts and the second is 5 watts, it can be assumed that 35 watts is being absorbed by the antenna and that 5 watts is being wasted in the transmission line. The loss, in addition to normal attenuation cable, is due to standing waves caused by impedance mismatches.

In the absence of an rf power meter; a field-strength meter can be used. The relative field strength is measured in the vicinity of the antenna, and the readings compared with those made previously.

An antenna that is exposed to the elements may need periodic replacement. The base insulator may become caked with dirt. This dirt will cause leakage. Because of skin effect, rust and accumulated film on the whip can become a path through which the rf current flows in preference to the actual whip.

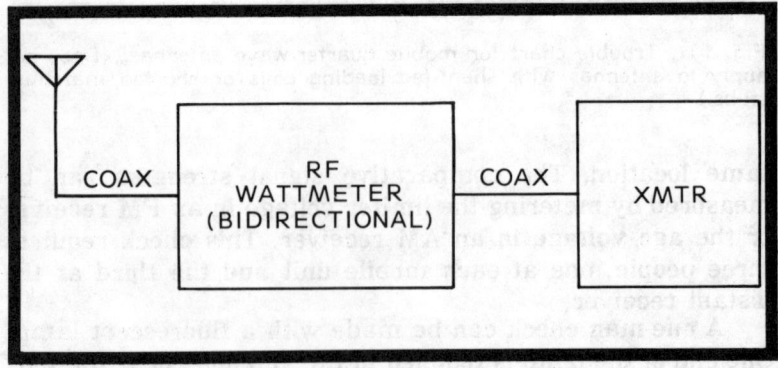

Fig. 5-18. Measuring rf power with a bidirectional wattmeter.

Poor connections and accumulated dirt and moisture at the antenna cables are a frequent source of trouble. Contact by the cable shield with the car body should be checked in particular.

FIXED-ANTENNA TROUBLESHOOTING

If both the talk-out and talk-in ranges are shorter than normal, the antenna system should be suspected. A quick check is to substitute another antenna system. A piece of wire connected to the antenna terminal will usually suffice.

A bidirectional rf power meter, connected in series with the antenna transmission line at the radio-unit end, as shown in Fig. 5-18, can be used to measure incident and reflected power.

An excessive difference between incident and reflected power indicates trouble in the transmission line, antenna, or connectors. If feasible, the power at the antenna end of the cable (with the antenna disconnected) should be measured with a termination-type rf wattmeter. If the power is less than anticipated—considering the cable length, attenuation of cable, and the operating frequency—the trouble apparently is in the cable.

The trouble may be due to improper transmitter tuning. The antenna tuning controls are there to balance out the reactance in the line so that the line (terminated in the antenna) looks like a pure resistance (50 or 72 ohms). If the transmitter is correctly tuned, the transmission line may be faulty.

A solid-dielectric cable that has been damaged or whose insulation has absorbed excessive moisture can be an extremely inefficient transmission medium, particularly at the higher frequencies. When this occurs, the cable should be replaced.

Another common fault is a short circuit or a high-resistance contact, resulting from improper installation of connectors.

When temperatures are extremely low, troubles may be caused by contraction of the inner conductor of the cable.

When an antenna system is checked with an ohmmeter at the radio end of the cable, an open circuit is generally indicated between the inner conductor and the shield of the cable. However, some antennas are provided with a matching stub, or are otherwise so designed that a short circuit will be indicated. This is a dc short circuit; but to the signal, the circuit looks like 50 ohms at the operating frequency.

The best test of the performance of an antenna system is an actual field test. By driving around in a mobile unit to determine the range, one can find out for sure how effective the antenna actually is. The minimum required antenna height (the critical height) for a given range can be determined during a field survey by using an antenna support like the one in Fig. 5-19, the height of which can be adjusted.

ANTENNA FARMS

In many large cities, the antennas of several remotely controlled base stations are installed on the roof of a tall building or a hilltop. Since all of the antennas are located in proximity to each other, it is often necessary to employ a cavity filter (Fig. 5-20) in series with the transmission line of each antenna to minimize mutual interference and intermod problems. In spite of the requirement for more elaborate antenna systems, this is an excellent way to make maximum utilization of an outstanding antenna site.

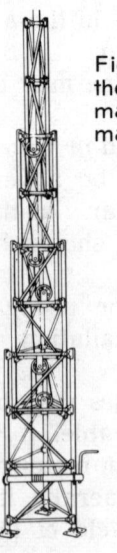

Fig. 5-19. A crank-up tower offers the advantage that antenna height may be easily adjusted by one man.

Fig. 5-20. A simple cavity improves receiver (or transmitter) selectivity.

ANTENNA SHARING

Separate receiving and transmitting antennas can be used at a two-frequency simplex or duplex base station or at the repeater station of a mobile relay system. But this requires two transmission lines as well as two antennas. Only one antenna and one transmission line are required when an antenna diplexer, such as the one shown in Fig. 5-21, is used. The diplexer has three ports, one for the transmitter output, one for the receiver input, and one for the antenna transmission line. The three ports (for coaxial cable) are connected as shown in Fig. 5-22.

In addition to diplexers, antenna multiplexers are available which make it possible for several transmitters to utilize a single antenna. These multiplexers cause only a small insertion loss but high isolation between transmitters.

ANTENNA GAIN AND RANGE

Base station antenna gain affects both transmission from the base station to mobile units and transmission from mobile

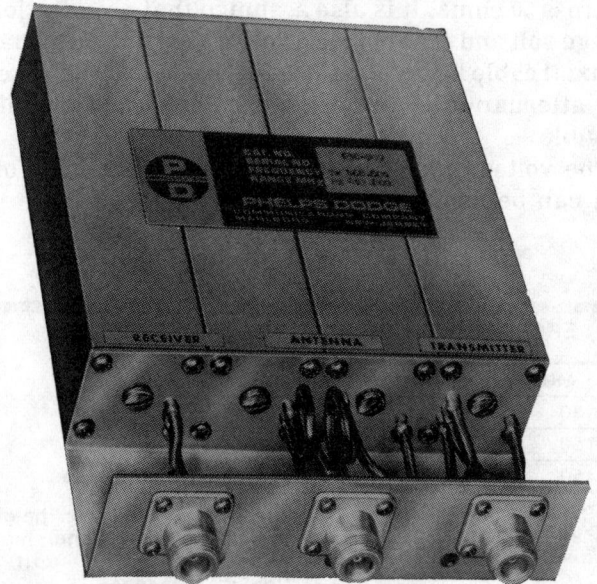

Fig. 5-21. A diplexer allows simultaneous transmission and reception using a single antenna.

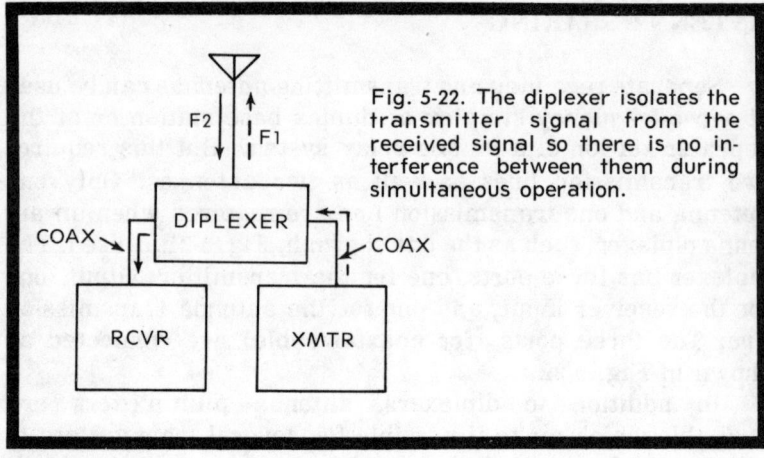

Fig. 5-22. The diplexer isolates the transmitter signal from the received signal so there is no interference between them during simultaneous operation.

units to the base station. A simple method for calculating range is to convert field strength given in microvolts per meter to microvolts across the feed point of the antenna. Since irregular terrain may be encountered in the transmission path, "shadow loss" due to obstructions must be considered.

It is assumed that the required input voltage for adequate receiver quieting for both the base station and mobile unit be 1 uV across 50 ohms. It is also assumed that propagation is over average soil and that polarization is vertical. Attenuation due to coaxial cable loss will be considered only at the base station, since attenuation of the coaxial cable in the mobile unit is negligible.

The voltage developed at the input terminals of an antenna can be expressed as follows:

$$V(uV) = hE$$

EFFECTIVE HEIGHT
h_{eff} (meters)

Freq. MHz	$\lambda/4$ Whip	Omni-6
30	1.35	7.5
150	0.32	1.5
450	0.1	0.49

Voltage at base of whip
$V(\mu v) = h_{eff} \times E$
E given μ v/m

Fig. 5-23. Effective heights (in meters) for low-band, high-band, and UHF—with "unity" and "gain" antennas.

where h is the effective height in meters, and E is field strength in microvolts per meter. In Fig. 5-23, the effective heights are given for a quarter-wave whip and an antenna providing about 6 dB of gain at the frequencies in question. If the above equation is rearranged and the required receiver voltage of 1 uV is inserted at the appropriate effective heights for the quarter-wave whip, the field strength should be 3.3 uV╱m. This is +9.6 dB above 1 uV╱m. In the case of the gain antenna, the field strength required to develop 1 uV at the input is 0.66 uV╱m. This is −3.6 dB referred to 1 uV╱m.

When considering transmission from the base station to the mobile unit at a frequency of 150 MHz, assume the base station antenna height is 100 ft and the gain of the transmitting antenna is 5.8 dB. The field strength indicated in Fig. 5-24 is based on 1 watt (1W) radiated: Fig. 5-25 gives the power correction factor. From this graph, it can be noted that for 50W the correction factor is 17 dB. If it is assumed that the coaxial feed system is slightly greater than 100 ft, the loss introduced by a ½ in. 50-ohm Spir-O-Foam (or equal) cable will be approximately −1.2 dB. Collecting the power, antenna gain, and coaxial loss (17.0 + 5.8 −1.2), the total correction is 21.6 dB. In the case of 1W radiated, it is indicated that +9.6 dB above 1 uV╱m is required. The curve in Fig. 5-24 shows this distance to be approximately 15 miles. However, due to the transmitter power and antenna gain with line loss subtracted,

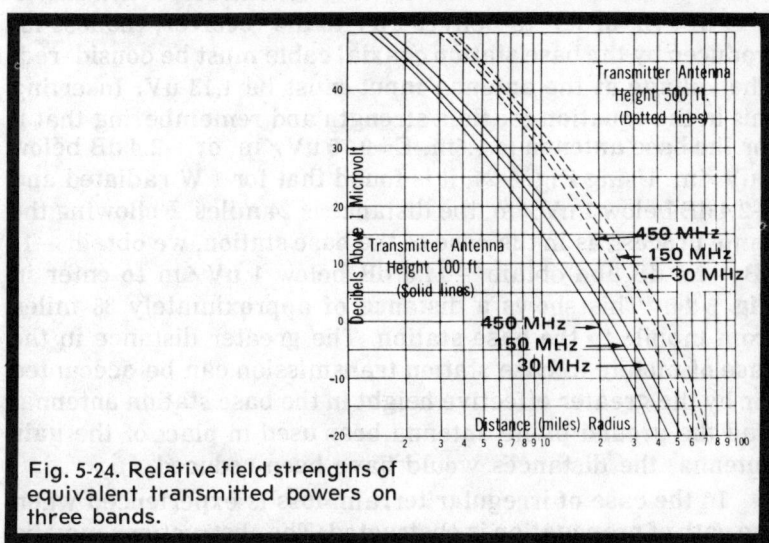

Fig. 5-24. Relative field strengths of equivalent transmitted powers on three bands.

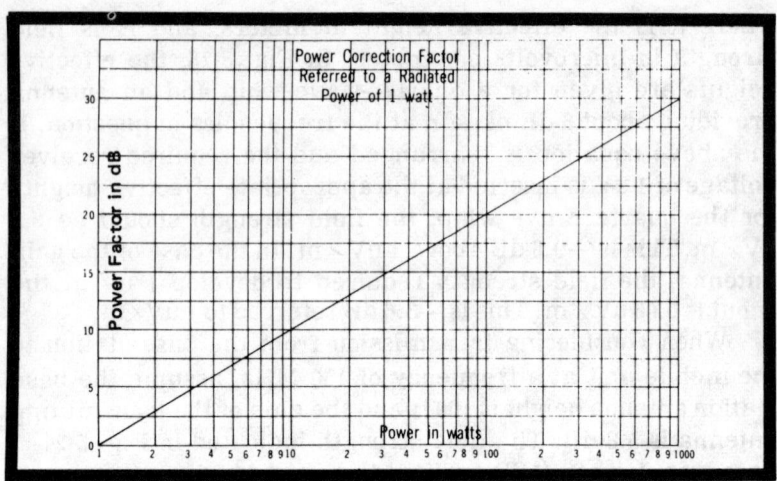

Fig. 5-25. Power correction factor, in decibels, for various rf power levels.

the propagation conditions have been improved; −21.6 dB + 9.6 dB = −12 dB below 1 uV/m. In Fig. 5-24, −12 dB below 1 uV/m indicates a distance of 35 miles over flat terrain.

Now, consider transmission from a mobile unit to the base station. Assume that the output of the mobile units is 30W. Referring to Fig. 5-25, the power correction factor for 30W is 14 dB. In considering a whip antenna at the mobile unit, −3 dB must be used as a correction factor. The total correction factor is 11 dB. In order to deliver 1 uV to the receiver, the loss introduced by the base station coaxial cable must be considered. The voltage at the antenna input must be 1.13 uV. Inserting this in the equation for field strength and remembering that h for the base antenna is 1.5m, E=0.75 uV/m, or −2.4 dB below 1 uV/m. Using Fig. 5-24, it is found that for 1 W radiated and −2.4 dB below 1 uV/m, the distance is 24 miles. Following the same process as in the case of the base station, we obtain −11 dB −2.4 dB abd obtain −14.6 dB below 1 uV/m to enter in Fig. 5-24. This shows a distance of approximately 38 miles from mobile to the base station. The greater distance in the case of mobile to base station transmission can be accounted for by the greater effective height in the base station antenna. Had the ground plane antenna been used in place of the gain antenna, the distances would have been reduced.

In the case of irregular terrain, loss is experienced when the path of propagation is obstructed. The obstructions may be buildings, hills, etc. The nomogram of Fig. 5-26 gives the shadow loss in decibels for the frequencies in question, where the construction lines are drawn according to the parameters as shown in the diagram. The example taken is for an obstruction 500 ft in height at a distance of 5 miles from the transmitter. The construction line indicates a loss of approximately 11 dB. In the case of the base station transmitting to the mobile unit, the loss in coverage is some 13 miles.

DIRECTIONAL GAIN

The approximate amount of gain can be determined by considering known theoretical patterns and known gains for these patterns, namely omnidirectional, bidirectional, and unidirectional. In the case of the omnidirectional high-gain antenna, the gain is due to a narrowing of the beam in the vertical plane yet maintaining 360 deg horizontal coverage. In the bidirectional case, increased gain is obtained by considering two wedges less than 360 deg of equal strength in diametrically opposite directions. In the unidirectional case, gain is obtained by reducing the vertical angle of radiation as well as directing most of the energy in only one direction. The half-power (3 dB) level in the pattern can be used to determine gain. Let **n** indicate an arbitrary number relative to a given half-power beamwidth in the vertical plane and **m** indicate an

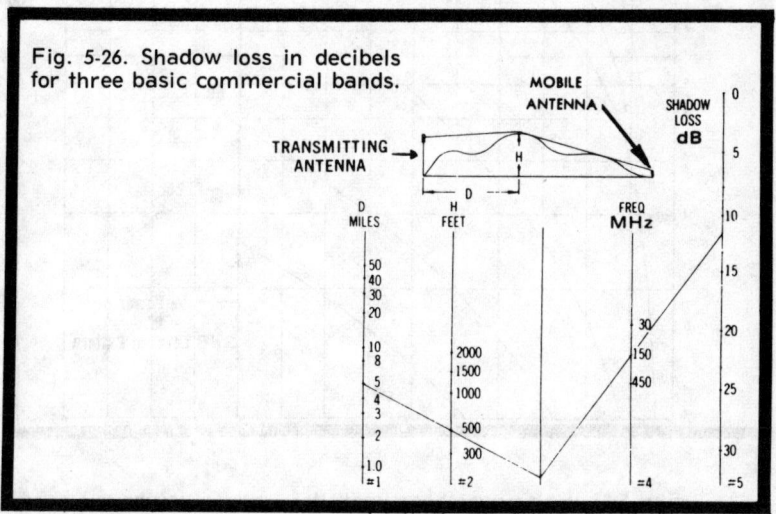

Fig. 5-26. Shadow loss in decibels for three basic commercial bands.

arbitrary number relative to a given half-power beamwidth in the horizontal plane.

The Prodelin Omni-6 antenna, for example, has a half-power beamwidth angle in the vertical plane of approximately 16 deg. Referring to the curves in Fig. 5-27, it can be noted that 16 deg intersects the half-power line for n or m equal 65. If we now enter on n or m as equal to 65 (Fig. 5-28), it can be seen that the gain over a half-wave dipole is approximately 6 dB.

In case B, consider that two half-wavelength dipoles are spaced one half-wavelength apart and fed in phase. In this case, the vertical pattern is that of a half-wave dipole

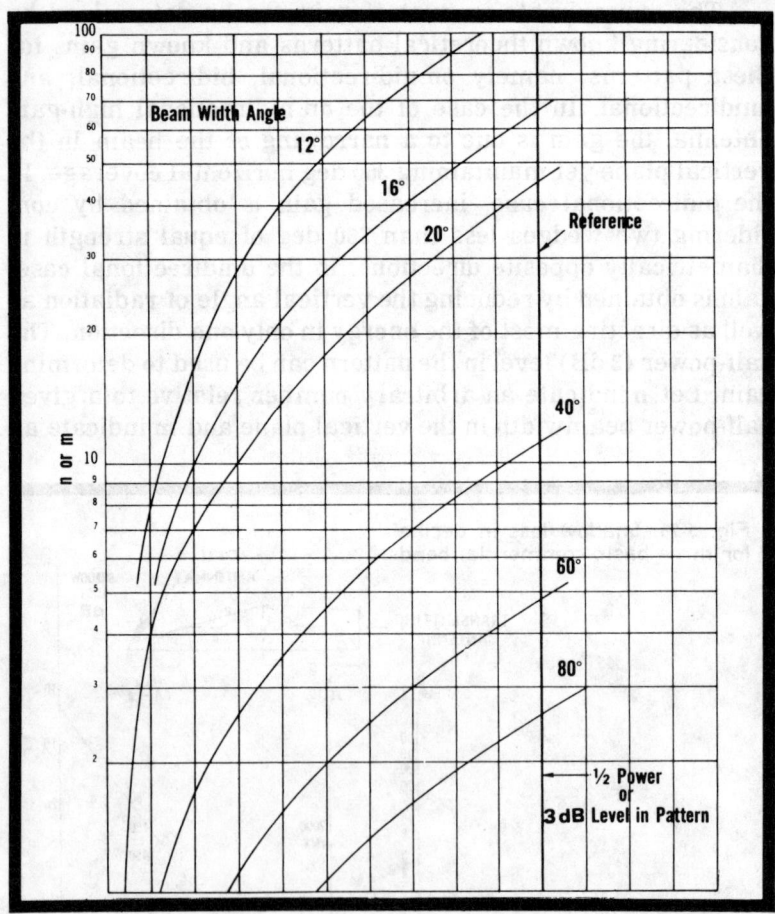

Fig. 5-27. Half-power beamwidth for various antennas.

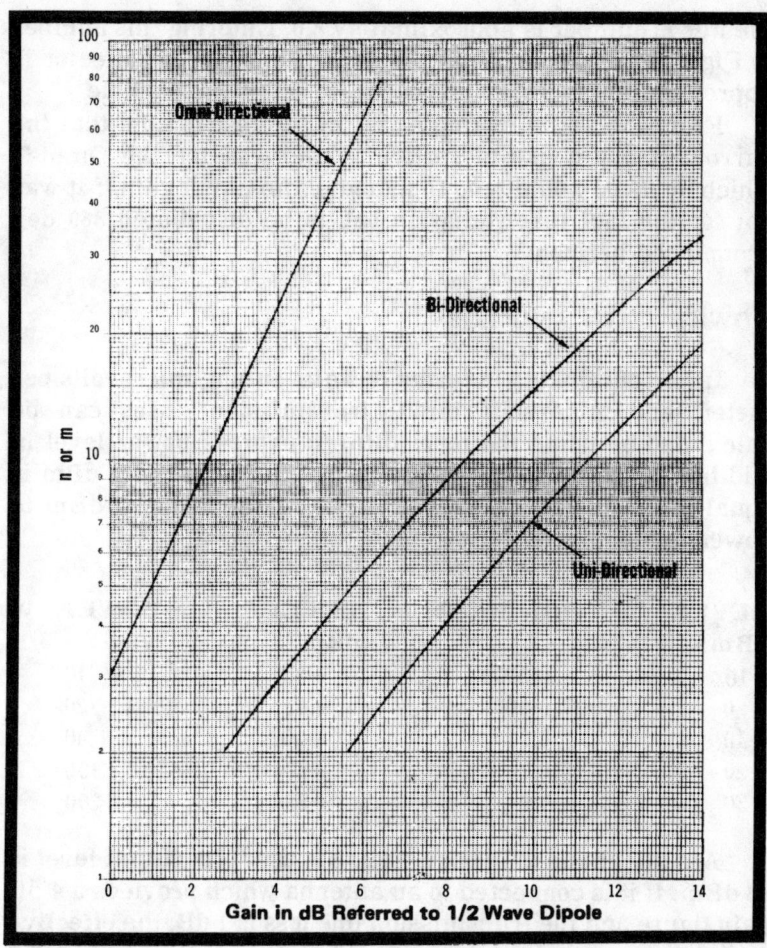

Fig. 5-28. Half-power vertical and horizontal beamwidths for antennas of various directivities.

having a half-power beamwidth of approximately 100 deg, and horizontal half-power beam width is 60 deg. The average value is approximately 80 deg, which gives **n** or **m** number of 2.5. In Fig. 5-28, an **n** or **m** number of 2.5 indicates 3.5 dB of gain.

In the unidirectional case, consider the corner reflector. The vertical half-power beamwidth is 50 deg, slightly less than that of the half-wave dipole. The horizontal half-power beamwidth is 40 deg. If **n** represents the characteristics in the vertical plane and **m** the characteristics in the horizontal plane, the average with **n** equal to 50 deg vertical and **m** equal to 90 deg horizontal, is 45 deg. Estimating 45 deg in Fig. 5-27,

119

the n or m number is approximately 8.0. Entering this number in Fig. 5-28, it is found that the gain of the corner reflector is approximately 10.5 dB with respect to a half-wave dipole.

From the above example it is of interest to note that the narrowest beam in the vertical plane was for the Omni-6, which by itself would tend to indicate maximum gain if it was not for the fact that radiation has to be distributed 360 deg around the horizon.

POWER GAIN AND LOSS

In lieu of thinking in terms of watts output, microvolts per meter, and microvolts input, transmission losses can be calculated by using the term dBm to express power level in addition to the term dB to express gain and loss. Zero dBm is equal to 1 milliwatt (0.001 watt). The relationships of dBm to power levels are as follows.

LEVEL, dBm	POWER, W	LEVEL, dBm	POWER, W
—10	0.0001	+40	10
0	0.001	+43	20
+10	0.01	+46	40
+20	0.1	+50	100
+30	1.0	+53	200

Assume that a 20W base station is used. Its output level is 43 dBm. If it is connected to an antenna which provides a 4 dB gain figure and the transmission line loss is 1 dB, the effective radiated power will be 40 watts (43 dBm + 4 dB —1 dB, for a net gain of 3 dB) or 46 dBm.

If the free-space transmission loss is 86 dB, the power level at the receiving antenna will be —40 dBm (—86 dB minus + 46 dBm is equal to —40 dBm). The received power level will be 0.1 uW.

The free-space attenuation at 150 MHz is approximately 100 dB over a 10-mile line-of-sight path. When the distance is doubled, the attenuation is 6 dB greater; when halved, it is 6 dB less. When the frequency is doubled, attenuation is 6 dB greater and, when halved, it is 6 dB less. When the frequency or distance is tripled, free-space attenuation is increased about 9 dB. And when reduced to one-third, attenuation is decreased by 9 dB. The above estimates are rough, with no shadow and absorption losses taken into consideration. The approximate free-space losses are as follows.

DISTANCE, Miles	LOSS AT 50 MHz, dB	LOSS AT 150 MHz, dB	LOSS AT 450 MHz, dB
5	85	94	103
10	91	100	109
20	97	106	115

It can be noted from the above that the free-space attenuation at 50 MHz is 9 dB less than at 150 MHz and 18 dB less than at 450 MHz. But this does not mean that transmission at 50 MHz is that much superior to transmission at higher frequencies since noise and easily attainable antenna gain must be taken into consideration. The signal levels at the input of a receiver are approximately as follows.

LEVEL, dBm	SIGNAL, uV	LEVEL, dBm	SIGNAL, uV
+40	7,000,000	-40	700
+20	700,000	-60	70
0	70,000	-80	7
-20	7,000	-100	0.7

Assume that the ambient noise level at 50 MHz is 1.75 uV (—92 dBm), 0.7 uV (—100 dBm) at 150 MHz, and 0.35 uV (—106 dBm) at 450 MHz. The following signal levels will be obtained at the receiver input terminals over a 10-mile line-of-sight path when using a 20W transmitter.

SIGNAL	LEVEL 50 MHz	LEVEL 150 MHz	LEVEL 450 MHz
Transmitter output	43 dBm	43 dBm	43 dBm
Coaxial cable loss	0.5 dB	-1 dB	-2 dB
Power to antenna	42.5 dBm	42 dBm	41 dBm
Antenna gain	0 dB	6 dB	10 dB
Effective radiated power	42.5 dBm	48 dBm	51 dBm
Free-space loss	91.0 dB	-100 dB	-109 dB
Intercepted power	-48.5 dBm	-52 dBm	-58 dBm
Noise level	-92.0 dBm	-100 dBm	-106 dBm
Signal-to-noise ratio	43.5 dB	48 dB	48 dB

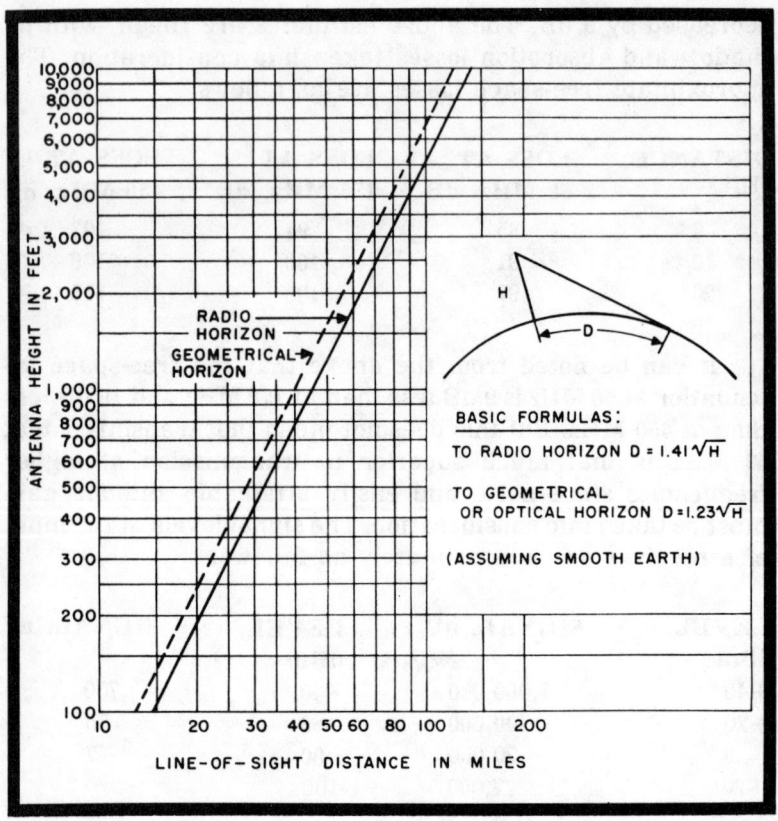

Fig. 5-29. Height versus line-of-sight range.

It can be seen that the 150 MHz and 450 MHz signals are superior to the 50 MHz signal when ambient noise levels at the receiving location are taken into consideration. The above applies only when transmission is over a line-of-sight path. Figure 5-29 shows the distance to the radio horizon for various antenna heights. Under many conditions, an allowance of 6-40 dB for shadow losses must be considered. However, in the 450 MHz band in particular, the signals are often reflected by solid objects and the losses are lower than when grazing is encountered.

Power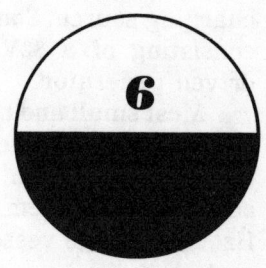

The power consumption of solid-state mobile radio units is substantially less than that of tube-type and hybrid mobile units. A solid-state mobile unit does not require a high-voltage power supply. Since no tubes are used, no filament current is required. A hybrid mobile unit which employs one or more tubes in the transmitter (none in the receiver) does require a high-voltage power supply; and a small amount of filament current is required. The standby battery current is small when quick-heating tubes are used in the transmitter. The filaments of these tubes draw no current until the microphone or handset is removed from its hangerswitch or until the push-to-talk switch is pressed. A tube-type mobile unit, on the other hand, requires high plate voltage and draws filament current even when in standby.

The power consumption of a base station is seldom important except in regard to the cost of ac power. Of course, the average power consumption of a tube-type base station is greater than that of a hybrid or solid-state base station. In any case, it is necessary to convert ac line power into dc.

Very important is the need to understand electric power sources, both on vehicles and at base stations.

VEHICULAR POWER SOURCES

Most modern automobiles and trucks have a 12V dc electrical system consisting of a 12V lead-acid storage battery, a voltage regulator, and either a dc generator or an alternator-rectifier system for charging the battery. Some models still have 6V dc electrical systems.

Most diesel-electric railroad locomotives have a 72V dc electrical system which employs a generator as the charging current source. Railroad cabooses mostly have a 12V dc electrical system, which employs an axle-driven or air-driven charging source. Some cabooses have a 32V electrical system consisting of a 32V passenger-coach battery and an axle-driven generator.

Most small and medium-size powered pleasure boats have a 12V electrical system. Larger boats have either a 24V or 32V dc electrical system. Many commercial vessels have 115-120V ac electrical system with a power-line frequency of 60 or 400 Hz. Some large vessels have only a 110-volt dc electric power system.

DC GENERATOR CHARGING SYSTEM

The electrical power system of an automobile consists of a storage battery, charging generator, and regulator, as shown in Fig. 6-1. Since the engine drives the generator at varying speeds, its output voltage would vary widely if there were no regulator.

The voltage across a fully charged 12V lead-acid battery is 12.6V. When a load is applied across the battery, the voltage will drop. How much it drops depends on the load and the internal battery resistance.

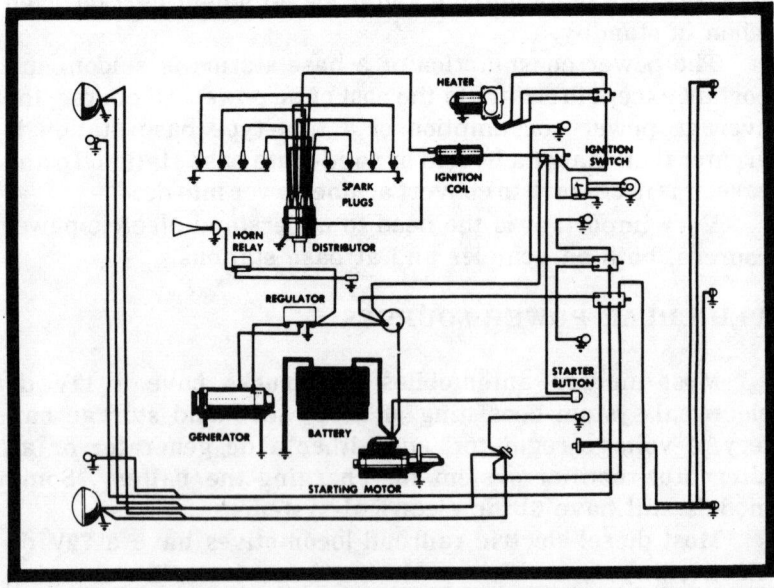

Fig. 6-1. Automobile electrical system.

The regulator unit consists of a voltage regulator, cutout relay, and current limiter. The voltage regulator controls the generator output voltage. The cutout relay prevents current flow from the battery to the generator when the generator is idle or running at lower than threshold speed. It does this by automatically disconnecting the generator from the battery. The current limiter prevents the generator from being overloaded.

As the generator speeds up, the cutout relay is energized, and the battery is connected to the generator output. The voltage regulator starts to vibrate, opening and closing the top contact and the armature contact. As the speed increases, the vibration stops, and the output voltage reaches maximum. The armature of the voltage regulator is now pulled in closer to the pole piece. Vibration again occurs, except that the bottom and armature contacts open and close rapidly. This occurs when the output voltage is around 14V (7V for 6V systems). The maximum output voltage, as determined by the voltage regulator, can be adjusted by varying the core gap. The gap is widened to raise the voltage or narrowed to lower it. This is done by loosening the contact block locking screw and moving the carrier up or down.

When the current from the generator to the battery and the load exceeds the capacity of the generator, the current flow through the coil of the current limiter becomes great enough to open the limiter contacts. A resistor is then inserted in series with the generator field coil. The resistor reduces the field current, and, hence, limits the generator output.

Figure 6-2 shows the internal circuitry of a typical regulator. When the generator is idle or running slowly, cutout relay M1 is deenergized and its contact is open, preventing current flow from battery into the regulator and generator. As the generator picks up speed, the cutout relay is energized. It then closes its contacts because of the current flow from the generator output through the series coil of the cutout relay (which is in series with the coil of current limiter M2, ballast resistor R1, and the primary coil of voltage regulator M3). The cutout relay closes when the generator output voltage reaches a predetermined level (adjustable). The shunt coil of M1 holds the relay closed as long as the generator voltage remains above this level.

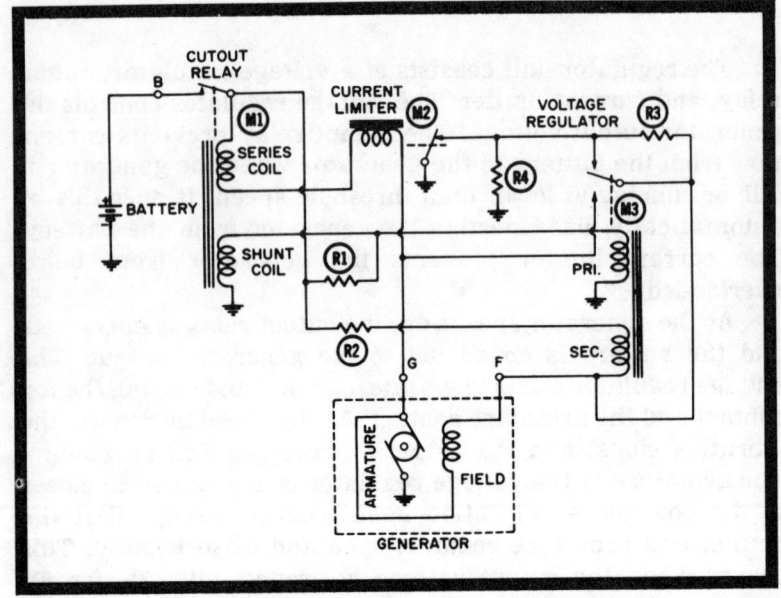

Fig. 6-2. Voltage regulator and generator system.

As the generator speed increases, the armature of voltage regulator M3 starts to vibrate when the output voltage rises to 13.0V or so (half that value for 6 volts). If earphones are connected across the F and G terminals, electrical sound created by this circuit interruption can be heard.

When the generator is not charging, power for the radio equipment is derived from the battery. At low speeds an alternator-type generator puts out enough current to take over most of the job. At higher speeds, the generator supplies the power for the radio equipment as well as the charging current for the battery.

When the battery is low and the generator is running, current flows from the generator into the battery. The amount of current is determined by the generator output and the state of charge in the battery. The positive terminal of the generator is connected to the positive terminal of the battery. As a result, the current flow through the battery is in the opposite direction from the discharge current. (See Fig. 6-3.) When the battery is fully charged, little or no charging current flows because the difference between the generator and battery voltages is now much smaller. If the voltage regulator is set too high, the battery might be damaged. Excessive voltage will also be

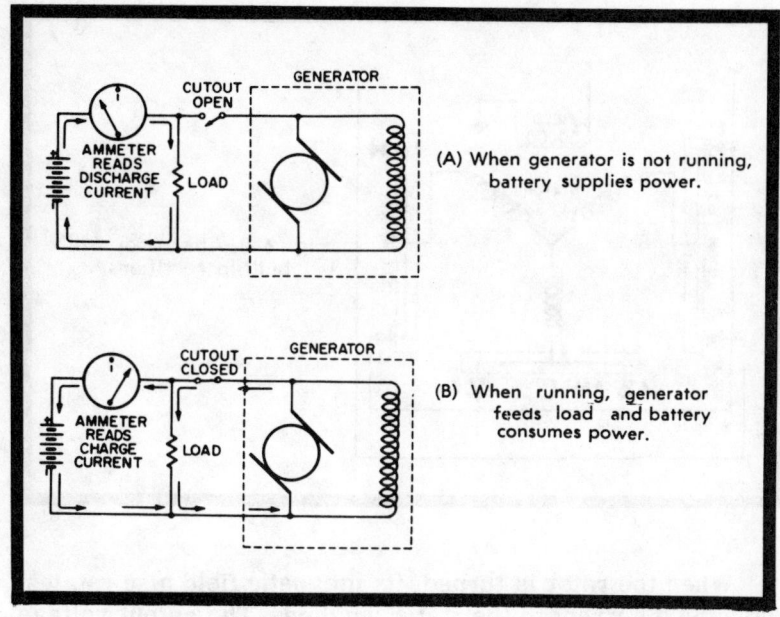

Fig. 6-3. Current flow with generator idle and running.

applied to the radio equipment, shortening the life of the components.

The battery would not be needed if the vehicle engine were running all the time. It is used to supply power for starting, and for the load when the engine is not running.

When trouble is experienced because the generator is unable to replenish the current taken out of the battery by the radio equipment, a larger generator should be installed. If the trouble is due to the vehicle being operated regularly at low speeds, or if the engine is idling much of the time, replacement of the generator driving pulley with one of a smaller diameter will speed up the generator and, hence, increase its output.

Figure 6-4 is a schematic of an alternator-rectifier. The generator is a three-phase alternator in which the power-output windings are part of the stator, and the field is the rotor. Since power is derived directly from the stator windings, no heavy current-carrying moving contacts are required. Only two slip rings are needed, and the current flow through them is very small. The six silicon rectifier cells, comprising a full-wave three-phase bridge-rectifier system, are contained in the stator housing.

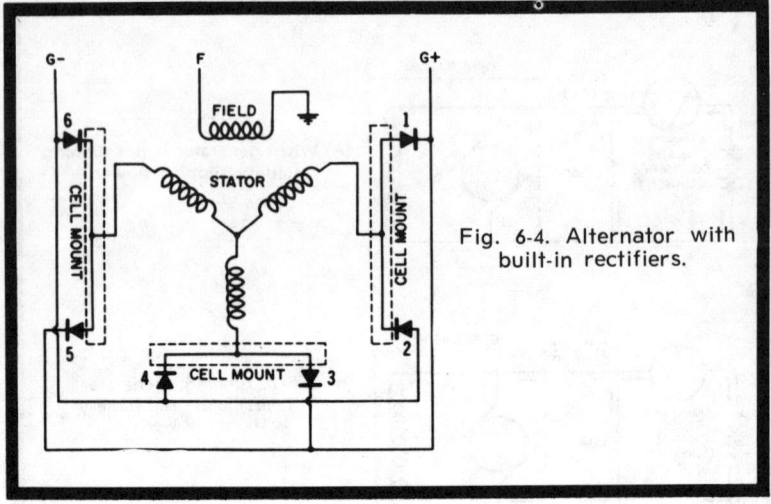

Fig. 6-4. Alternator with built-in rectifiers.

When the rotor is turned, its magnetic field also rotates, inducing a current in the stator windings. The output voltage is three-phase ac, which varies in frequency with the rotor speed. The rectifiers convert the ac to dc. The dc output has a very high ripple frequency, which is eliminated when it is shunted by the battery. A regulator varies the field current to maintain the dc output voltage constant.

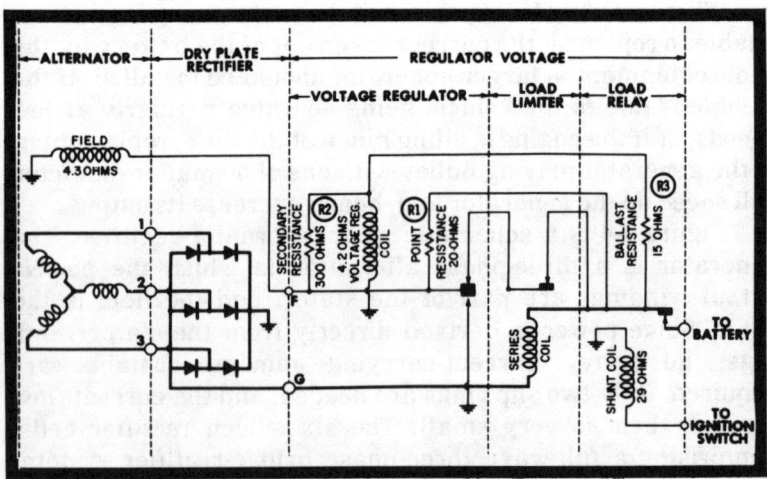

Fig. 6-5. Schematic, alternator-rectifier system.

AC Generator Charging System

Figure 6-5 shows the circuitry of a complete add-on alternator-rectifier system and its associated regulator, and Fig. 6-6 shows a function drawing of the regulator alone.

A cutout relay is not used, since dc from the battery cannot flow back into the generator output windings because of the rectifiers. However, the field (rotor) is energized by the vehicle battery. If a means is not provided for disconnecting the field coil when the engine is not running, the field will continue to draw current.

A load relay automatically connects the field to the battery when the ignition switch is turned on. The relay connects the "hot" side of the battery to the ungrounded end of the field coil through R2 and R3.

When the alternator is running, the dc output of the rectifier is fed, through the coil of the load limiter and through R3, to the voltage-regulator coil. This causes the voltage-regulator armature to vibrate, opening and closing the top contact and the armature contact when regulation starts, and the bottom and armature contacts when the voltage reaches maximum. The switching action controls the field current by pulsing it.

As shown in Fig. 6-7 (a simplified schematic of the voltage regulator), the battery is connected directly to the field when the armature contact of the voltage regulator touches the top

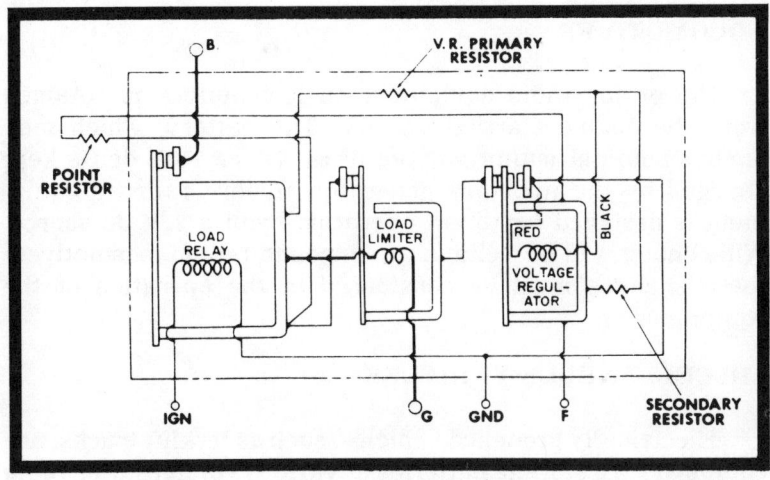

Fig. 6-6. Voltage regulator wiring diagram.

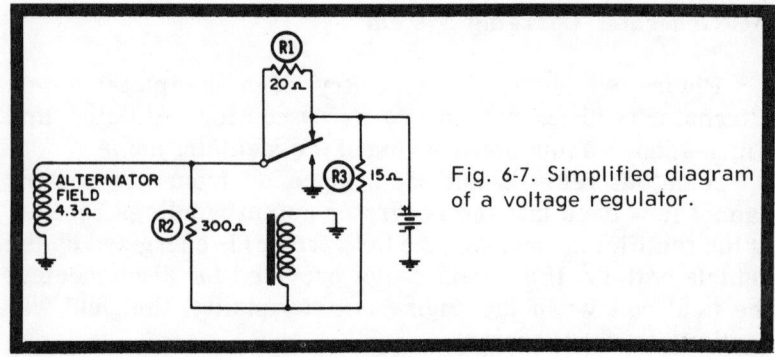

Fig. 6-7. Simplified diagram of a voltage regulator.

contact. When these contacts are open, R1 (a 20-ohm resistor) is in series with the field, limiting the field current to about one-fifth its maximum value. While vibrating, the top contacts alternately raise and lower the field current.

As the armature contact mates with the bottom contact, the field is shorted to ground. When these contacts vibrate, applied field voltage is alternately switched on and off.

The field current is steady only when the contacts are held open. As they make and break, the effective field current is determined by **time** as well as by resistance. Since neither zero nor maximum field current flows continuously, the effective field current is somewhere between, being determined by how much time each condition exists with relation to the other.

LOCOMOTIVES

Power for radio equipment on locomotives is obtained from the engine starting battery. The battery, which may have a nominal output voltage of 64, 72, or 110V dc, is kept charged by the auxiliary generator. Modern railroad equipment is designed for direct operation from a 72V dc source. Wide changes in dc voltage are encountered on locomotives; these changes must be considered in the operation of the equipment.

MISCELLANEOUS VEHICLES

Electrically propelled vehicles, such as forklift trucks, are equipped with storage batteries of various voltages. For radio equipment to be operated from such a source, or a dc-to-ac converter is required, or the radio unit must have a power supply designed to accommodate this voltage.

REVERSE-POLARITY PROTECTION

In most cars, the negative terminal of the battery is grounded (negative ground), but not in all (positive ground). A mobile unit designed for use only in a vehicle with negative ground may not be used in a vehicle with positive ground, and vice versa. Many mobile units are designed for use in vehicles with either negative or positive ground. In such units, the common ground buss is not grounded to the case.

If reverse-polarity dc voltage is applied, transistors could be destroyed. For this reason, some mobile units employ a protection circuit such as the one shown in Fig. 6-8. When battery lead X is connected to the positive negative voltage source, the diode is reverse-biased and does not conduct. But if the battery leads are inadvertently reversed (X is negative and Y is positive), the diode conducts and the fuse blows.

HYBRID MOBILE UNITS

In a hybrid mobile unit, low voltage dc to the transistors is usually derived from the battery through a voltage regulator. High voltage for the transmitter tubes is also obtained from the battery but through a mobile power supply which employs transistors in an electronic switching circuit, an example of which is shown in Fig. 6-9.

The transistors are used in a push-pull feedback oscillator circuit. The resulting ac voltage is stepped up by the power transformer. The ac output voltage is then fed to a rectifier.

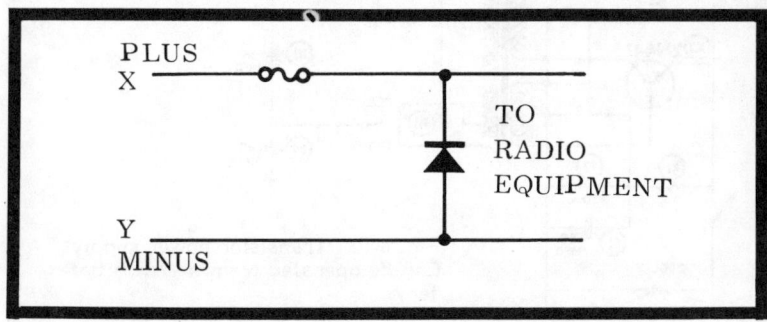

Fig. 6-8. Reverse-polarity protection circuit.

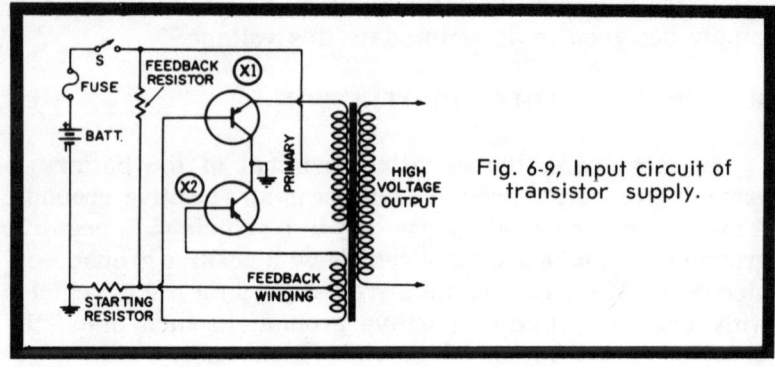

Fig. 6-9, Input circuit of transistor supply.

TUBE-TYPE MOBILE UNITS

The heaters of the tubes of a tube-type mobile unit are fed directly from the battery. The high dc plate and screen grid voltages are also furnished by the dc voltage source through a mobile power supply such as that shown in Fig. 6-10. The two transistors operate in a push-pull oscillator circuit. The high ac voltage at the secondary of the power transformer is fed to a full-wave voltage doubler rectifier. As can be seen in the diagram, a switch is used to provide higher B+ voltage when transmitting and a lower voltage when receiving.

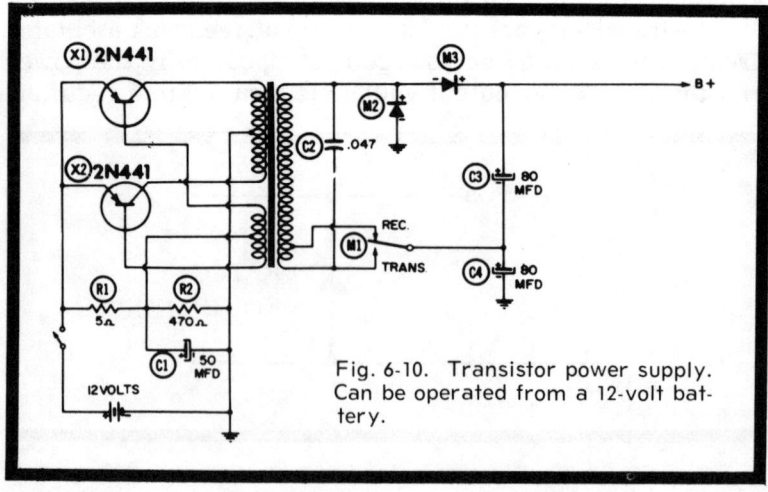

Fig. 6-10. Transistor power supply. Can be operated from a 12-volt battery.

Servicing

Mobile radio equipment servicing can be divided into preventive maintenance, field servicing, and shop servicing. Since it is impractical to make repairs to solid-state equipment employing printed circuit (PC) boards in the field, most of the work in the field consists of checking out the installation with repairs limited to the antenna system, battery cable, and control cable (the "umbilical" that links the control head to the transmitter-receiver unit).

Although most mobile radio systems operate on a single channel (single frequency or paired frequencies), many now operate on more than one channel. Therefore, in this chapter reference will be made to checking of equipment on various channels. The same basic information is applicable to single-channel equipment.

As in the television receiver industry, some mobile radio equipment manufacturers are starting to make use of plug-in PC boards and modules. If spares are carried by the technician, defective boards or modules can be replaced in the field, making it unnecessary to pull the set and take it to the shop for repair.

When PC boards are soldered to the other circuits, it often pays to replace an entire board that has a defective component. It requires time and money to locate the defective component and then replace it. Often, when a new component is being soldered in place, it is destroyed by the heat of the soldering iron.

The cost to the customer can be reduced if the customer buys spare mobile units that can be installed in place of a unit requiring shop repair. It will cost the customer less for technician time and, when two-way radio is used to save time and money, the customer will not have to have a mobile unit off the air while waiting for repairs.

The spares can be stored at the service shop, ready for use whenever required. The customer should also buy spare PC boards which can also be stored at the shop. On the other hand, if the shop services many units of the same type, the shop owner might find it advantageous to buy spare PC boards for use when required.

Some equipment manufacturers offer a PC board exchange and repair service. Defective boards are sent back to the factory for repair or replacement. When a manufacturer does not provide this kind of service, it still pays to replace complete boards to make a mobile unit operational in the shortest possible time. Then, when time permits, a technician can repair the board and put it back in inventory.

FIELD SERVICING

Servicing of a mobile radio installation in a vehicle is generally limited to determining if the trouble is in the transmitter-receiver unit itself and should be replaced with a spare or taken to the shop, and to checking out the antenna and cabling, as well as the control head (when used), microphone, etc.

If the mobile radio does not function at all, the trouble may be a blown fuse or defective wiring. Ordinarily, a lamp on the control head glows whenever the set is turned on. Another lamp glows whenever the transmitter is actuated by operation of the push-to-talk button on the microphone.

If the "power on" lamp does not glow, either there is no power or the lamp is burned out. Lack of power indicates a broken connection, a blown fuse, or a dead battery. Should the "power on" lamp glow, but the radio remains inoperative, the next step is to advance the squelch control to the fully unsquelched setting. If no noise is heard from the speaker, the receiver or the speaker connections may be out of order.

Antenna Troubles

Noise, but no or very weak signals, indicates trouble in the antenna system. Noise will ordinarily be heard, even with the antenna disconnected and the squelch set in the unsquelched position, because background noise in a sensitive receiver is generated within the set itself. This noise diminishes or disappears when a signal is received.

Antenna troubles could consist of a broken connection, a short between the inner conductor and shield braid in the coaxial cable, or excessive cable losses, which can occur when the inner insulation (dielectric) has absorbed an excessive amount of moisture. The antenna can be checked out quickly. A 12V lamp or pilot light, a socket for the lamp, a battery clip, a small alligator clip, and two lengths of wire will form a simple test set, as shown in Fig. 7-1. When the battery clip is connected to the "hot" (ungrounded) battery terminal, and the alligator clip is connected to the metal shell of the antenna plug at the set end of the coaxial cable, the lamp should light. (Disconnect antenna plug from set first.) If the lamp does not light, the shield braid of the cable may not be properly contacting the plug shell or the point at the antenna end where it grounds to the car body.

To determine that the center conductor of the coaxial cable is not open and is actually contacting the vertical antenna radiator, connect the test lead (with the small alligator clip) to the antenna whip. The lamp should not light. If it does, there is a short in the cable or plug, or at the antenna. Now short the center pin of the antenna plug to the shell with a screwdriver blade. The lamp should light. If it doesn't, the center conductor of the cable is open, or there is an open connection at the plug or at the base of the antenna.

A test made with a field-strength meter is more conclusive. When connected to a short piece of wire which serves

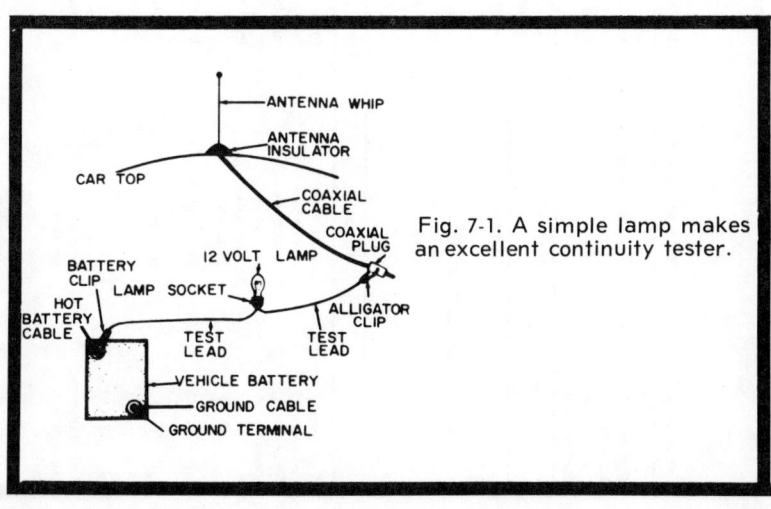

Fig. 7-1. A simple lamp makes an excellent continuity tester.

TABLE 7-1. MOBILE INSTALLATION TROUBLESHOOTING

SYMPTOM	POSSIBLE CAUSE	WHAT TO CHECK	HOW TO CHECK	RESULT OR NEXT STEP
Unit does not operate; "power" light does not glow.	No input power	Fuse	Try new fuse	If new fuse blows, replace mobile unit with a spare.
	Open cable	Input voltage at mobile unit	With VOM	If no voltage, check and repair cable
	On-off switch defective in control head	Switch terminals	With VOM	If voltage present with switch in either position, replace control head with a spare.
	On-off switch defective (in dash-mount unit	Input voltage at mobile unit	With VOM	If voltage present, replace mobile unit with a spare.
	Pilot lamp	Pilot lamp	Try new lamp	New lamp should glow
Unit does not operate; "power" light glows	Short within mobile unit power circuits	Plate or collector voltage	With VOM	If no voltage, replace mobile unit with a spare.
	Short within mobile unit	Input current	With ammeter	If current higher than rated, replace unit with a spare.
	Input voltage polarity reversed	Input voltage polarity (at mobile unit)	With VOM	If polarity reversed, transpose input leads. If unit does not operate because it has been damaged, replace with a spare.
Unit transmits but does not receive	Squelch set too tight	Squelch control	Adjust squelch control through entire range; disable tone squelch if used.	If no noise heard, proceed to next step.
	Defective rf amplifier tube (if used)	Rf amplifier tube		Try new tube. If operation not restored, replace unit with a spare.
	Defective	Transmit-receive	Short antenna and	If operation restored,

136

Symptom	Probable cause	Check	Remedy
Unit receives but does not transmit	PTT switch defective or mike cable open	PTT circuit	Try new mike or short PTT terminals at mike receptacle with test lead. Monitor transmitter output with an rf wattmeter or field strength meter. If operation restored, replace mike with spare or repair PTT switch or mike cable. If operation not restored, replace unit with a spare.
Short transmit range; noisy reception	Defective tube (if tubes used)	Transmitter tubes	Try new tubes, one at a time.
	Antenna system defect	Antenna system	Disconnect antenna and insert test lead probe into aztenna receptacle (do not turn transmitter on) If reception improves, check antenna system.
	Antenna system defect	Antenna system	Check as shown in Fig. 7-1 If antenna system okay, proceed with next step.
	Wrong antenna for band used	Antenna	Determine if antenna is of correct type for the band Replace antenna if of the wrong type and retune input circuits of unit.
Short transmit range; normal reception	Antenna system mismatch	Vswr	Connect in-line rf wattmeter in series with antenna; measure vswr and adjust transmitter for minimum vswr. If vswr cannot be reduced to less than 1.3:1, replace antenna or coaxial cable.
	Low output power	Output power	Measure output power with rf wattmeter. If power too low, proceed with next step.
	Weak tube (if tubes used)	Tubes	Replace tubes in transmitter one at a time. If power output not increased, replace unit with a spare.
	Power supply adjustment (if transistors used)	Collector Voltage	Measure collector voltage at output of voltage regulator with VOM. If voltage too low, adjust voltage regulator for correct voltage. If this can't be done, replace unit with a spare.

137

as a pickup antenna, the meter should indicate current flow when placed within a few feet of the radio antenna (transmitter turned on). If the test is negative, chances are the transmitter is inoperative or the antenna system is defective.

An even better approach is to use an in-line rf wattmeter in series with the coaxial cable transmission line. This allows measurement of transmitter output power and voltage standing-wave ratio (vswr). If the vswr is higher than 1.5:1, the transmitter output circuit should be adjusted. If it is impossible to reduce the vswr to less than 2:1, the antenna may be of poor design or cut for the wrong frequency. Other possibilities are open, shorted, or crimped coax, bad connections, and the like.

Table 7-1 is a mobile installation troubleshooting chart. It covers the basic symptoms and possible causes and explains what and how to check.

Defective Tubes

Although most new mobile radio equipment employs no tubes, many in service employ both tubes and transistors (hybrid) and many all-tube units are still in service. In fact, old-model tube-type units are being sold for use in new systems after modification to meet current FCC technical standards.

Since it is impractical to use a tube tester on a vehicle when no ac power source is available, tube testing in the field usually consists of replacement of tubes, one at a time, to find one that is faulty. In the case of a nonfunctioning transmitter, or one that delivers lower power than normal, the unit should be connected to an rf wattmeter. The rf output is monitored as tubes are replaced to note any increase in rf output power as a new tube is installed. After a new tube has been installed in place of a defective one, it may be necessary to realign the stage in which the tube is used because of probable differences in interelectrode capacitances of the tubes.

Using the tube substitution method when checking a receiver, any improvement or restoration of operation should be evident simply by listening to the signals being reproduced by the speaker. Again, particularly in the rf amplifier and mixer stage, it may be necessary to realign the affected stage to compensate for differences in interelectrode capacitances.

Power Supply Transistors and Vibrators

Many tube- and hybrid-type mobile units employ switching transistors in the high-voltage power supply rather than a vibrator. Replacement of one or both of these transistors in the field is usually impractical. However, it can be determined in the field if they are at fault, in which case the unit should be taken to the shop and replaced by a spare. Using a multimeter to measure ac volts, the absence of ac voltage across the secondary of the power transformer is an indication of a fault in the primary circuit, usually an open or shorted switching transistor. When the transistors are operating, a whine can sometimes be heard by placing the ear close to the power transformer. The whine is the oscillating frequency of the dc-to-ac inversion circuit and is normally quite high-pitched.

Since the vibrator is a mechanical device, its contacts may fail. Although anyone can replace it, a new vibrator can be quickly damaged if defective equipment is causing excessively high current to flow through it. If a new vibrator does not restore performance, some other part or parts within the set are to blame.

SHOP SERVICING

All repairs requiring the use of a soldering iron (other than the antenna system and cabling) should be performed in the shop, where adequate test equipment is available. When a defective mobile unit is brought to the shop, a quick way to diagnose the basic trouble is to measure input current. If a metered dc power supply is not available, this can be done by connecting a dc ammeter in series with one of the power cable leads. Table 7-2 lists the meanings of various off-normal current indications.

When checking a solid-state or hybrid mobile unit, the ammeter should indicate low current with the unit set to receive and squelched and with no signal being received. When a signal is received or the squelch is open (noise in speaker), current should rise and increase as volume is turned up (assuming that the receiver employs a class B a-f amplifier). When the transmitter is turned on, current should rise.

When checking a tube-type mobile unit, current should be high when first turned on and then vary as tube heaters warm

TABLE 7-2. INPUT CURRENT CHECKS

Ammeter Indication	Possible Trouble	
	Solid State Unit	Tube-type Unit
Higher than rated current at all times, but unit does not operate	Shorted transistor or capacitor	Shorted capacitor, stuck vibrator, or shorted power switching transistor
Lower than rated current at all times, and unit does not operate	Open transistor	Defective tube or open rectifier
High current on receive, normal on transmit; unit transmits but won't receive.	Shorted transistor in receiver or short in power distribution network	Short in receiver power distribution network
Higher than rated current on transmit, normal on receive; unit receives but won't transmit	Shorted transistor in transmitter or short in power distribution network	Shorted transmitter tube or capacitor, or short in power distribution network
Lower than normal current on receive normal on transmit; won't receive	Open receiver transistor or resistor	Defective tube or open resistor or switching circuit
Lower than normal current on transmit normal on receive; won't transmit	Open transmitter transistor, resistor or coupling capacitor	Defective rf power amplifier tube
Current varies at all times; (after warmup, won't operate	Leaky capacitor	Leaky capacitor or worn-out vibrator
Current very high initially (won't operate), drops later (unit operates)	Marginal capacitor	Marginal capacitor
Current normal initially (unit operates), rises later (won't operate)	Marginal capacitor	Marginal capacitor
No current at any time (won't operate)	Blown fuse or open main power circuit	Blown fuse or open main power circuit

up and receiver plate current rises to normal. Current should not vary significantly when a signal is received or the squelch is open (assuming that the receiver employs a Class A a-f amplifier). When set to transmit, the current should rise significantly except in the case of a low-power transmitter whose power input is essentially the same as that of the receiver.

Table 7-2 is a basic mobile unit checkout chart. It lists the steps to check functioning. Figure 7-2 shows a typical bench test setup.

Operating power for the mobile unit is obtained from a variable output dc power supply. If the power supply has a built-in ammeter, the ammeter (A) shown in the diagram isn't needed. An af output meter (dB meter or ac voltmeter) is connected across the speaker terminals. A dc voltmeter is connected to various test points specified by the manufacturer.

The antenna connector of the mobile unit is connected through a coaxial jumper cable to the rotor of a three-position coaxial switch. The poles of the coaxial switch are connected

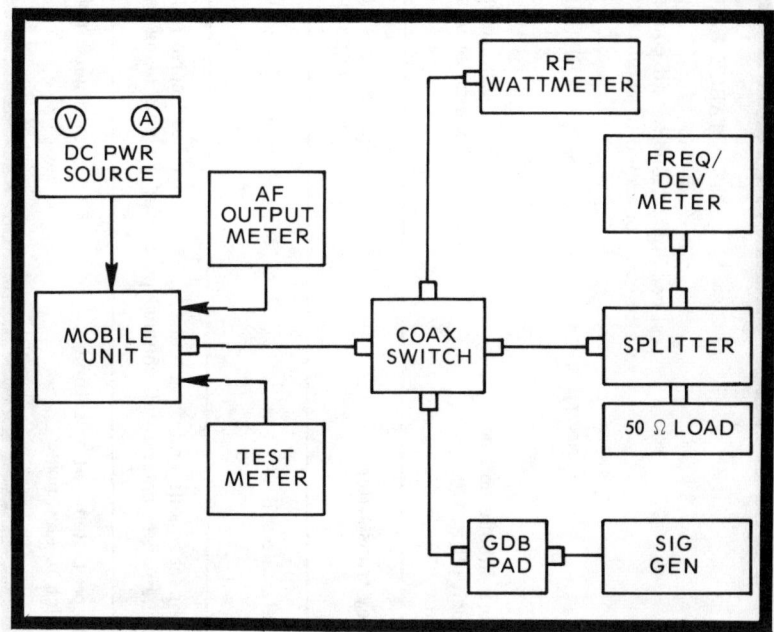

Fig. 7-2. Bench test setup for mobile-unit checkout.

TABLE 7-3. BASIC CHECKOUT

Test conditions: Mobile unit connected to power source. Rf wattmeter connected to antenna terminal

DO THIS	THIS SHOULD HAPPEN	IF NOT, DO THIS
1. Turn mobile unit on, squelch off and volume up.	Pilot lamp lights Loud noise in speaker	Check fuse, power cord See Table 7-4
2. Key transmitter	Speaker is silenced Power output indicated by wattmeter	Check mike switch and PTT circuit
3. Talk into mike	Power output rises (AM sets only)	Check mike connections, and transmitter tuning
4 Connect mobile unit to antenna; set channel selector to all channel positions.	Loud noise on all channels when no signal being received	Try new crystal for dead channels
5. Repeat step 4 after setting squelch to stop noise	Loud noise not heard on any channel	If squelch cannot be set to stop noise, see Table 7-5

through coaxial jumper cables to an rf wattmeter, a frequency and FM deviation meter, and rf signal generator. The frequency and FM deviation meter is connected through a splitter which is terminated in a dummy load. The rf signal generator is connected through a 6 dB pad, which provides the required interface between the receiver input and signal generator output.

The use of a coaxial switch eliminates the need for frequent disconnection and reconnection of coaxial jumper cables. However, care must be exercised to avoid turning the transmitter on when the switch is set to the signal generator position.

INOPERATIVE RECEIVER

If the receiver is dead, the obvious points to check first are (1) availability of power, (2) vibrator, (3) tubes, (4) crystal, and (5) control system, consisting of cables, speaker, microphone, volume and squelch controls, and on-off switch.

A blown fuse indicates internal trouble, such as a shorted capacitor or transistor or stuck vibrator. If the fuse blows with the vibrator removed, there may be a short in the input power circuits, which include the wiring, relays, and input-voltage bypass capacitors. If the fuse blows only when the vibrator is in place, try a new fuse again, but remove the rectifier tube if there is one. (Most sets use silicon rectifiers.)

If the fuse blows with the vibrator in place and the rectifier tube out of the set, the trouble is apparently due to (1) a blown buffer capacitor across the high-voltage winding of the power transformer, or (2) a defective power transformer.

With both the vibrator and the rectifier in place, blowing of fuses indicates (1) a short or overload in the receiver circuits, (2) a shorted tube, or (3) a shorted capacitor. If it is (3), the radio should be taken to the shop.

When the squelch is set to the fully unsquelched position, noise should be heard from the speaker, even with no antenna connected. If no sound is heard, a defective tube or transistor could be the reason. New tubes can be tried, one at a time, until the trouble is corrected. At this time, the background noise should burst through the speaker.

A defective receiver crystal can disable the receiver, of course. If available, a spare can be tried.

Inoperative Transmitter

A dead transmitter can be caused by lack of power, even if the receiver is working. When the push-to-talk button on the microphone is pressed, the "transmit" pilot lamp should glow. As the button is pushed in and out, input current should vary. If it doesn't the trouble could be in the push-to-talk switch or the microphone cord.

If the transmitter is of the tube type and employs a vibrator, a new one should be tried. The trouble also could be in the relay through which the input power is applied. Measure the transmitter plate voltage with a dc voltmeter at the output of the rectifier, a metering tip jack, or a metering socket.

Using a suitable test meter, drive should be noted at all stages (except the oscillator, of course). If none exists at the first multiplier stage and the dc operating voltage is normal, the trouble is in the oscillator. In FM transmitters it could be in the phase modulator, which is usually between the oscillator and the first frequency multiplier.

The crystal could be at fault. In multichannel transmitters, the trouble can be localized to a particular crystal or oscillator by trying the other channels. The defect could be in the frequency-selector circuit which, if open, could disable one or all oscillators.

Drive on the first multiplier stage, but none on a succeeding stage, indicates trouble in the driven stage or the one preceding it. If all stages from the first multiplier to the final amplifier have drive and the final rf amplifier draws current, tuning of the tank circuit of the final amplifier should produce a dip at the resonant point and an increase in collector current as the antenna trimmer is adjusted.

With rf wattmeter (see Fig. 7-2) connected, the final amplifier and antenna circuits should be tuned for maximum rf output.

If any repairs or tuning adjustments are made which could affect the frequency of transmission or widen its modulation deviation (FM), the transmitter frequency and modulation deviation should be measured.

Transmitter frequency measurements should be made with a calibrated heterodyne frequency meter, frequency synthesizer, of electronic frequency counter. Frequency deviation can be measured with an F, deviation meter or a communication monitor (such as Cushman or Singer-Gertsch, which are designed to measure both carrier frequency and FM deviation). The modulation level of an AM transmitter can be measured roughly be observing the indication of an rf wattmeter. When modulated 100 percent by a sine-wave audio test signal, a rf power output of an AM transmitter should rise 50 percent.

The modulation test can be made by talking or whistling into the microphone and watching the indicator of the FM deviation meter or rf wattmeter when checking an AM transmitter. However, more accurate measurements can be made by feeding a 1000 Hz test signal into the transmitter's microphone input circuit. Figure 7-3 shows how to assemble an adapter which enables connection of an audio signal generator to the transmitter's audio input circuit through a microphone plug.

Table 7-4 lists basic transmitter checkout steps. In step 6 it is suggested that a separate receiver be used for checking carrier hum and audio distortion. A good receiver for this purpose is a three-band tunable FM monitor receiver such as the Realistic **Patrolman** PRO-3A which covers the low, high, and UHF bands.

It is required by the FCC that FM communication transmitter frequency deviation be limited to ± 5 kHz. Most FM transmitters have a deviation control which should be adjusted to limit FM deviation so it will not exceed the

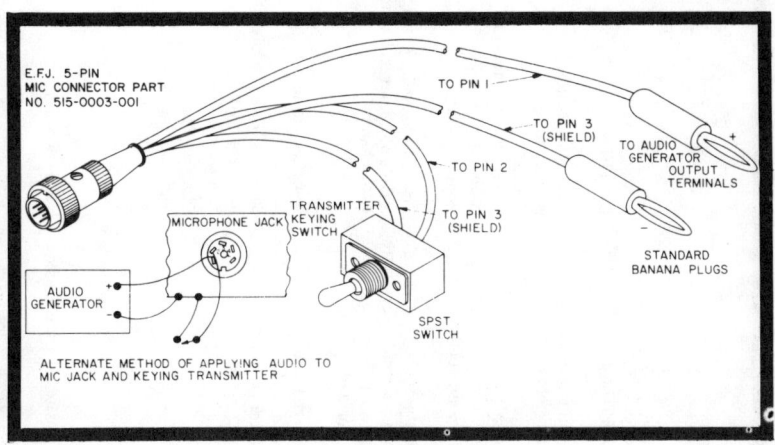

Fig. 7-3. A mike adapter simplifies signal-generator interconnection.

TABLE 7-4. TRANSMITTER CHECKOUT

Test conditions: Mobile unit connected to power source. Rf wattmeter connected to antenna terminal.

SYMPTOM	DO THIS	IF THIS HAPPENS	CHECK THIS
1. Won't transmit on any channels	Turn transmitter on with mike switch	No indicated rf power output	Transmitter oscillator and rf amplifiers
2. Won't modulate	Wiggle mike connector cable, etc.	Intermittent modulation	Microphone cable connections
3. Low modulation	Replace mike	No improvement	Multiplier-stage tunings modulator circuit
4. Instability; won't transmit every time mike switch is operated	Test all channels, keying mike switch several times on each channel	No rf output every time	Transmitter oscillator tuning; if on only one channel try another crystal
5. Short range	Same as for step 1	Low indicated rf output	Transmitter tuning, tubes, power voltages
6. Hum on carrier	Same as above, while listening to carrier with another receiver	Steady hum when not modulating	Power supply modulator and tubes
	Same as above while talking into mike	Hum superimposed on voice when modulating, but not on unmodulated carrier	Modulator, microphone cable for effective shielding
7. Distorted transmission	Same as above	Distorted speech	Modulation level, modulator, aduio tubes

146

prescribed limit. When applying an audio test signal to the transmitter input, the deviation control can be adjusted while monitoring the rf output with an FM deviation meter. The audio signal level required depends upon the design of the transmitter with respect to the type of microphone used. As the level of the audio signal is increased, the FM deviation should increase until it reaches its maximum permitted value. A further increase in audio level should not cause an increase in FM deviation if the modulation limiter circuit of the transmitter is adjusted properly.

TRANSMITTER METERING

The following are generally provided to enable voltage and current measurements when the transmitter is operating: tip jacks into which a dc milliammeter, microammeter, or voltmeter, can be connected to reach various circuit points; test points to which a meter or scope can be connected; a multipole connector into which the plug of a special test set is inserted; or a phone jack into which a dc milliammeter or microammeter is connected and which is wired to a circuit-selecting switch.

It is necessary to be able to observe variations in drive in all stages except the oscillator, because the preceding stage is tuned; and in the collector, plate, or cathode current in the final rf amplifier stages, because its tank and antenna circuits are tuned. All stages except the final rf amplifier are ordinarily tuned for maximum drive in the following stage. The tank circuit of the final rf amplifier is tuned for minimum (dip) current. Antenna circuit tuning increases the final rf-amplifier current.

The FCC requires that the power input to the final rf stage be below the maximum value specified in the station license. Power input in watts is determined by multiplying the supply voltage by the plate or collector current (amperes).

Some base-station transmitters are equipped with built-in meters to facilitate tuning and provide continuous indication of transmitter performance. An external meter is required in all commercial mobile units and most base-station equipment.

Power output is of concern to the technician. It can be measured with an rf wattmeter connected across the antenna connector of the transmitter. Some rf wattmeters are of the in-

Fig. 7-4. Bird's "Termaline" terminal wattmeter serves as dummy load for high-power transmitters.

line type; others, of the termination type (Fig. 7-4), are provided with an internal dummy load to dissipate the power delivered by the transmitter. Wattmeters actually measure the voltage across the antenna load, even though their scales are calibrated in watts. If the signal across a 50-ohm load is 20 volts, the power will be 8 watts, since power in watts is equal to voltage squared divided by resistance.

RECEIVER CHECKOUT

A tip jack, test point, or metering socket terminal ordinarily is provided for measuring the first limiter voltage in

TABLE 7-5. RECEIVER CHECKOUT

Test conditions mobile unit connected to power source and antenna.

SYMPTOM	DO THIS	IF THIS HAPPENS	DO THIS
1. Won't receive.	Apply modulated rf test signal to input of receiver	No tone in speaker	Check antenna relay contacts. Check local oscillators; if trouble not there, apply test signal to input of each af, i-f, and rf stages working back from the speaker to identify dead stage
2. Receives only strong signals	Same as above	No tone in speaker on the dead channel	Try new crystal for that channel; check channel selector
3. Receives on all channels but one	Monitor limiter voltage (FM receiver) or agc voltage (AM receiver). Apply rf test signal to input of each i-f and rf stage, working back from detector, and watch for increase in voltage as each stage is included in the chain.	No increase in output voltage at particular stage	Check the stage which provides no gain; if no defect found, realign all stages
4. Receives with heavy background noise	Same as for step 1	Tone modulation heard in background noise	Check antenna relay contacts and input coil
5. Squelch won't unsquelch (continuous noise)	Measure avc voltage,	Voltage rises when signal received	Check squelch circuit voltages and tubes
6. Distorted sound	Connect headphones to detector output	Speech is clear	Check audio amplifier and speaker
7. Hum in speakers	Turn volume down to minimum	Hum still heard	Check power supply and af tubes.

FM receivers, or in the agc, avc voltage in AM receivers. This is the most important test point in the receiver, since it provides go / no-go as well as qualitative information. Other test points include oscillator-multiplier circuits, discriminator, and sometimes the second-limiter.

Limiter voltage exists in a high-gain receiver even when no signal is being received. This is due to the noise generated in the front end of the receiver. This noise is a signal, as far as the limiter is concerned.

When a signal is received, the limiter voltage increases proportionally to the signal level. In an AM receiver, the same is true: the avc voltage increases or decreases with signal strength.

Discriminator

All FM receivers employing a discriminator as an FM detector have (or should have) some means for external metering of the discriminator balance (TP1 in Fig. 7-5). L2 is tuned for zero voltage at TP1, and L1 is tuned for maximum reading at TP2. Connecting a meter at TP2 gives the technician a reference against which he can make receiver adjustments.

The secondary of the discriminator transformer ordinarily is adjusted for zero when the signal is exactly at the desired frequency. In a superheterodyne receiver, this is the i-f fed without modulation to the discriminator. This measurement is best made with an electronic voltmeter, which can be set to zero at center scale so that positive and negative variances from zero can be noted.

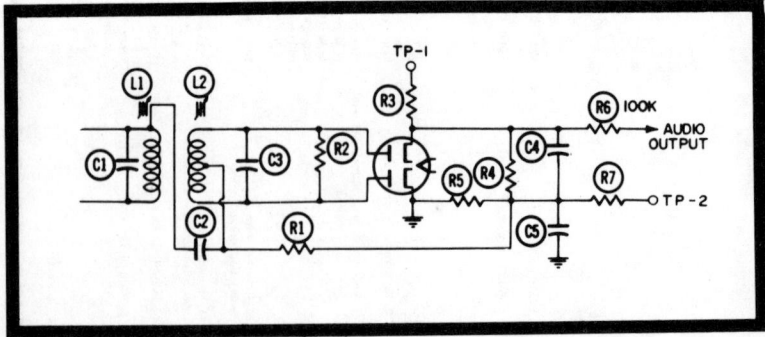

Fig. 7-5. Typical tube-type discriminator circuit.

Oscillator Adjustment

When the local oscillator consists of more than one stage and tuning adjustments are provided, it has the same basic circuitry a transmitter has. Provision is usually made for metering the drive. The oscillator is tuned for maximum drive to the next stage and then backed off a bit, since the circuit might tend to be unstable when set to the top of the peak. Drive is measured at the succeeding stages as tuning adjustments are made. (Follow the procedures in the appropriate instruction manual.)

AM Receivers

The same basic metering is required in AM receivers. Instead of limiter voltage, avc voltage is metered to measure the relative signal level, which rises to a peak when all circuits are tuned to an on-frequency signal.

When an avc metering point is not provided, a high resistance voltmeter can be connected to the avc bus and ground.

RECEIVER I-F ALIGNMENT

The alignment instructions published in the appropriate service manual should be followed.

The i-f circuits are aligned first, starting with the limiters or discriminator (or AM detector) and working toward the front end of the receiver. A signal generator that can be accurately tuned to the various intermediate frequencies is required for this alignment.

For FM receivers, a signal generator with means for frequency modulation is preferred, although an AM signal generator (operated unmodulated) can be used. With an FM signal generator, an ac voltmeter can be placed across the receiver audio output to indicate the output. With an AM signal generator, a 20,000-ohm-per-volt voltmeter should be used as the output indicator and the limiter voltage monitored. Adjustment of the discriminator usually requires an electronic voltmeter.

When i-f circuits are aligned, the oscillators are generally disabled to prevent interaction and consequent misleading results. This can be done by pulling the receiver crystals. Obviously, the second local oscillator must be reactivated before the mixer, or i-f or amplifier preceding it can be tuned. The signal-generator output is fed through a small isolating capacitor to the input of the mixer immediately preceding the i-f amplifier section to be aligned (unless the service manual specifies otherwise). The signal-generator output should be kept very low and should be reduced as the receiver output increases, to prevent overloading of the receiver. The alignment tool should be insulated to prevent body capacity effects.

Mixer-Oscillator

Again it is stressed that the appropriate service manual be referred to for specific instructions on how to align the mixer and heterodyne oscillator circuits. The results of mixer tuning adjustments are, as with i-f alignment, monitored at the receiver output or limiter circuit. Although it is possible to observe the results of tuning at some other point, it is customary to adjust tuning circuits with respect to the overall receiver performance.

This is not true, however, with oscillators. Here the adjustment is critical in regard to oscillator stability, but has only a slight effect on receiver sensitivity. When local oscillator stages are tuned, the results are monitored by measuring the rf signal level within the oscillator-multiplier circuits.

The local oscillator circuits are aligned first, before the mixer input is resonated to the desired frequency. A mixer (as many as two in a signle receiver) can actually serve as a complete i-f amplifier section in a double-conversion receiver. The mixers are tuned for maximum output, each to its designated frequency. In some receivers, one of the intermediate frequencies may be different for various operating frequencies. Therefore, refer to the appropriate service manual before making any adjustments.

RF Stages

The rf stages are tuned for maximum audio output or limiter (or avc) voltage in the receiver. The signal, at the lowest usable level, is fed to the antenna receptacle through a coaxial cable and with an appropriate load or pad, as specified by the receiver as well as the signal-generator manufacturer. Only a laboratory-grade signal generator will do. Low-priced signal generators intended for servicing home AM or FM radios will not do, even if they can be tuned to the appropriate mobile band. In the first place, the accuracy of frequency calibration, frequency stability, and ability to attenuate the output signal to a low enough level (less than a microvolt) without excess signal leakage leave much to be desired. Chapter 8 provides detailed information on various suitable signal generators.

Even with a top-grade signal generator, the calibration of the tuning dial should not be depended upon. Some shops employ crystal-controlled signal generators.

After the rf stages and all receiver tuning circuits have been aligned as specified in the instruction manual, the antenna adjustments (if provided in the receiver) and tuning circuits of the first rf stage input should be retrimmed. The receiver must be connected to an antenna. Although the final adjustment is preferably made with the receiver connected to its own antenna, this is not always feasible. Antenna systems can be provided in the shop, one for each band, and the final input trimming made against a signal from a distant station. The discriminator adjustment can now be rezeroed against an off-the-air signal from a local station, if this is practical.

SENSITIVITY MEASUREMENT

The overall sensitivity of a receiver can be measured by applying a signal to the input and noting the result at the output. FM receivers are rated according to the amount (generally 20 dB) of quieting (or for 12 dB SINAD) with a certain signal level applied at the input.

The squelch is disabled by adjusting it so it will remain open with no signal applied. An ac voltmeter is connected to the receiver audio output (with no signal applied), and the noise level is measured. An unmodulated input signal is applied and its level increased until noise level drops 20 dB (voltage drops to 10 percent of the original value).

Receiver performance (AM or FM) can also be determined by applying a modulated signal and measuring the resultant audio output. This will give information on the number of microvolts (or fraction of a microvolt) that will produce so many milliwatts (usually 10 to 50 mW) audio output. If the signal input is advanced, the amount of signal required to produce full rated audio output can also be determined. AM receivers are also rated according to the microvolts of input required for a 10 dB signal-to-noise ratio to be obtained.

If the audio output of a receiver is rated at 1W, the voltage across a 4-ohm output (with a speaker or 4-ohm dummy load connected) will be 2V since voltage is equal to the square root of power times resistance. At 10 mW the voltage is 0.2V, and at 50 mW, 0.45V.

SELECTIVITY MEASUREMENT

An overall selectivity test is sometimes difficult to make because of the problem of accurately determining the output frequency of the rf signal generator. For instance, when determining the width of the flat top of the resonance curve, one must be able to set the signal generator accurately to a few kilohertz on each side of the center operating frequency.

Therefore, selectivity of the i-f amplifier can be measured more readily, because the signal generator is more easily set at the lower frequencies. For instance, in checking out a 455 kHz i-f amplifier with a 10 kHz bandpass, it should be possible to set the signal generator accurately to 450 and 460 kHz.

The measurement is made by feeding the signal to the input of the mixer ahead of the i-f amplifier. The limiter voltage is then measured or the ac audio output voltage can be monitored with an ac voltmeter. The signal generator is set to the i-f center frequency. The signal level required to produce a certain amount of limiter or audio voltage is then noted. The signal generator (unmodulated) is next set 5 kHz higher than the center i-f, and the signal level is adjusted to produce the same limiter reference voltage. The signal generator is then set 5 kHz lower, and the signal level is again adjusted to produce the same limiter voltage. If the curve is symmetrical, the input signal level should be the same.

The tests should proceed further, of course, so that the amount of attenuation can be determined at various increments of frequency. At ±30 kHz, for example, the signal-generator output is advanced to produce the same limiter or agc voltage as the one at the center frequency. For instance, if the output voltage of the signal generator must be increased 1000 times, the attenuation of signals ±30 kHz removed from the center frequency will be 60 dB.

BANDPASS SYMMETRY

The bandpass of a highly selective FM receiver is only 12 to 15 kHz wide. The carrier frequency (rf and i-f) should be centered within this passband. For example, in a single-conversion receiver with a 10.7 MHz i-f amplifier, the i-f signal should be centered at 10.7 MHz so that the available band space for each sideband will be equal. And in the case of a double-conversion receiver with a 455 kHz low i-f, the i-f amplifier should be able to pass signals from 450 to 460 kHz when receiving an FM signal deviated ± 5 kHz. If the i-f is not correctly centered, clipping of one of the sidebands could result.

The frequency of the i-f signal depends upon the frequency of the intercepted signal with respect to the assigned channel frequency and the frequency of the local oscillators within the receiver. Both the frequency of the distant transmitter and of the local oscillator are subject to some drift and, therefore, cause a small change in the frequency of the i-f signal. Although this small drift cannot be prevented, every effort should be made to tune the i-f amplifier stages so that the bandpass will be symmetrical and that the i-f signal will be correctly centered.

Since it is difficult to set a tunable rf signal generator precisely 5 kHz above and below the carrier frequency or the frequency of the i-f signal, a crystal-controlled signal generator will make the job easier. Figure 7-6 is a schematic of a signal generator equipped with crystals for 450, 455, and 460 kHz and for use in checking the symmetry of a 455 kHz i-f amplifier. For other intermediate frequencies, a similar signal generator can be used. For checking a 10.7 MHz i-f amplifier, for example, it should be equipped with crystals for 10.695, 10.700, and 10.715 MHz.

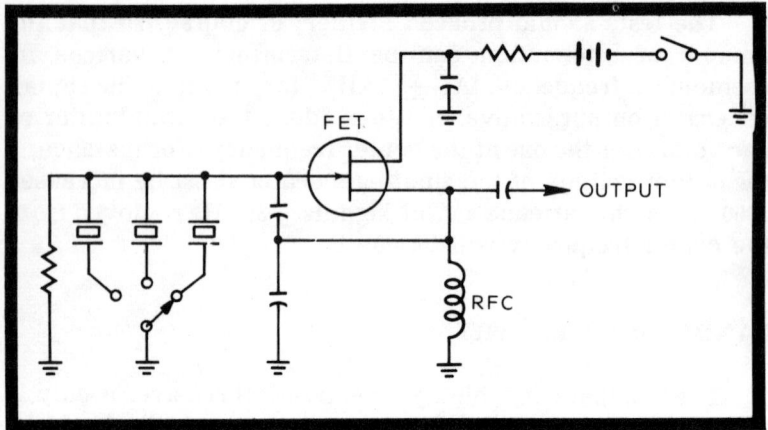

Fig. 7-6. Stable three-frequency signal generator uses crystals for the operating channels.

The output of the signal generator is loosely coupled to the output of the mixer ahead of the i-f stages to be checked. If the center frequency of the i-f amplifier to be checked is 455 kHz, for example, the signal generator is set to 455 kHz and the discriminator is zeroed. Then the signal generator is set to 450 kHz and then to 460 kHz and the discriminator output voltage is noted. It should be the same at either frequency.

The same kind of check can be made at the limiter test point to determine that the preceding stages are tuned to be symmetrical. Since the bandpass of the i-f stages is not actually flat, the voltage indications at 450 and 460 kHz will be lower than at 455 kHz. The same techniques are used at other frequencies. And, of course, the signal generator should be designed for and equipped with crystals for the appropriate frequencies.

To check the bandpass of an AM receiver, the same techniques are used except that avc voltage is monitored.

TROUBLESHOOTING

Signal tracing is a good system for localizing receiver troubles. An easy way is to open the squelch and apply an audio signal (from a signal generator) to the input of the first audio stage (through a capacitor to prevent possible conflict with dc conditions), and note whether a tone can be heard from the speaker.

Then, working back from the discriminator (or detector) to the mixer, feed a modulated i-f signal to the inputs of the various stages, changing the signal-generator frequency as required. To determine whether the local oscillators are functioning, feed an unmodulated signal (tuned to the applicable local-oscillator injection frequency) to the input of each mixer, starting with the last one.

A frequency meter of an electronic counter can be used for determining the existence and frequency of each local oscillator signal. The signal is picked up through a small capacitor at each mixer input.

Receivers should be checked with the normal input voltage applied, as well as at reduced and higher-than-normal voltages, to simulate actual operating conditions.

RELAY MAINTENANCE

A relay, like any other device with moving parts, is subject to wear. In simplex radio systems, transmitter control and antenna relays as well as the keying relays used in remote-control circuits, are operated frequently. Unless hermetically sealed, they will gather dust, which impairs their electrical as well as mechanical function.

Relay contacts exposed to air will become contaminated. When contacts carry enough current that sparking occurs, the dust will be burned off. Eventually the contacts may become pitted.

Contacts exposed to air must be cleaned regularly. They should never be sandpapered or filed. Instead, a burnishing tool should be used.

When using a burnisher, be careful not to bend the relay contact springs. If the contacts are burned or pitted, the relay should be replaced.

Relays can also be cleaned ultrasonically by immersing them in a suitable detergent. If the relays are not of the plug-in type, they must be removed from the equipment, unless the assembly on which the relay is mounted is small enough to fit into the cleaning tank.

The adjusting screws, which affect the sensitivity and dropout threshold of the relay, should not be touched except by someone who knows what he is doing. Relay maintenance is a skill unfamiliar to most radio technicians. Moreover, whenever in doubt about the reliability of a relay, it is better to replace it than to chance failure of the equipment.

PREVENTIVE MAINTENANCE

The FCC requires that the frequencies, degree of modulation, and power input to the final-amplifier stage of all transmitters be measured and the findings recorded in the station's log at regular intervals. This is a bare necessity to avoid suspension of a station license, or punishment. The equipment deserves more.

The vehicle in which a mobile radiotelephone is installed is part of a mobile station. The body of the vehicle is part of the antenna system. The battery, charging generator, and even the engine are part of the radio system, since they are necessary components of the electrical power source.

Therefore, one phase of a preventive-maintenance program is inspection of the vehicle. The procedures include:

1. Measure battery voltage with engine not running, but with receiver turned on.
2. Repeat step 1 with transmitter operating.
3. Measure battery voltage with engine running fast enough to charge the battery.
4. Inspect radio power-input cable connections and fuse.
5. Inspect cable to control head.
6. Inspect speaker and its cable.
7. Inspect microphone, its cable, and connector plug.
8. Inspect antenna cable and connector.
9. Inspect antenna, particularly where it connects to coaxial cable and the bond to the car body or bumper.
10. Inspect distributor and spark-plug suppressors (if used), and bypass capacitors used for noise reduction.

If the battery voltage falls appreciably when the transmitter is operating (engine not running), the battery may be nearing the end of its life, or the charging system is not doing an adequate job with the engine running at a fair clip.

Frayed cables should be repaired by taping over worn insulation. If too frayed, the cables should be replaced. If the microphone cable or the connections at the plug or at the other end are in poor shape, it is easier to replace the complete microphone assembly with a spare and make repairs later in the shop, where it is more convenient to do so.

If the antenna looks as if it has been exposed to the elements for too long, replace it. Remember that HF, VHF, and UHF signals travel on the surface of a conductor, not through the core. If the surface of the whip is coated with "gunk," or if it is corroded or rusted, it will be an inefficient radiator.

If the insulator at the base of the antenna whip is cracked, replace it. If it is coated with dirt, scrub it clean with a stiff brush and a good solvent. Too many watts and microvolts may be leaking off to ground.

Although it is the auto mechanic's job to keep a car running, it is the radio technician who is often blamed if dirty spark plugs or a noisy charging generator impairs the radio performance. It takes only a few minutes to wipe the dirt from the insulation of spark plugs. Should generator brushes or commutator need service, the owner should be so advised, since this is clearly beyond the duties of the radio techinican.

After the vehicle itself and the radio antenna, cabling, and control devices have been checked out, attention should be devoted to the radio equipment. When spares are available, a freshly serviced communications unit (transmitter-receiver-power supply) should be installed and the original unit taken to a shop for routine preventive maintenance.

If this is not feasible, the vehicle should be driven to the shop, where the required equipment is available. The paces through which the radio equipment should be put include:

1. Clean chassis, using compressed air to remove accumulated dust.

2. Test tubes (when used) and replace those that do not meet standards.

3. Test vibrators (when used). If in service more than three months, replace.

4. Retune transmitter.

5. Peak up receiver, antenna, and rf and mixer trimmers.

6. Measure the transmitter frequency.

7. Measure transmitter modulation.

8. Measure transmitter power input to the final rf stage.
9. Measure transmitter output with rf wattmeter.
10. Reconnect mobile unit to antenna, and tune transmitter for maximum output while watching indication on field-strength meter. Also repeak receiver antenna trimmers.

Setting Up the Shop

Since FCC technical standards and operational requirements are increasingly being tightened, the mobile radio shop must be equipped with sophisticated test instruments of high precision (see Fig. 8-1) and manned by adequately trained technicians. "Wet finger" voltmeter techniques used by old-time home radio technicians are no longer adequate. Now, it is necessary to be able to measure frequencies to an accuracy of better than a few parts per million or even more. It is also necessary to generate stable rf signals at levels that are but a fraction of a microvolt.

Ideally, the mobile radio repair bench should be inside of a "screen room" that excludes outside interference and minimizes radiation of radio energy when testing transmitters. A truly effective screen room requires total shielding of all four walls, the ceiling and floor. The power lines fed to the screen room should be appropriately filtered.

Enclosing the test area in a copper-screened room will go a long way toward reducing outgoing and incoming in-

Fig. 8-1. Example of a well-equipped shop.

161

terference. All pieces of the screening material should be bonded together electrically. One point of the shield should be grounded through the shortest heavy conductor.

Most shops, however, are not shielded. For this reason, care must be exercised, when transmitters are tested, to minimize radiation of signals which might cause illegal (or unneighborly) interference.

Workbenches of the proper height should be provided. Compressed air should be available, so that technicians can blow away dirt from equipment prior to servicing. If compressed air is not available, a pair of fireplace bellows will do.

LIGHTING

Without adequate lighting, it is difficult to see into tight corners inside equipment. Although fluorescent lighting permits better identification of color codes, incandescent lights do not produce radio interference as the cooler-running flourescent lights do. Fluorescent lights may be all right for overall lighting, but they should not be placed near a receiver being tested. An illuminated magnifying glass can also be of

POWER

Power should be available at all work locations for operation of test equipment, soldering irons, and portable lighting, as well as ac radio equipment to be serviced. Strip-type outlets just above the bench level provide outlets every few inches along the bench.

One or more dc voltages must also be made available for operation of mobile units. Most vehicles are now equipped with 12V batteries. Both 6V and 12V power can be provided from a pair of 6V storage batteries floated by a charger or a rectifier. Rectifier power supplies are available in many voltage and current ratings. Most have controls for setting the output voltage, and meters for reading the current and voltage. Some contain automatic voltage regulators which hold the output voltage to as close as 0.01 percent.

TEST EQUIPMENT

In a shop in Concord, California, the test equipment is installed on an overhead conveyor which can be slid to any position over a long workbench. Thus, one set of test equipment can be used at several work positions. Some shops put equipment on double-decked carts. One cart can be equipped with a frequency meter, modulation meter, and rf wattmeter for transmitter checking; and another, with signal generators and other equipment for checking and aligning receivers. Shelf space on which test equipment can be placed should be provided above the benches.

Tube and Transistor Testers

In addition to a general-purpose tube tester, the mobile radio shop should have some means of checking tubes for grid emission and leakage. At a military electronics shop, the reliability of airborne radar equipment was bettered by more than 400 percent when tubes were checked on a special grid-circuit tester, as well as on a general-purpose tester. Many tubes that checked "good" on a general-purpose tester failed to pass the grid-emission test.

There are many kinds of tube testers on the market, some more critical than others. All of them test for short circuits and indicate the relative merit in terms of dynamic mutual conductance, transconductance, plate conductance, or emission. The simplest test is for cathode emission: a meter indicates the amount of current flow in the cathode. In some testers, an ac signal is applied to the tube. The performance of the tube under simulated operating conditions is then measured in terms of dynamic mutual conductance.

Some technicians feel they can get by with a simple emission-type tube tester. To weed out the bad tubes that were undetected by the tube tester, they also perform an operating test in the set. This is done by substituting new tubes, one at a time, and noting any change in performance. A weak rf signal is applied to the receiver input. Performance changes are then observed with a meter connected to the limiter (avc bus in AM sets) or audio output. Obviously, more tubes can be culled during the first part of the operation if a highly critical tube tester is used.

Unfortunately, no transmitter tube testers are available through service industry channels. Most transmitter tubes are therefore tested on regular tube testers. However, rf amplifier tubes operate at high voltages. For this reason, they do not get much of a test in an ordinary tube tester. These tubes are generally tested on a transmitter, by measuring the transmitter output with an rf wattmeter and noting any change.

One of the leading radio-TV manufacturers stated in its instruction manuals that no known "adequate" transistor testers were available. Since then, many commercial transistor testers have appeared on the market. In a typical transistor tester, a signal from a reference oscillator is applied to the transistor as shown in the block diagram in Fig. 8-2. The transistor is biased for class-B operation because of the impedance across its base-emitter junction will conduct only when the input-signal level exceeds the work function of the emitter-base diode. In addition to **beta** testing of transistors such instruments will also measure the collector-current parameter with the transistor removed from the equipment.

Frequency Meters

Transmitter frequency can be measured roughly with Lecher wires, a calibrated receiver, or with a simple absorption-type wavemeter like the one in Fig. 8-3. Coil L and tuning capacitor C1 are tuned to resonate at the transmitter frequency by observing the meter reading. When they are tuned to the transmitter frequency, the meter reading will be

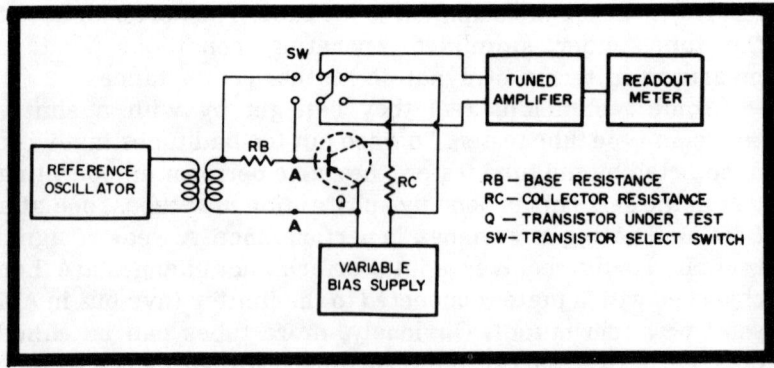

Fig. 8-2. Block diagram of an in-circuit transistor tester.

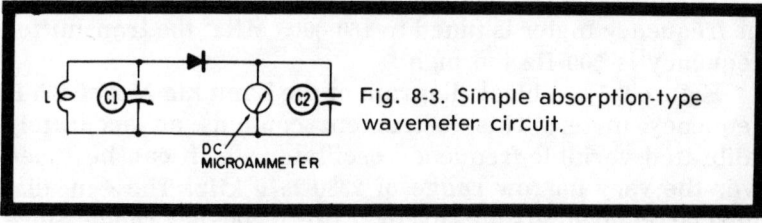

Fig. 8-3. Simple absorption-type wavemeter circuit.

maximum. The dial can be calibrated in megahertz: however, it cannot be calibrated accurately enough, nor read as closely as required. Thus, such an instrument is useful only for approximate measurements.

The FCC requires that the frequencies of transmitters operated between 50 and 1000 MHz be maintained within 0.00025 or 0.0005 percent of the assigned frequency, and those in the 25-50 mHz band, within 0.002 percent. However, transmitters operated at less then 3W input to the final rf amplifier, between 25 and 1000 MHz are required to maintain a frequency stability of only 0.005 percent.

Measurement of frequencies to determine that they are within these tight limits requires precision apparatus. The measuring instrument must have an even higher frequency stability, so that any errors in the instrument will not lead to erroneous readings.

Heterodyne Frequency Meters. Frequency can be measured precisely with a heterodyne frequency meter. The transmitter signal, picked up by a simple receiver, is compared with the frequency of a variable oscillator, as illustrated in Fig. 8-4. When the two signals are on the same frequency, no beat note will be heard. Any difference between the two will result in a beat note. For instance, if the transmitter is supposed to be tuned to 160 MHz, but zero beat is obtained when

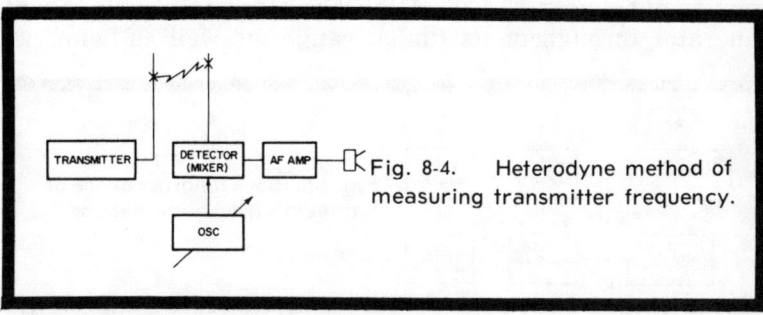

Fig. 8-4. Heterodyne method of measuring transmitter frequency.

165

the frequency meter is tuned to 160.0005 MHz; the transmitter frequency is 500 Hz too high.

Figure 8-5 is a block diagram of the Lampkin Model 105-B frequency meter. This instrument contains an accurately calibrated variable-frequency oscillator which can be tuned over the very narrow range of 2330-2670 kHz. The 4-in. dial must be revolved 40 times to cover this frequency range. Since the dial has 200 divisions, 8000 separate markings can be indicated.

The transmitter signal is picked up by a short wire "antenna" connected to the rf input jack. The transmitter signal and a harmonic of the oscillator signal are mixed in the detector. When they are close in frequency, an audible beat note will be heard in the headphones. This beat note is amplified by the audio amplifier within the instrument. When the oscillator is tuned to zero-beat with the transmitter signal, the dial is read and the frequency determined by referring to a calibration chart. A 7.5 MHz crystal calibrator is provided, against which the tunable oscillator dial calibration can be checked near the middle of the tuning range. The instrument can also be checked against a standard signal from the Bureau of Standards radio station WWV.

This instrument is intended for measurement of transmitter frequencies from 2.3-175 MHz. However, it can be used at higher frequencies by measuring the frequency of one of the multiplier stages within the transmitter. It can also be used as a signal generator for measuring the frequency of a signal being intercepted by a radio receiver. This is done by beating the oscillator signal of the instrument against the received signal.

The Gertsch frequency meter (Fig. 8-6), also of the continuously tunable types, can be used for measuring any frequency between 20-1000 MHz. It is also useful as a signal generator throughout its tuning range, as well as below 20

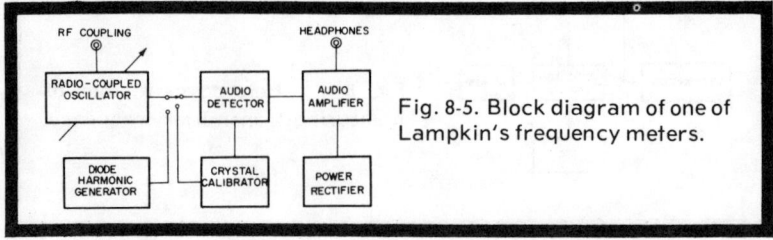

Fig. 8-5. Block diagram of one of Lampkin's frequency meters.

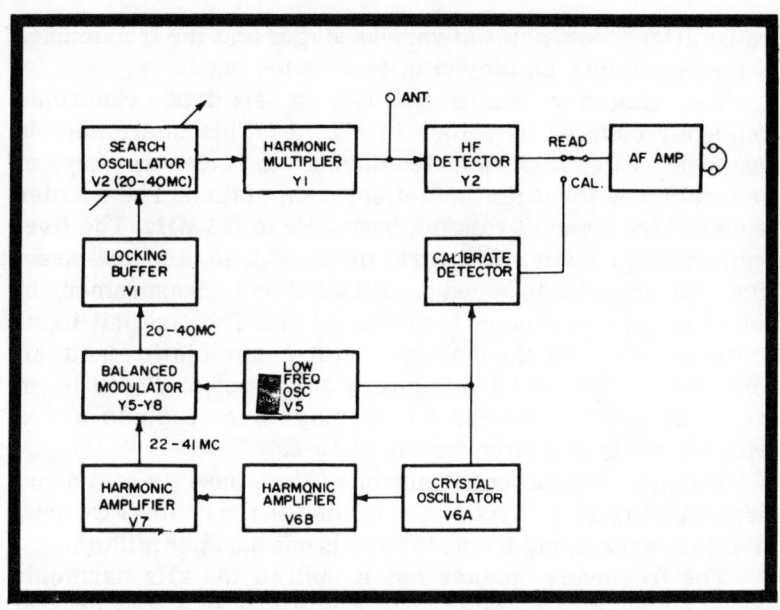

Fig. 8-6. Block diagram of popular Gertsch frequency meter.

MHz. The instrument indicates frequency by interpolating between known crystal harmonic frequencies by means of a calibrated oscillator (V5), which is tunable from 1-2 MHz. Another oscillator (V2), knwon as the search oscillator, tunes from 20-to-40 MHz. Its output is fed, through a diode-type harmonic multiplier (Y1), to the antenna terminal and the high-frequency diode detector (Y2).

The search oscillator is tuned so that its fundamental signal (20-40 MHz) or one of its harmonics is matched to the incoming signal. This is done by listening for a beat note as the oscillator is tuned past the transmitter frequency to be measured, and then adjusting for **zero** beat. By means of a selector, the proper **crystal** harmonic is selected and the low-frequency oscillator is tuned, until the difference frequency from the balanced modulator (Y5-Y8) approaches the search-oscillator frequency. The tuning is continued until zero beat is obtained. The frequency is then read directly from the tuning dials.

Frequency Counters. One of the most useful instruments for mobile radio servicing is the electronic frequency counter which directly displays the measured frequency in illuminated numerals. A counter can be used for measuring transmitter frequencies at various stages and the frequencies of the oscillators employed in tone-coded encoders.

The Regency Model EC-175, a six-digit electronic frequency counter, is shown in Fig. 8-7. This instrument is designed to enable the technician to measure crystal frequencies without mathematical computation. The counter reads out frequencies ranging from 5 Hz to 175 MHz. The five-position range switch with gate times of 1, 10, and 100 msec, plus 1 second and 10 seconds, allows direct measurement of any in-range frequencies to within 0.1 Hz. The six-digit light-emitting-diode (LED) display features automatic decimal-point positioning and leading-zero suppression. There is an overrange LED indicator for readings over 6 digits and a separate LED indicator for count rate.

The proportional oven-controlled time base gives a short term stability of 2 parts in 100 million per day for FCC certification work. Long-term stability is one part per million.

The frequency counter has a built-in 100 kHz harmonic generator for direct calibration to WWV. A 10.7 MHz crystal oscillator for afc locking and i-f alignment work is also a built-in feature. A metal-oxide-semiconductor preamp provides sensitivity of 100 mV at 100 MHz. It operates on both 120 V (ac)

Fig. 8-7. Regency EC-175 frequency counter.

and 12V(dc) so it can be used to test units in cars without having to remove the radio from the vehicle.

The Ballantine Model 5700A counter, shown in Fig. 8-8, counts directly to 220 MHz and only prescales by two for its 512 MHz operation. The counter measures from 5 Hz to 512 MHz and has a sensitivity at 500 MHz of 10 mV. The instrument incorporates a frequency offset capability. This optional capability enables the user to offset the counter's displayed frequency by a fixed number of cycles from the frequency being measured. Typically, in an application where the counter is measuring the output of a receiver's local oscillator, the input frequency to the receiver can be read out directly on the display by initially setting into the counter an offset equal to the receiver's i-f by means of a prewired board.

Other features in all modes of operation of the instrument are a quick recognition display achieved by logical grouping of the display numerics, and front-panel pushbutton blanking of unused or unwanted digits. With the blanking feature, the **number of digits** display can be selected to show 5, 6, 7, 8, or 9 places by pushbuttons directly under the display digit.

Modulation and Deviation Meters

FCC regulations require measurements to be made to determine that the bandwidth of a transmitted signal does not exceed the bandwidth authorized for the station. In

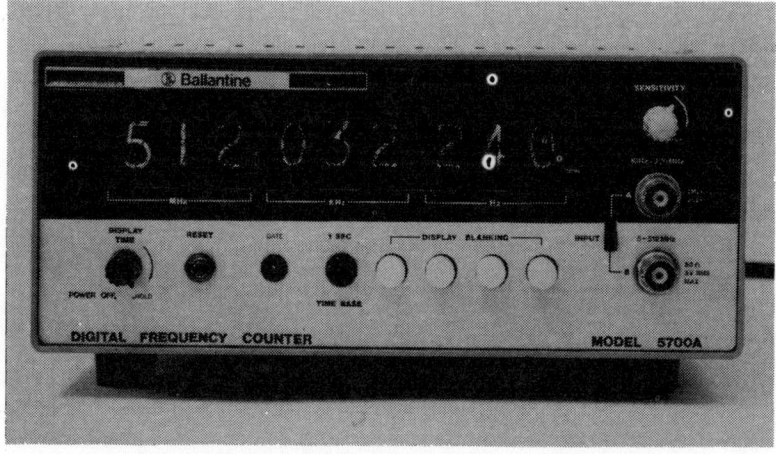

Fig. 8-8. Ballantine 5700A frequency counter.

narrowband systems, maximum transmitter deviation is ±5 kHz for FM. If the assigned frequency is 162.525 kHz, the signal will vary from 162.520 (—5 kHz) to 162.530 (+5 kHz). Allowing ± 0.0002 percent maximum center-frequency drift, the edge of the FM signal could drop as low as 162.5192 MHz and swing almost to 162.531 MHz when the transmitter center frequency drifts to its maximum limit on the high side.

Deviation measurement. Several instruments are available for measuring the deviation of FM transmitters. Some are incorporated into frequency meters, others are separate instruments. Figure 8-9 is a block diagram of the Lampkin Model 205A FM modulation meter (actually a superheterodyne) receiver equipeed with a vacuum-tube voltmeter). It will measure the modulation of FM transmitters operating on any frequency from 25-500 MHz. Instantaneous peak deviation is indicated on a direct-reading 0-25 kHz (peak) meter. Its local oscillator, tuned from 26-49 MHz, relies upon harmonics for operation at higher frequencies.

The instrument reads positive frequency deviation from center frequency when the metering circuit is connected to the discriminator. A switch reverses connections X and Y to enable reading of the negative deviation peaks. An audio amplifier and speaker are also included for aural monitoring of the signal being measured.

Amplitude Modulation Measurement. The AM transmitter bandwidth depends upon the modulation frequency. With voice modulation (limited to 3000 Hz) the signal includes the basic carrier (operating frequency) plus the upper and lower

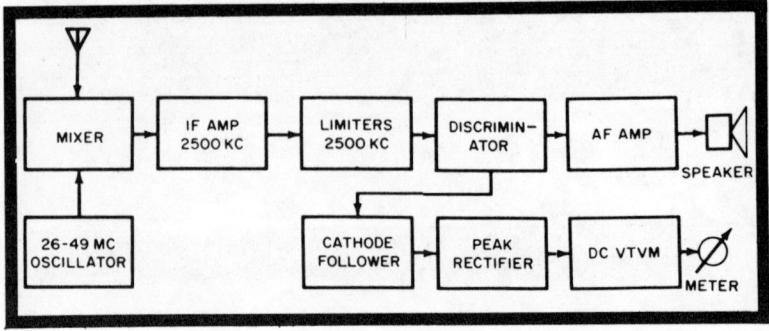

Fig. 8-9. Block diagram of Lampkin 205-A modulation meter.

sidebands, each 3 kHz wide. Thus, the transmitted signal, when modulated at 3000 Hz is 6 kHz wide. To allow for some frequency shift, an AM transmitter is assumed to occupy a bandwidth of 8 kHz.

Overmodulation in an FM transmitter causes the signal to deviate more widely, and thus, to occupy a wider band. On the other hand, splatter and distortion occur when an AM transmitter is overmodulated. The signal may then occupy a much wider band than it should and thus cause interference. AM voice transmissions become louder as the modulation is increased, an increase in power. However, there is a limit to how much the power can be increased by modulation before heavy distortion will occur. When the power is fully modulated, the effective range of the transmitter is at maximum.

Modulation can be checked by watching for an increase in power output, as indicated by an rf wattmeter or field-strength meter, while speaking into the microphone.

The percentage of modulation can be measured with an oscilloscope. The vertical deflection plates of the scope are fed rf from the transmitter. This is done by placing a pickup coil near the final rf tank, as shown in Fig. 8-10. The horizontal plates are connected to the output of the modulator. When modulation is 100 percent, a sharp-pointed, straight-sided triangle will appear on the scope screen. The af and rf signals are fed directly to the deflection plates of the crt, not through the scope amplifiers.

RF POWER METERS

Transmitter output power can be measured with an rf wattmeter. Some wattmeters act as a dummy load in place of the antenna; others can be inserted into the antenna transmission line. Figure 8-11 is a schematic of the Sierra Model 185A termination wattmeter. R1 is the dummy load into which

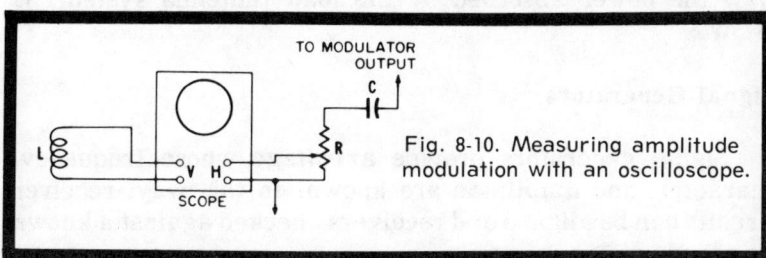

Fig. 8-10. Measuring amplitude modulation with an oscilloscope.

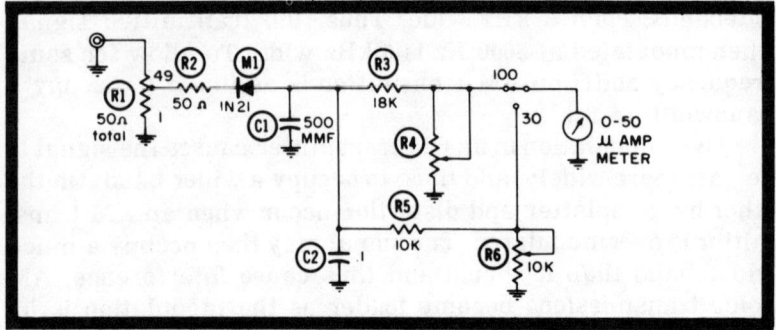

Fig. 8-11. Circuit of a termination-type rf wattmeter.

the transmitter output is fed via a coaxial line. A portion of the voltage developed across R1 is obtained at a tap 2 ohms above ground. This voltage is fed to a rectifier, which converts the rf to dc so it can be read with a dc microammeter (the scale of which is calibrated in watts). A two-position switch enables selection of full-scale readings of 30 or 100W. R4 and R6 are variable calibration resistors.

A bidirectional power monitor such as the Bird Model 43 Thru-Line (Bird Instruments) shown in Fig. 8-12 can be used for measuring reflected and incident power up to 1000 watts, at frequencies from 2 to 1000 MHz. The voltage standing-wave ratio and power absorbed by the antenna can also be determined from the incident and reflected power readings. The instrument consists of a peak voltmeter which measures the voltage across a 50-ohm impedance.

Various plug-in elements determine the frequency range and the full-scale metering ranges. When set one way the element measures incident power; set the other way it measures reflected power.

The power absorbed by the antenna system is equal to the difference between the incident and the reflected power. If the incident power is 50W for example, and the reflected power is 5.5W the power absorbed by the load (antenna system) is 44.5W.

Signal Generators

Signal generators provide a voltage whose frequency, character, and amplitude are known. In this way, receiver circuits can be aligned and receivers checked against a known standard.

Fig. 8-12. Bird **Thru-Line** wattmeter.

In the early days of radio the signal generator was a crude affair. Almost any device which generated a radio signal of approximately the proper frequency was used. As the art developed, the standards for test signals became more rigid. During World War II, radio service technicians at military bases became indoctrinated into the use of precise signal sources. They were required to align receivers so that the dial calibrations agreed with the frequencies received. Receivers had to meet specified standards of sensitivity in terms of so many microvolts input for so many audio volts output. Selectivity, avc action, and image rejection were among the

173

tests that had to be made. Any receivers not conforming to these standards were rejected for military use.

The same thinking applies to mobile radio. Receivers are expected to provide a usable output with signal levels of less than one microvolt. The receiver bandpass must be adequate to accept an FM signal without excessive distortion, but with ample rejection of adjacent and cochannel signals.

In the hands of an expert, even an electric shaver will do as an emergency signal generator. When held close to the antenna lead-in, an electric shaver creates enough "hash" to enable an expert to align the circuits so that the receiver will be highly sensitive. Given the proper tools, the expert can do a far better job.

Three known frequencies are required to align a dual-conversion superheterodyne receiver. ("Known" means that the frequency of the test signal must be known within very close limits.)

To align the front end to a specific channel, a laboratory-grade signal generator is required because it is necessary that (1) the test signal can be reduced to less than 1 uV, (2) its frequency can be set accurately, and (3) it will remain put long enough for the alignment to be made.

Figure 8-13 is a block diagram of the Measurements Model 80-R standard signal generator. Two meters are provided. One indicates the modulation percentage, and the other, the reference output level above the amount of attenuation caused by the attenuator. The output is taken through a cable terminated in a 50-ohm load. The cable has binding posts which can be connected to the receiver under test. The manufacturer recommends the use of a 6 dB pad at the output to isolate the attenuator system from the effects of standing waves, which may be present when the load is of uncertain impedance.

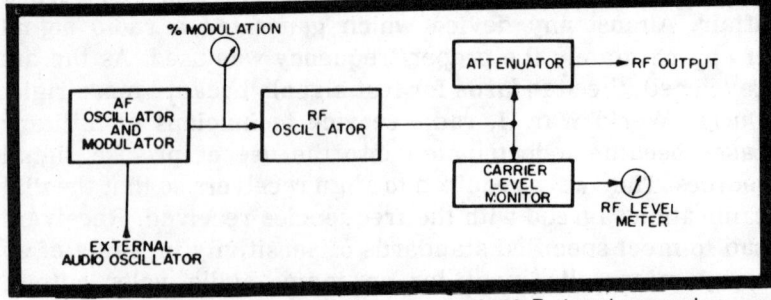

Fig. 8-13. Block diagram of Measurements 80-R signal generator.

Figure 8-14 is an external view of another Measurements signal generator, the Model M-560. It has six bands. Three bands provide continuous coverage from 25 through 54 MHz. The other three cover 140-174, 400-470, and 890-960 MHz. The signal for the last band is the second harmonic of the oscillator when tuned between 445-480 MHz. The dial calibration is accurate within 0.5 percent. The output voltage can be adjusted from 0.1 to 100,000 microvolts by the use of a mutual-inductance attenuator.

The signal generator is frequency modulated (FM) at 1000 Hz, the signal deviation being adjustable from 0 to 16 kHz peak. FM can be obtained at other modulating frequencies by using an external audio oscillator.

Signal generators are generally recalibrated by the manufacturer or at a specialized instrument service depot. However, spot calibrations can be against signals from WWV on 2.5, 5, MHz. A typical calibrator provides direct, calibrated measurements of the rf voltage at 25, 50 and 100 millivolts, plus serving as a calibrated source of rf voltage at 0.5, 1, and 2 microvolts. The calibrator also measures the modulation percentage of the signal generator.

FIELD-STRENGTH METERS

The transmitter output can be gaged and the radiation pattern of an antenna determined with a field-strength meter. This can be a very simple device, as is the instrument in Fig.

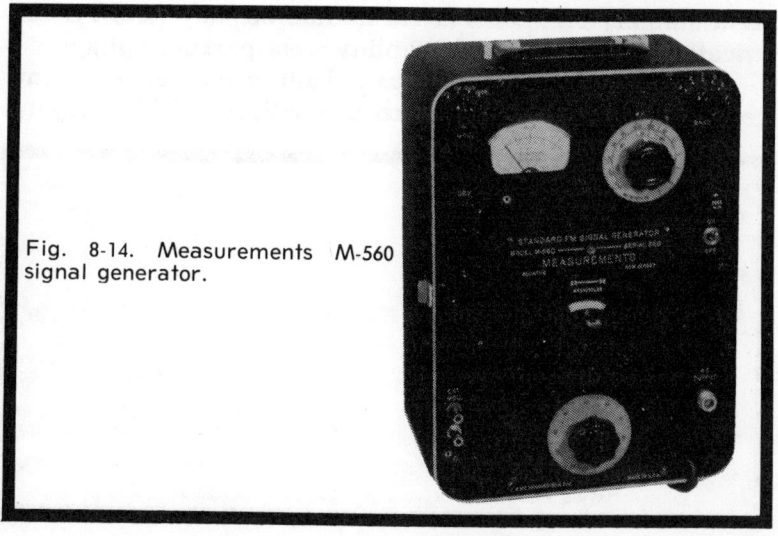

Fig. 8-14. Measurements M-560 signal generator.

8-15, which consists of a 0-50 or 0-100 dc microammeter shunted by a crystal diode. For the 152-174 MHz band, an 18-inch piece of wire can be extended from each of the two meter terminals to serve as a dipole antenna. For the 450 MHz band, the elements need by only six inches long.

Frequency Counters

One of the most useful instruments for mobile radio servicing is the electronic frequency counter which directly displays the measured frequency in illuminated numerals. A counter can be used for measuring transmitter frequencies at various stages and the frequencies of the oscillators employed in tone-coded squelch encoders.

The Regency Model EC-175, a six-digit electronic frequency counter is shown in Fig. 8-7. This instrument is designed to enable the technician to measure crystal frequencies without mathematical computation. The counter reads out frequencies ranging from 5 Hz to 175 MHz. The five-position rnage switch with gate times of 1, 10, and 100 msec, plus 1 second and 10 seconds, allows direct measurement of any in-range frequencies to within 0.1 Hz. The six-digit light-emitting-diode (LED) display features automatic decimal-point positioning and leading-zero suppression. There is an overrange LED indicator for readings over 6 digits and separate LED indicator for count rate.

The proportional oven-controlled time base gives a short term stability of 2 parts in 100 million per day for FCC certification work. Long-term stability is one part per million.

The frequency counter has a built-in 100 kHz harmonic generator for direct calibration to WWV. A 10.7 MHz crystal

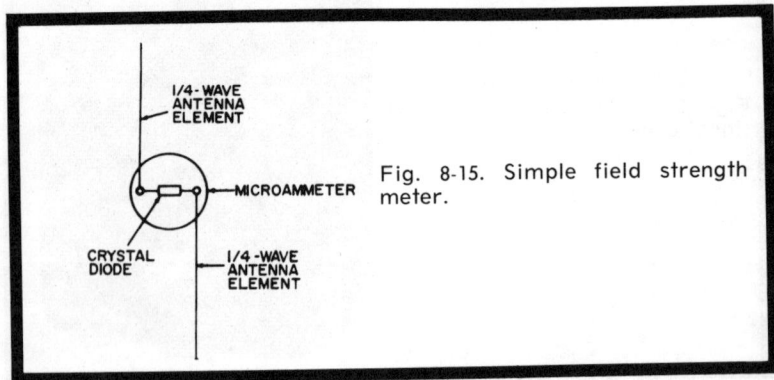

Fig. 8-15. Simple field strength meter.

oscillator for afc locking and i-f alignment work is also a built-in feature. A metal-oxide-semiconductor preamp provides sensitivity of 100 mV at 100 MHz. It operates on both 120V (ac) and 12V (dc) so it can be used to test crystals in cars without having to remove the radio from the vehicle.

The Ballantine Model 5700A counter, shown in Fig. 8-8 counts directly to 220 MHz and only prescales by two for its 512 MHz operation. The counter measures from 5 Hz to 512 MHz and has a sensitivity at 500 MHz of 10 mV rms. The instrument incorporates a frequency offset capability. This optional capability enables the user to offset the counter's displayed frequency by a fixed number of cycles from the frequency being measured. Typically, in an application where the counter is measuring the output of a receiver's local oscillator, the input frequency to the receiver can be read out directly on the display by initially setting into the counter an offset equal to the receiver's i-f by means of a prewired board.

Other features in all modes or operation of the instrument are a quick recognition display achieved by logical grouping of the display numerics, and front-panel pushbutton blanking of unused or unwanted digits. With the blanking feature, the **number of digits** display can be selected to show 5, 6, 7, 8, or 9 places by pushbuttons directly under the display digit.

SPECIAL MOBILE RADIO INSTRUMENTS

The portable Racal 9054 HF/VHF/UHF calibrator, shown in Fig. 8-16, checks both frequencies and FM deviation. Frequency range is 100 kHz to 512 MHz. This instrument allows the preset tuning of mobile radio telephones to be accurately and quickly adjusted in their vehicles. FM deviation may also be measured to insure that interference is not being caused to adjacent channels by excessive modulation.

The principle of operation is based on the fact that frequencies of mobile equipments are harmonically related to the channel spacing employed. A harmonic from a frequency standard within the 9054 is compared with the transmitted frequency of the radiotelephone. If an audible tone is heard from the loudspeaker of the instrument, the radiotelephone is off frequency. The transmitter's oscillator trimmer is then adjusted for zero-beat and the final calibration carried out visually with the aid of the front panel meter of the calibrator.

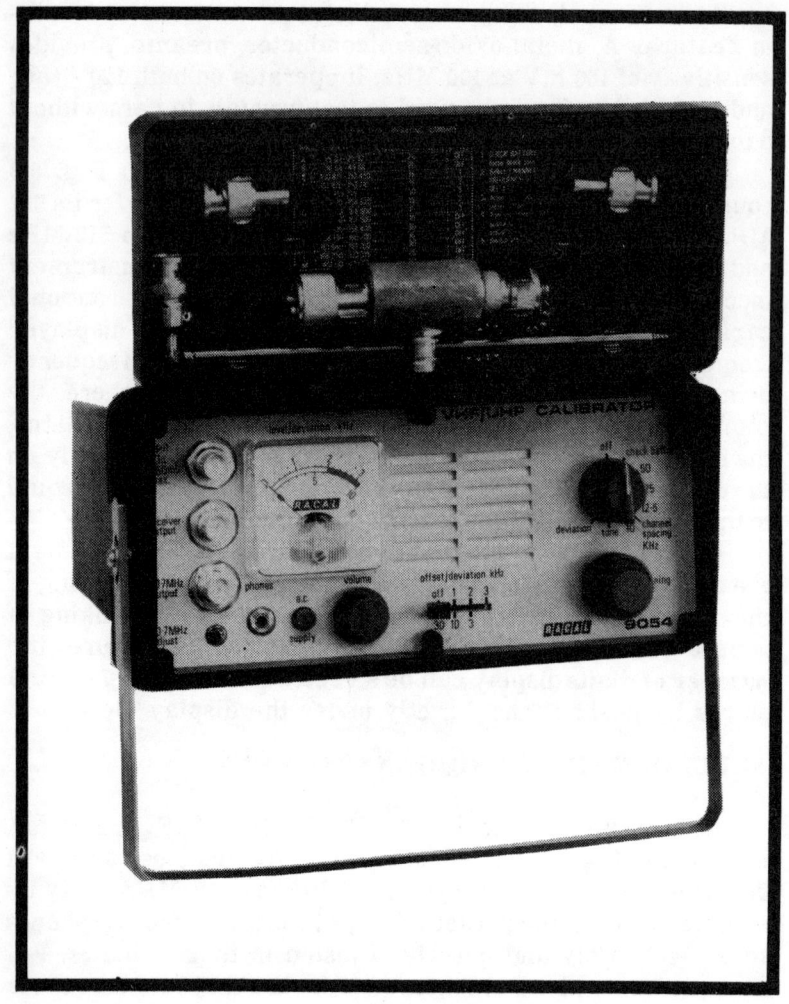

Fig. 8-16. Racal calibrator.

This accuracy is achieved without having to use separate crystals for different frequencies.

The Marconi generator/synchronizer combination is shown in Fig. 8-17. The basic signal generator, Model 2002B, covers the wide range of 10 kHz to 88 MHz and provides full AM and FM facilities. The synchronizer unit, 2170B, digitally sets the carrier frequency in 10 Hz steps with crystal stability, and presents a 6-digit display of the radio frequency. The

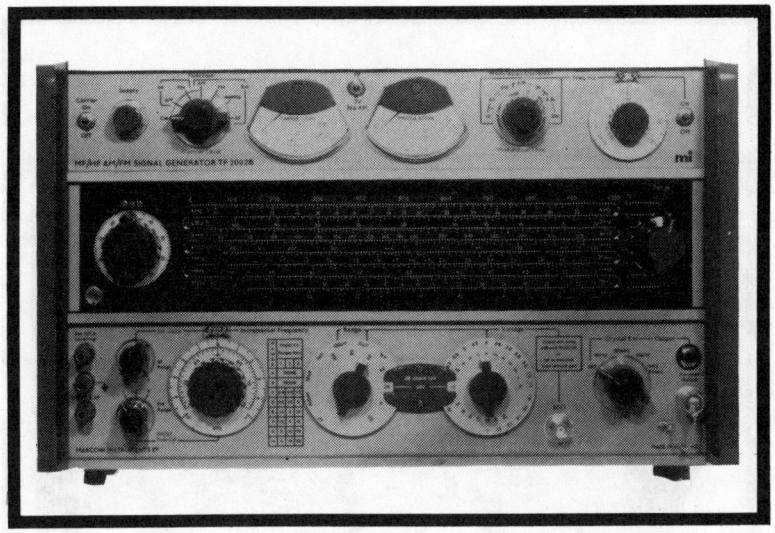

Fig. 8-17. Marconi generator/synchronizer.

major benefit from this system is that a carrier with the frequency precision and stability normally associated with synthesizers is produced but it is derived from a spectrally pure source which is free from spurious outputs. Another benefit is the ease, speed, and repeatability with which precision bandwidth measurements may be made.

A portable battery-operated communication monitor which can be used to service all FM / AM / SSB equipment in the 50 kHz to 512 MHz range is the Gertsch Model FM-10C is shown in Fig. 8-18. The digital readout frequency controls are easy to read and set up. Plug-in modules expand the capabilities of the monitor. For example, plug-ins provide oscilloscope and meter readout of FM deviation and oscilloscope readout of AM modulation percentage. Carrier frequency and modulation can be measured simultaneously. The FM-10C has provisions for an external time base input, i-f output for spectrum analysis, and an internal time base for calibration.

The Gertsch Model TG-1, four-tone generator, shown in Fig. 8-19, is used for testing tone-selective receivers. Systems which can be tested with this instrument include: Bellboy, Quik-Call, Sel-Call, Secode, Private-Line, Tone Alert, and Group Call. All tones can be remotely programmed for use in automated base stations. The instrument generates groups of

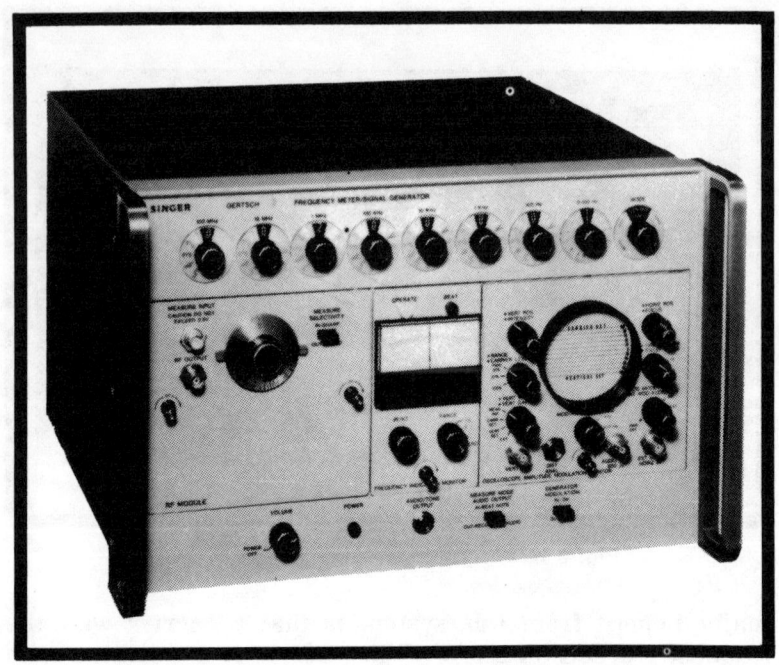

Fig. 8-18. Gertsch FM-10C communication monitor.

up to four frequencies anywhere in the 0-10 kHz range. Frequencies can be set on thumbwheel controls to the nearest 0.1 Hz. All tone durations are calibrated and repeatable in all modes of operation (continuous, burst, sequential, simultaneous, etc.). Tone groups, including first and second burst times and pause times, can be preset and an entire group can be repeated indefinitely at precise intervals. The frequency accuracy of the TG-1 is ± 0.005 percent and the tone output amplitude can be varied from zero to 5V.

The Lampkin 107B digital frequency meter / generator can be used to pull all transmitters, receivers, i-f and discriminators in a system exactly on frequency well within all present and proposed FCC accuracies. It generates and measures frequencies from 1000 Hz to 1000 MHz. It can accurately provide a signal continuously variable from 1 mV to less than 0.1 uV rms, with leakage less than 0.07 uV. The output can be amplitude- or frequency-modulated by either an external source or a 50-6000 Hz internal audio oscillator.

The Hewlett-Packard Model 9540, shown in Fig. 8-20, performs all of the usually required tests for production and

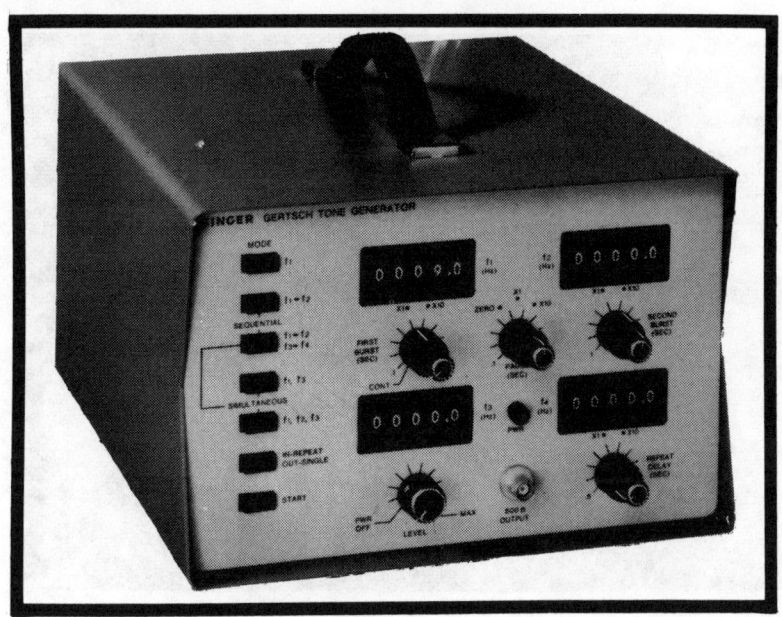

Fig. 8-19. Signal generator for testing tone-selective receivers.

maintenance of mobile transceivers. It automatically tests transceivers operating in any of the mobile communications bands (including citizens band) from 10 to 1000 MHz. A typical transceiver can be tested to EIA standards in less than 3 minutes. A data record may be printed out and displayed at the same time. A computer, integral with the system, operates in easy-to-use HP BASIC programming language. Test engineers and technicians can set up test sequences without outside programming assistance. Tests are run using simple pushbutton commands with results displayed on the control panel. An optional keyboard crt display terminal is available on which full instructions for tests can be displayed on the screen.

    A dual-connector rf test head connects the transceiver to the system. With two connectors, one transceiver warms up while the other is being tested. In addition, the two connectors can be used for input and output in module testing. A test probe for troubleshooting is also part of the test head. It connects directly to the counter in the system. Troubleshooting instructions may be on a printed list, or displayed on the optional crt display.

Fig. 8-20. Hewlett-Packard mobile transceiver testing systems.

Transmitter tests include: carrier power output, carrier frequency and stability, AM and FM hum and noise, AM modulation, FM modulation, audio distortion, audio frequency response, and audio sensitivity.

Receiver test include: SINAD sensitivity, quieting sensitivity, audio sensitivity, squelch operation, channel setting accuracy, audio power output, audio distortion, audio frequency response, FM modulation acceptance bandwidth, AM selectivity, hum and noise levels, image channel rejection, and i-f rejection. Modules and subassemblies that can be tested include: local oscillators, frequency synthesizers, i-f amplifiers, audio amplifiers, filters, selective signaling circuits, and power supplies.

SCHEMATICS

The following pages contain schematic diagrams that should prove helpful in servicing transistorized VHF/FM equipment. The schematics shown represent applicable portions of the standard communications Corp. Model SR-C851TR FM remote mobile radiotelephone unit.

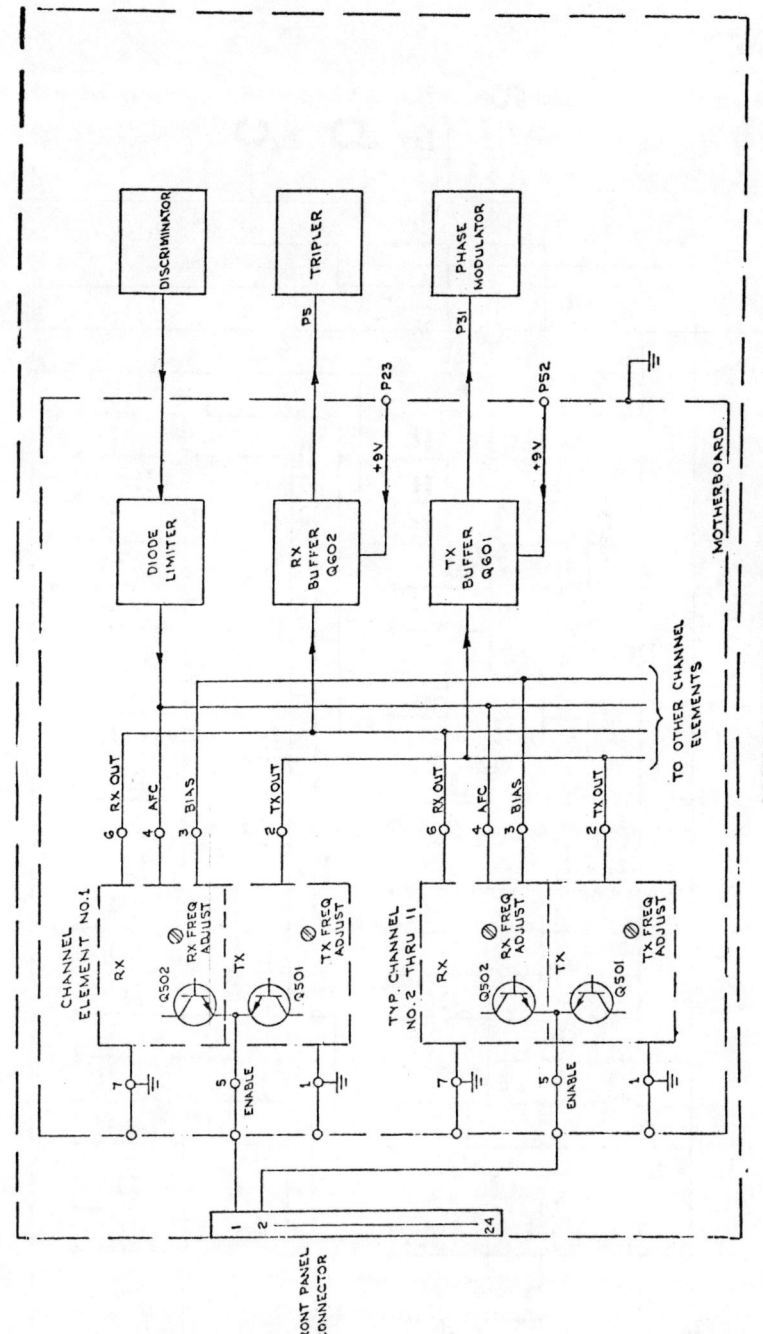

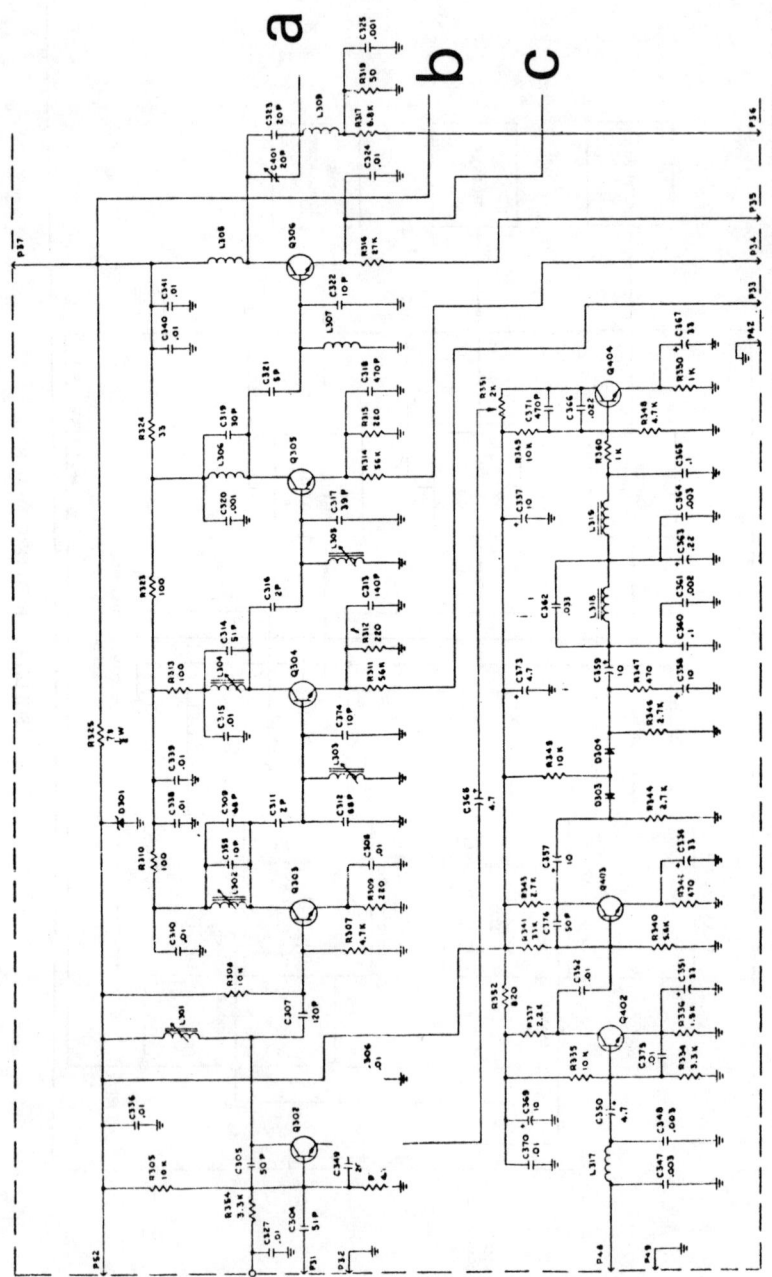

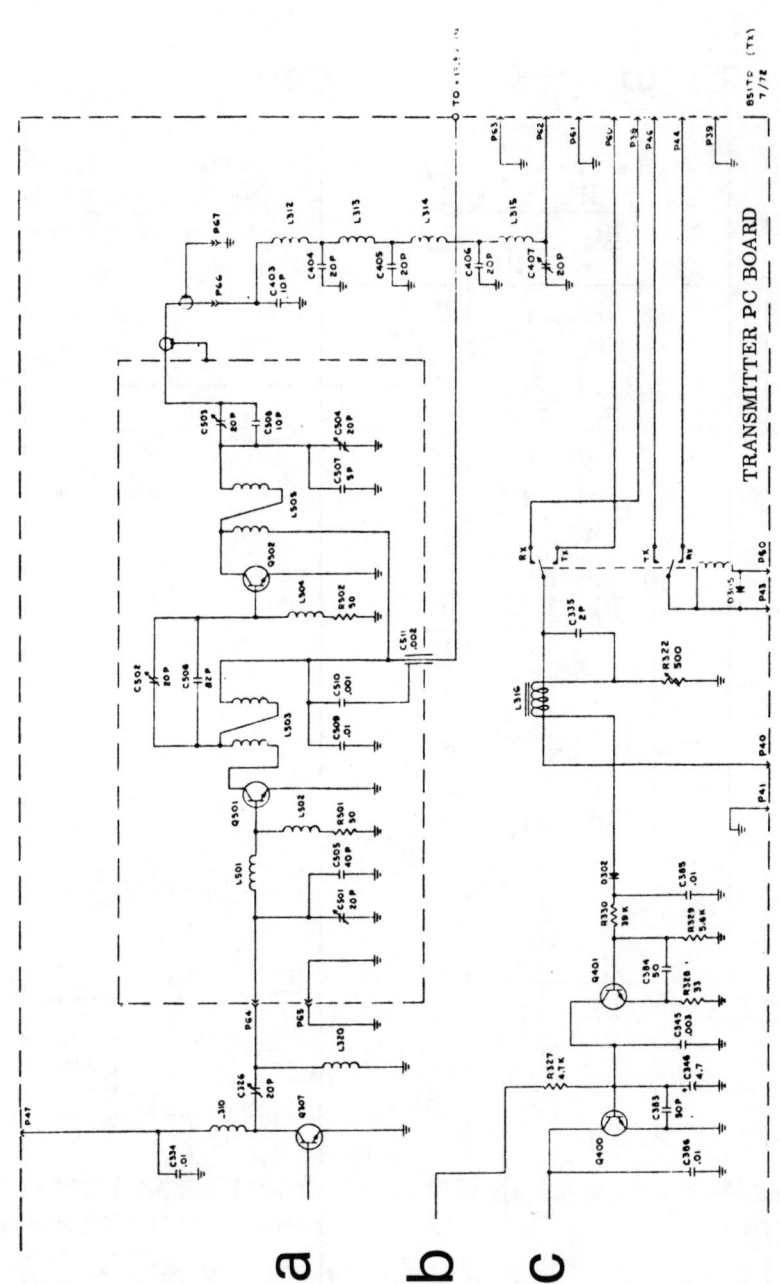

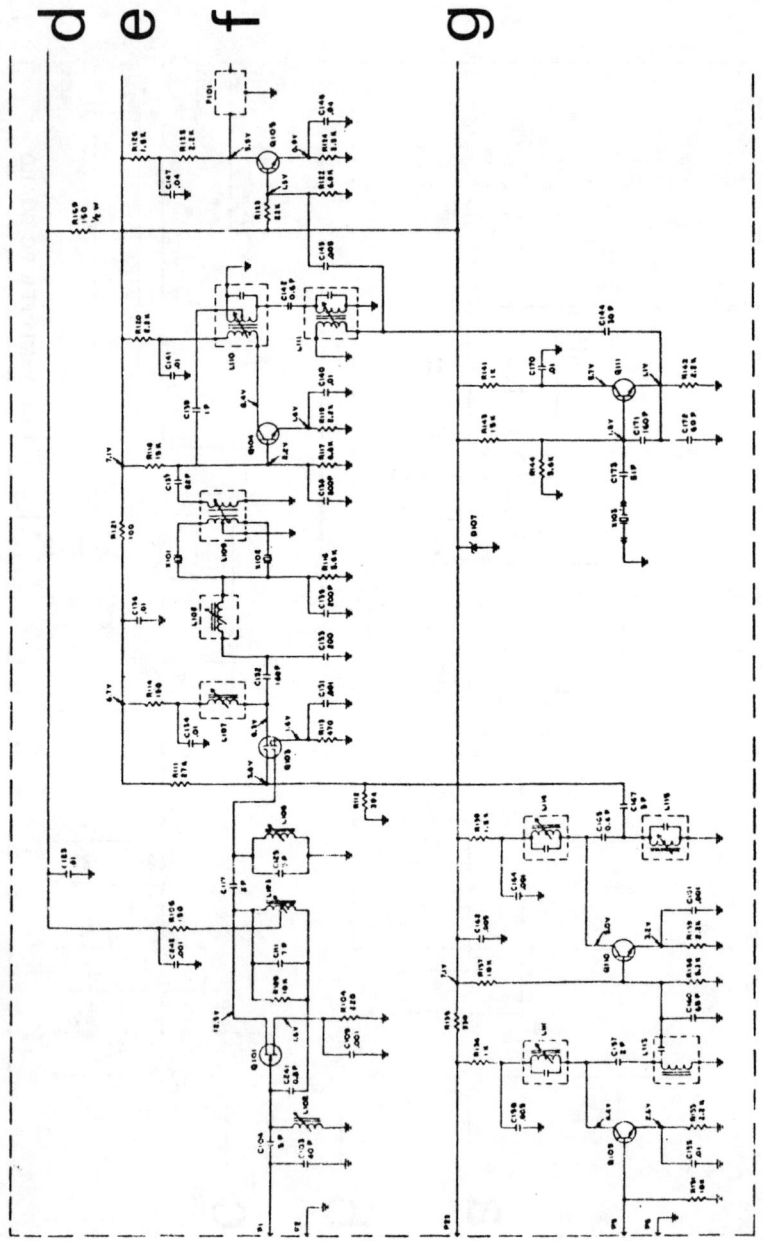

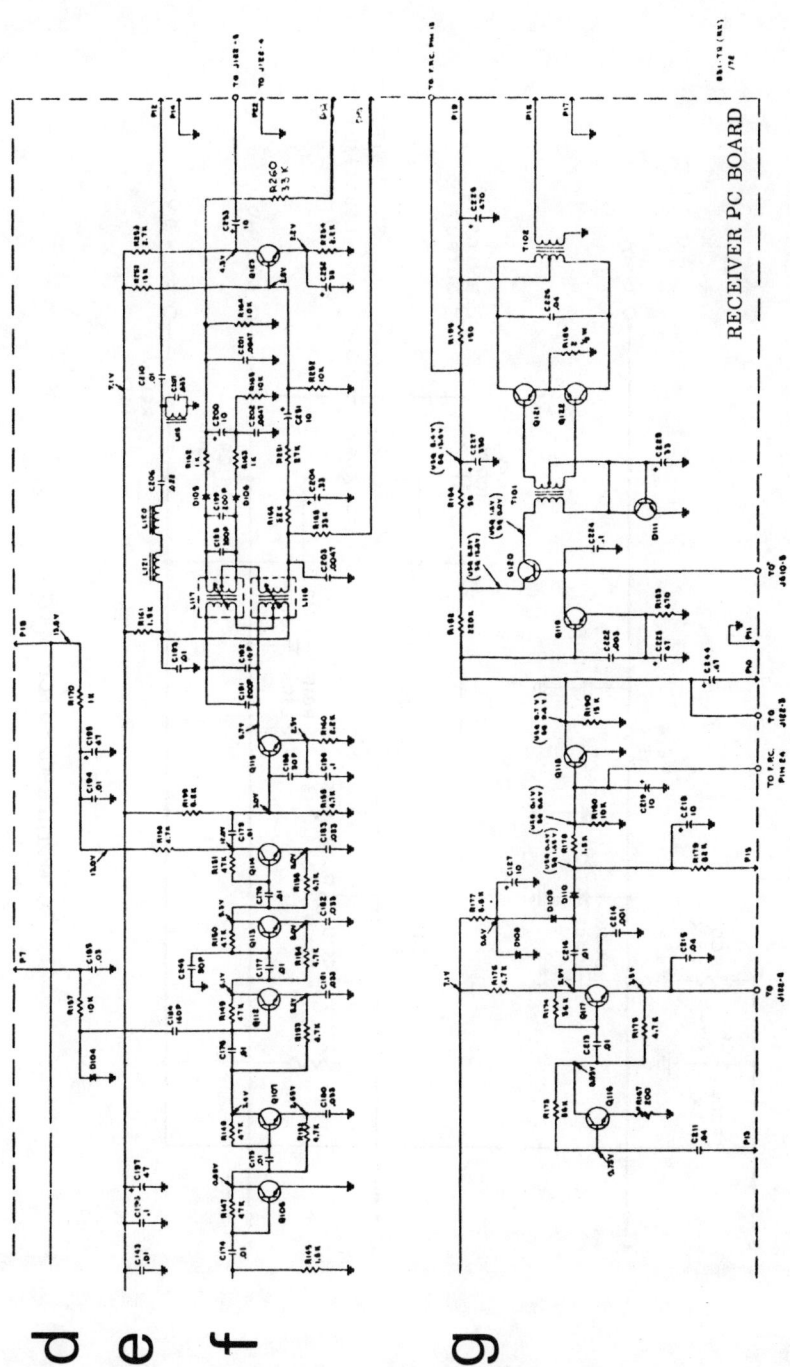

RECEIVER PC BOARD

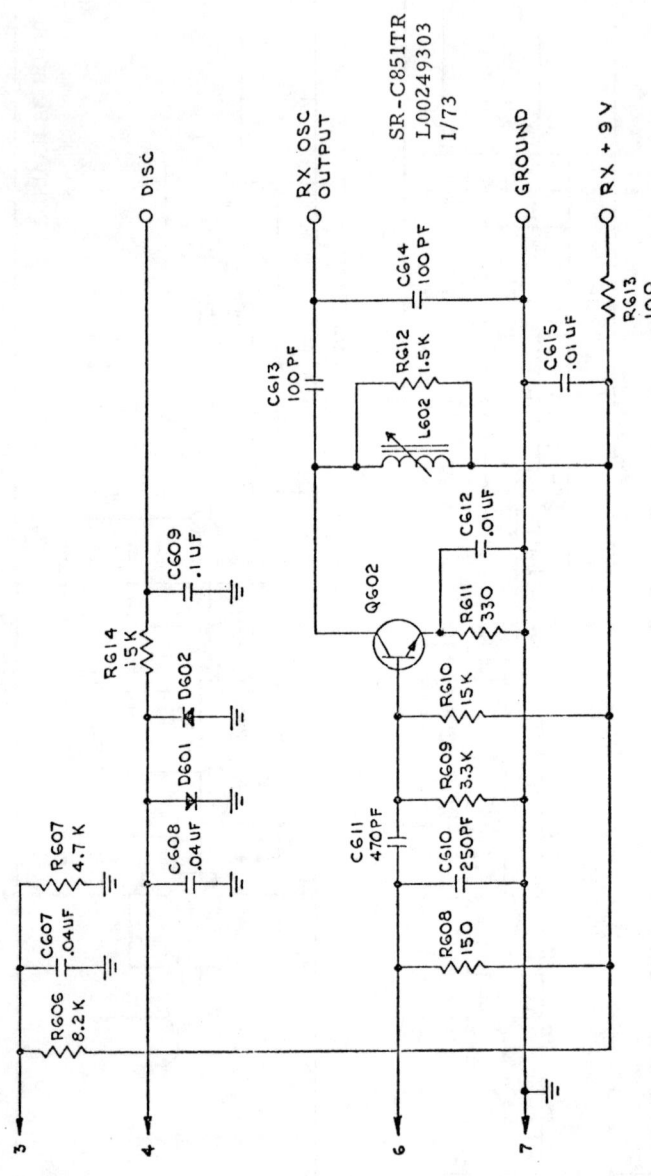

MOTHERBOARD SCHEMATIC

Index

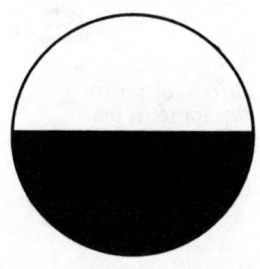

A

Ac generator charging system	129
Af amplifiers	80
AM	
—detectors	66
—receivers	151
—transmitters	32
—vs FM	20
Amplifier, driver	42
Amplifiers	
—af	80
—booster	31
—i-f	61, 77
—linear	44
—rf	50, 71
—rf power	27, 43
Amplitude modulation measurement	170
Antenna	
—farms	112
—gain	113
—range	113
—sharing	113
—systems	98
—troubles	134
Antennas	
—base station	100
—fixed-station	100
—mobile	100
Automatic frequency control	69

B

Band	
—high	52
—low	50
—UHF	54

Bandpass

—filters, rf	72
—symmetry	155
Booster amplifiers	31
Base station	7
—antennas	100

C

Calling, selective	93
Charging system	
—ac generator	129
—dc generator	124
Checkout, receiver	148
Circuits	
—mixer	73
—solid-state transmitter	36
—squelch	65
Communicating range	11
Control	
—multifunction	88
—systems	81

D

Dc generator charging system	124
Detectors	
—AM	66
—FM	63, 79
Deviation	
—measurement	170
—meters	169
Dial systems	95
Dialing, two-way	19
Directional gain	117
Discriminator	150
Dispatching services, radio	17
Driver amplifier	42

189

E

Effects of power	12
Equipment, test	163
Extended local control	90
Extended range systems	14

F

Farms, antenna	112
FM	
—detectors	63,79
—vs AM	20
Field servicing	134
Field-strength meters	176
Filters, rf bandpass	72
Fixed-antenna	
—troubleshooting	111
—supports	105
Fixed station	7
—antennas	100
Frequency control, automatic	69
Frequency	
—counters	167
—meters	164
—meters, heterodyne	165
—multipliers	26,40
Front ends	47

G

Gain	
—antenna	113
—power	120
Generator charging system	
—ac	129
—dc	124
Generators, signal	172

H

Heterodyne	
—frequency meters	165
—oscillator	57
High band	52
Hybrid mobile units	131

I

I-f	
—alignment, receiver	151

—amplifiers	61,77
—systems	60
Impulse noise silencers	67
Inoperative transmitter	144

L

Lighting	162
Lightning protection	106
Limiters	62,78
Linear amplifiers	44
Local oscillators	74
Locomotives	130
Loss, power	120
Low band	50

M

Maintenance	
—preventive	158
—relay	157
Metering, transmitter	147
Meters	
—deviation	169
—field-strength	176
—modulation	169
—rf power	171
Mixer circuits	73
Mixer-oscillator	152
Mixers	55
Mobile-antenna installations	108
Mobile antennas	100
Mobile radio	7
—instruments	176
Mobile telephone service	19
Mobile unit	7
Mobile units	
—hybrid	131
—tube-type	132
Modulated oscillator	38
Modulation meters	169
Modulator, phase	25,39
Monitoring	93
Multifunction control	88
Multiple-frequency operation	60
Multipliers, frequency	26,40

N

Noise silencers, impulse	67

O

Oscillator
—adjustment 151
—heterodyne 57
—modulated 38
Oscillators 22,37
—local 74

P

Paging, radio 16
Phase modulators 25,39
Point-to-point radio 15
Power 123,162
—gain 120
—loss 120
—sources, vehicular 123
Power supply transistors 139
Preventive maintenance 158

R

Radio
—dispatching services 17
—instruments, mobile 176
—mobile 7
—paging 16
—point-to-point 15
Range
—antenna 113
—communicating 11
Range systems, extended 14
Receiver
—checkout 148
—circuits, solid-state 71
—i-f alignment 151
—inoperative 143
Receivers 46
—AM 151
—tube-type 46
Relay
—maintenance 157
—system 15
Remote control,
  two-wire 91
Reverse-polarity
  protection 131
Rf
—amplifiers 50,71
—bandpass filters 72
—power amplifiers 27,43

—power meters 171
—stages 152
Right-of-way systems 87

S

Selective calling 93
Selectivity measurement 154
Sensitivity measurement 153
Servicing 133
—field 134
—shop 139
Sharing, antenna 113
Shop
—servicing 139
—setting up 161
Signal generators 172
Silencers, impulse noise 67
Simplex basis 8
Solid-state
—receiver circuits 71
—transmitter circuits 36
Squelch circuits 65,79
Stability 60
Station
—base 7
—fixed 7
System, relay 15
Systems, basic 7

T

Telephone service,
  mobile 19
Test equipment 163
Transistor testers 163
Transistors, power
  supply 139
Transmission lines 103
Transmitter
—circuits, solid-state 36
—inoperative 144
—metering 147
Transmitters 21
—AM 32
—tube-type 21
Troubleshooting 90,156
Tube testers 163
Tube-type
—mobile units 132
—receivers 46
—transmitters 21
Tubes, defective 138

Two-way dialing	19
Two-wire remote control	91

U

UHF band	54

V

Vehicles, miscellaneous	130
Vehicular power sources	123
Vibrators	139